Just Skin and Bones?
New Perspectives on
Human-Animal Relations in the
Historical Past

Edited by

Aleksander Pluskowski

BAR International Series 1410
2005

I0096056

Published in 2016 by
BAR Publishing, Oxford

BAR International Series 1410

Just Skin and Bones? New Perspectives on Human–Animal Relations in the Historical Past

ISBN 978 1 84171 853 8

© The editors and contributors severally and the Publisher 2005

The authors' moral rights under the 1988 UK Copyright,
Designs and Patents Act are hereby expressly asserted.

All rights reserved. No part of this work may be copied, reproduced, stored,
sold, distributed, scanned, saved in any form of digital format or transmitted
in any form digitally, without the written permission of the Publisher.

BAR Publishing is the trading name of British Archaeological Reports (Oxford) Ltd.
British Archaeological Reports was first incorporated in 1974 to publish the BAR
Series, International and British. In 1992 Hadrian Books Ltd became part of the BAR
group. This volume was originally published by Archaeopress in conjunction with
British Archaeological Reports (Oxford) Ltd / Hadrian Books Ltd, the Series principal
publisher, in 2005. This present volume is published by BAR Publishing, 2016.

Printed in England

BAR
PUBLISHING

BAR titles are available from:

BAR Publishing
122 Banbury Rd, Oxford, OX2 7BP, UK
EMAIL   info@barpublishing.com
PHONE   +44 (0)1865 310431
FAX   +44 (0)1865 316916
www.barpublishing.com

Contents

Preface

This volume of papers is derived from two sessions focusing on current research in British zooarchaeology; the first of which took place on Wednesday 17th October 2003, at the meeting of the Theoretical Archaeology Group in Lampeter, entitled 'Just Skin and Bones? New Perspectives on Human-Animal Relations in the Historical Past', organised by the editor and from which the title of this volume originates; and the second of which took place on Thursday the 9th September 2004, at the annual meeting of the Association of European Archaeologists in Lyon, entitled 'Advancing Zooarchaeology – Beyond Socio-Economics in Faunal Research', organised by Krish Seetah.

Unfortunately only a limited number of papers from these two sessions could be included in this volume, and additional contributions were sought from scholars working with new ideas, methodologies and materials in the field of historical zooarchaeology. The resulting collection therefore represents a snapshot of current historical (and predominantly medieval) animal studies, including comparisons with prehistoric contexts. Although the geographical focus is on the British Isles, the issues raised by the contributors have international relevance. The papers cover a diverse range of topics and are arranged chronologically. Krish Seetah begins with a survey of changing methods of butchering cattle in Neolithic, Iron Age and Romano-British societies, suggesting how they may be linked to transformations in cultural values attached to these animals. James Morris continues with a long-term perspective but shifts the focus from domestic to wild fauna, comparing treatments of red deer in the Neolithic, Iron Age and medieval period in the Scottish Isles. Like Seetah, he also links the changing treatment of animal bodies with conceptual shifts. The rest of the papers in the volume concentrate on significantly shorter timeframes, starting with three contributions on specific types of early medieval animal-related material culture. Howard Williams explores the multiple facets of human-animal relations in early Anglo-Saxon cremation rituals, Steven Ashby summarises work in progress which investigates the physical and conceptual aspects of bone comb production in Viking Age England and Scotland, and Chris Fern presents an exhaustive survey of equestrianism in early Anglo-Saxon England, situating the horse in the broader context of elite culture. The chronological focus of the volume then shifts to the high medieval period with a particular emphasis on predators and prey. Naomi Sykes examines the impact of the Norman Conquest on hunting culture and relates the treatment and control of deer to expressions of Anglo-Norman identity. Pluskowski's paper focuses on the other primary hunters of deer in the north – wolves – linking their biogeography with ecological and cultural factors in a comparative study of medieval Britain and southern Scandinavia. The final two papers shift our attention to the later Middle Ages. Richard Thomas surveys a range of evidence for pets from the medieval to early modern periods in England, tracking changes in attitudes and animal value. Sue Stallibrass likewise combines a diverse number of sources in her interpretation of fish vertebrae from Chevington Chapel, tracing the 'life history' of these remains from animal to artefact.

The term 'zooarchaeology' is not included in the title because of the perceived hermeneutic boundaries traditionally drawn around the discipline; virtually all the papers in this volume have drawn on other disciplines or forms of evidence in varying degrees, whether directly or indirectly, and whilst faunal remains continue to provide a focus for archaeological understanding of human-animal relations in the past, they are becoming increasingly incorporated into broader interpretative frameworks, a number of which are represented by the nine papers in this volume. Multi-disciplinarity is nothing new in the field of historical archaeology, but interdisciplinary syntheses are less common, perhaps because the sheer amount of data seems unwieldy, or because such an approach requires familiarity with a diverse range of practical and theoretical tools, a familiarity that needs to be continuously updated. Yet any study of human interactions with animals and their shared environments in the past is rooted in ecological and ethological science, in environmental anthropology, economics, philosophy and psychology. Modern understandings of taxonomy are employed to identify the excavated remains of animal species, and modern ethological analogues are used to model their behaviour. In this respect the foundations for interdisciplinarity in the field of historical animal studies have already been laid. Moreover, these studies can be approached from any number of zoocentric or anthropocentric perspectives, which, with the aid of multi-disciplinary databases (such as *The Medieval Animals Database* being developed by Gerhard Jaritz, Alice Choyke and Laszlo Bartosiewicz at the Central European University in Budapest), will ultimately converge, and syntheses of primary sources at different spatial and temporal scales, focusing on specific research questions, will become more common.

It is hoped this collection will stimulate further debate in, and enthusiasm for, research into human-animal relations in the historical past from multiple and integrated perspectives. The editor is extremely grateful to Krish Seetah for his continuing advice and support – both inside and outside the academic sphere – and to each of the contributors for offering their papers and for their patience. Finally, I would like to thank Dr David Davison and his colleagues at BAR for their continuing interest, support and assistance.

Aleksander Pluskowski
Cambridge, January 2005

Editor and Authors

Aleksander PLUSKOWSKI
Dr Aleksander Pluskowski, Department of Archaeology, University of Cambridge, Downing Street, Cambridge CB2 3DZ, United Kingdom

****

Steven, P. ASHBY
Steven, P. Ashby, Department of Archaeology, University of York, The King's Manor, York, Y01 7EP, United Kingdom

Chris FERN
Chris Fern, University College Winchester, Hampshire, SO22 4NR, United Kingdom.

James, T. MORRIS
James, T. Morris, School of Conservation Science, Bournemouth University, Dorset House, Talbot Campus, Poole, BH12 5BB, United Kingdom

Krish SEETAH
Krish Seetah, Department of Archaeology, University of Cambridge, Downing Street, Cambridge, CB2 3DZ, United Kingdom

Sue STALLIBRASS
Dr Sue Stallibrass, English Heritage Archaeological Science Adviser for North-West England, Department of Archaeology, Hartley Building, University of Liverpool, Liverpool, L69 3GS, United Kingdom

Naomi SYKES
Dr Naomi Sykes, Department of Archaeology, University of Southampton, Avenue Campus, Highfield, Southampton, SO17 1BF, United Kingdom

Richard THOMAS
Dr Richard Thomas, School of Archaeology and Ancient History, University of Leicester, Leicester LE1 7RH, United Kingdom

Howard WILLIAMS
Dr Howard Williams, Department of Archaeology, University of Exeter, Laver Building, North Park Road, Exeter, EX4 4QE, Devon, United Kingdom

Figures & Tables

Butchery as a Tool for Understanding the Changing Views of Animals: Cattle in Roman Britain

Krish Seetah

Introduction

One of the main jobs of the zooarchaeologist is to understand the the patterns of exploitation used by past cultures (Zimmerman Holt 1996) The domestication of *Bos primigenius* is certainly one of the most significant animal exploitations to have occurred in human history, and can be considered one of the defining moments in prehistoric man's taming of nature (Davis & Dent 1966: 65-66). This statement is made without the intention of detracting from other advances in agricultural development or animal husbandry. However, it would be a mistake not to recognise the significance of cattle domestication as being of paramount importance to the establishment of a sustained meat supply for early human societies and throughout history.

This point having been made it must be remembered that cattle are not always the most important domesticate to any given society, nor are they always kept solely or even predominately for their meat. It is likely that cattle have been valued for secondary products from early in their domestication (Milisauskas & Kruk 1991), and consequently have always been seen as a multipurpose animal (Bartosiewicz *et al*, 1997). It has even been speculated that the secondary products attainable from cattle are in fact the main reasons for their domestication (Urquhart 1983: 78), and when both osteological and historic evidence is evaluated this proposition is certainly plausible. Indeed it has been suggested that up to and including the Roman period cattle were kept mainly for traction and other secondary products, and culled for meat only at the end of their working life (Maltby 1984).

This paper briefly evaluates some of the changes that are evidenced in the archaeological record relating to changing priorities in the use of cattle. It will then go on to explore issues that are rarely analysed from archaeological data, focusing on butchery analysis from the Romano-British period as a foundation for evaluation of non-economic attitudes to cattle within this period. Whilst Holt (1996) is accurate in stating that the determination of *exploitation* is a key function of zooarchaeology, this need not be the sum of what faunal analysts can do with animal bones. We need only look at the multitude of viewpoints that contemporary humans have towards animals to see that this is certainly an area worth further exploration. However, while we are clearly able to make direct observations of modern attitudes, as archaeologists we are very limited when attempting to analyse our ancestor's perceptions. This does not however imply that there is no starting point; on the contrary this paper will demonstrate we can use economic factors to increase our level of interpretation beyond the purely exploitative.

A brief history of cattle exploitation

Although the aim of this paper is to provide the reader with a sense of the broader interpretations that might be achieved with animal bone data, particularly the perceptions intrinsic to human / animal relationships, it is useful to outline the background to the key issues. This essentially relates to how attitudes may have changed from the initial appropriation of *Bos primigenius* to the period under investigation employing the economic data available.

The main underlying zooarchaeological perspective relates to whether the aurochs, the progenitor to all domestic cattle breeds, was originally domesticated for its secondary products or for meat. Secondary products can be taken from an animal while it is still alive without the need for its slaughter. The three main secondary products from cattle are dairy goods, traction and dung (Clutton-Brock 1981: 62; Bowman 1977: 9; Sherratt 1983; Charles *et al* 1998).

Until the domestication of equids, cattle played a pivotal role in land expansion (Bartosiewicz *et al* 1997; Bowman 1977: 5). Archaeological evidence for traction comes from a range of sources such as iconographic representation and even preserved plough marks (Sherratt 1983). More important are actual osseous deformities, either of the lower extremities (termed exotoses) (Fig 1), or of the horn cores and cervical / thoracic vertebrae (Fig 2) (Bartosiewicz *et al* 1997, Milisauskas & Kruk 1991, Sherratt 1983). Other sources of evidence include the presence of bones from castrated animals (oxen) (De Cupere *et al* 2000; Milisauskas & Kruk 1991) and characteristic age at death ranges favouring older animals.

As with traction, evidence for milking practice again comes from artistic sources as well as representation in the archaeological record. Sex ratios of bone assemblages that show a kill off pattern predominating in older female animals and juvenile males, have been taken to indicate dairying husbandry (humans seen as a competitor with the calf for milk) (McCormick 1992). Furthermore, a lack of adult males reinforces this notion as this is taken to indicate exploitation for traction was not a priority (Sherratt 1983), although these activities are not mutually exclusive.

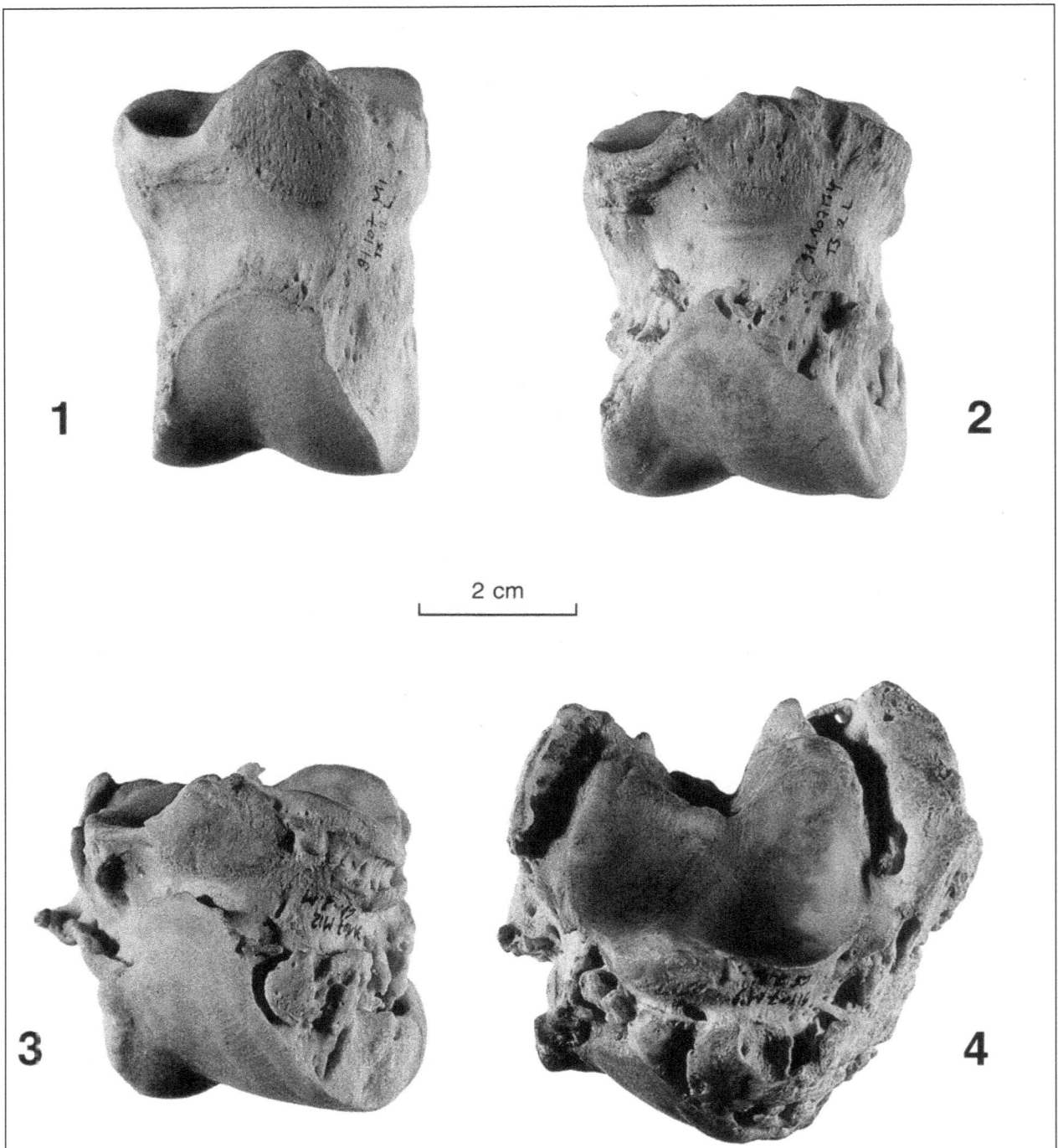

Figure 1.1: Range of deformities; 1 – normal, 4 – heavily deformed (Bartosiewicz et al 1997: 10).

Dairying is a highly efficient means of exploitation, yielding four or five times the protein of meat production (Sherratt 1981: 284), traction is not productive unless the results in agricultural gains outweigh the expense of maintaining the plough animal. This is convincing in its simplicity; it basically does not make economic sense to maintain older animals (especially large animals such as cattle) unless they can be productive in other ways. Therefore, changes in these factors should indicate a shift in priority, subsequent exploitation, and socio-cultural / ritual / symbolic perceptions from the Neolithic onwards.

Patterns of Exploitation over time

Cattle domestication is thought to have first occurred during the Neolithic with a subsequent 'secondary products revolution' taking place (Sherratt 1983). Cattle decreased in size from the archaic *Bos primigenius,* possibly as a result of night penning or by specific breeding and selective processes (Fries & Ruvinsky 1999: 15; Barker 1985: 30) (See fig 3 exhibiting decrease in size of astragalus and phalanx in Neolithic cattle; Jope & Grigson 1965: Pl Xb).

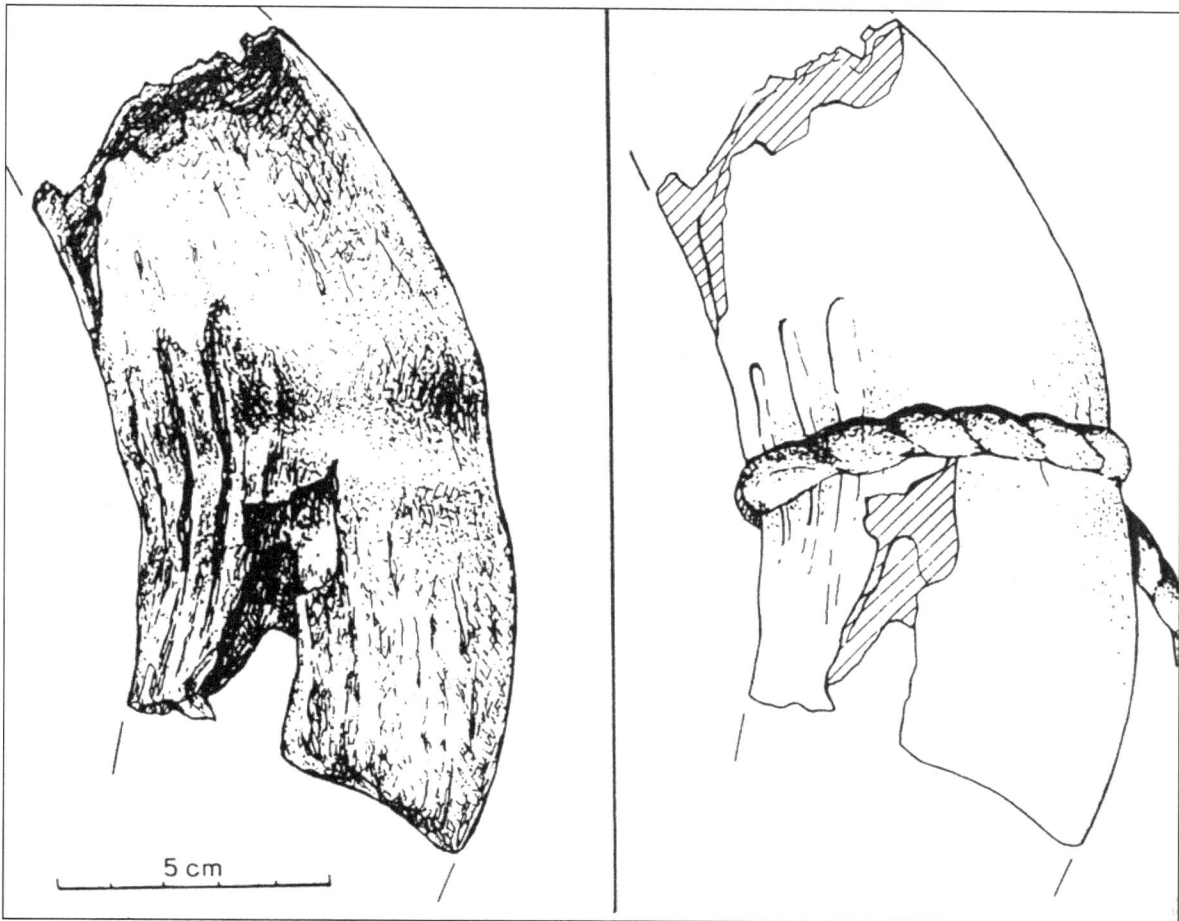

Figure 1.2: Rope marked horn cores (Milisauskas & Kruk 1991: 564).

Figure. 1.3. Bos primigenius (right) compared to Neolithic cattle (left) (Jope & Grigson 1965: Pl Xb).

Unfortunately while this reduction is noted from a number of Neolithic sites such as Maiden Castle, Dorset and Windmill Hill, Avebury (Jackson 1943: 362; Jope & Grigson 1965: 145), the possible implications are not discussed. A smaller animal may have a lower work capacity or produce less milk. However, a smaller animal should reach maturity earlier and is therefore able to work from a younger age. Diminutive animals would also be easier to house and importantly, to manage, while still maintaining the majority of their power.

Other evidence supporting the importance of secondary products comes indirectly from sites such as Stonehenge (Maltby 1990: 248; Serjeantson 1995: 440). Animals falling into an 'intermediate' size category are thought to be female aurochsen, however, it is feasible that these are castrates. The development of traction and dairying are likely to have occurred during this phase, although it is difficult to show the extent to which these activities were actually exploited from the archaeological record.

Sites such as Grimes Grave, Norfolk, give a valuable, if somewhat restricted (due to small sample size) view of the Bronze Age. Morphologically the cattle at Grimes Grave fall between Neolithic and Iron Age ranges, reinforcing the notion that size was an important aspect of husbandry and not coincidental. However, from an archaeological perspective the most salient features are the presence of a potential castrate, and the relatively high representation of adult females within the bone assemblage (Legge 1981: 81). While it can be speculated that the presence of a castrates indicates possible traction for this particular site, this in no way can be taken to represent an exploitation pattern for the Bronze Age as a whole. Furthermore, a single animal could actually reinforce notions of ritual activity more so than traction, as it might be hypothesized that this individual was of 'special' significance.

During the Iron Age the management of cattle for secondary products reaches a more advanced level. Excavations from Wessex suggest that cattle may have been calved in enclosed settlements such as Danebury, Hampshire, leading to the development of a dairy economy in that region, but with grazing taking place on lowlands (Hambleton 1999; Grant 1984: 107-10). Further to this is the proposal that castration was first used as an extensive management mechanism during this period and that there was an average increase in secondary products such as dairy and traction (Grant, 1991: 467). While the above supports secondary product exploitation, it has been suggested that Iron Age farmers employed a less 'intensive' cattle husbandry regime (Grant 1991: 470), and even shifted towards more primary product exploitation (Hambleton 1999).

The trend of size diminution, which had been seen from initial domestication in the Neolithic, is reversed during the Roman occupation (Allen 1990: 60). However, this has been attributed to the importation of larger animals, rather than specific breeding practices (Murphy et al 2000). Possible implications of this relate to an increased need for animals capable of prolonged ploughing, or for carrying heavier burdens then native cattle were capable of doing. This is supported by traction related pathologies from sites such as Great Holts Farm, Essex, and Frocester in Gloucester, (Murphy et al 2000; Noddle 2000: 236-7) which seem to indicate an increased need for traction, although in the absence of data relating to previous periods this is purely speculative. Also, it must be remembered that poor soil conditions and heavy terrain, as well as old age can lead to pathological abnormalities (Maltby 1993; Bartosiewicz et al 1997; Murphy et al 2000).

Indirect evidence for the possible increased need for traction comes from the fact that horses only account for 1-6% of fragments from Greyhound Yard, Dorchester. Even though only a small number would need to be maintained for traction purposes, this is still a low value when one takes into account that cattle accounted for between 22 and 47 % (average 35 %) (Maltby 1994: 87-89).

Furthermore, it is naïve to analyse the Roman assemblage without taking into account the cultural context of the invading peoples. It has been suggested that cattle in Italy were valued predominately as beasts of burden and for dairy produce (Grant 1975: 384). This is supported by the various trends identified by King (1984) where the *Coloniae* sites, with strong military associations and Romanised settlements, show the greatest numbers of cattle, and the unromanised settlements demonstrating a pattern closer to that seen in the Iron Age.

The problem of actually deciphering secondary exploitation of cattle from the Roman period arises from the sheer variability of husbandry patterns. Aside from the trends highlighted by King, evidence for large-scale cattle processing makes comparisons between sites hard to interpret (Maltby 1994: 88). How many of the animals from the processing sites were important for traction? If numbers of cattle have increased proportionally with the Roman occupation it is possible that animals are being killed earlier, following a period of secondary exploitation. Sites such as Pasture Lodge Farm, Lincolnshire, report some 50 percent of animals being slaughtered before full maturity (Leary 1998: 51). Therefore it is highly likely that the remaining 50 percent are being kept for secondary products. Dairying during this period is also likely to have been important due to the storage potential of cheese.

Linking Functionality with Perceptions

It can be seen that the trends in exploitation of cattle secondary products has seen considerable change over the time frame in question, generally with greater reliance on one type or another depending on the period. Secondary exploitation during the Neolithic to Iron Age seems to indicate an even dichotomy between dairying and traction, although the need for traction seems to become more important from the Romano-British period onwards. The greatest advancements in relation to 'improvement' of cattle also appear in this period where animals are evidently imported from overseas; also it appears that trade and specific exploitation, for example through butchery sites, and 'knackers yards', occurred (Done 1986: 145).

Issues of trade and specialisation have recently been reinforced by research into the butchery practice from the Romano-British period (Seetah 2004; Seetah in prep). The main methodology involved the replication of cut marks from a number of archaeological assemblages in order to identify the patterns of butchery from this period. The Romano-British period was of particular value as urban Romano-British sites tended to show a great deal of uniformity in how the animals were apparently processed. The results indicated a principle of butchery clearly based on a need for quick and efficient carcass dismemberment.

Implement and technical specialisations were apparent and it was speculated that a degree of cross trade interaction must have taken place in order for the level of tool specialisation to have occurred (Seetah 2004).

Linking this into the information highlighted in earlier sections of this paper it is clear that the Romano-British period shows evidence of a significant shift in the level, if not the diversity, of exploitation. Clearly it can be seen that secondary products had played a major role in the exploitation of cattle up to this point, not only influencing the morphology of the animals, but also the numbers of animals kept and their overall value as a symbol of wealth. However, there is tangible evidence for a dramatic shift in the level of exploitation for meat, and the way this resource itself was used.

Up to the Romano-British period it might be argued that cattle were indeed seen as primarily a beast of burden. Despite evidence from the Continent to suggest that cattle in the rest of the Empire were kept principally for traction (Murphy *et al* 2000), it would appear that in the urban and military enclaves (both of which exhibit a similar, systematic method of butchery) of Roman Britain, cattle were mainly a source of meat.

This is the point at which the current research potentially has the means to make the furthest reaching contributions. The patterns of butchery seen, and the tools associated with what is arguably a burgeoning if not already established trade, point towards a set of socio-cultural factors that are not generally discussed when looking at faunal remains from a purely economic standpoint. While we might be able to speculate from the numbers of bones found on Romano-British sites that certain socio-economic developments were being made, the fact that tangible results from the butchery experimentation point to clearly visible patterns of dismemberment, as well as specific trade implements (Seetah 2004), could signify a potential transition that is indicative of further reaching attitudes.

Looking back at the periods previous to the Romano-British, it is apparent that secondary products, in particular traction and dairying were of particular importance. Cattle would appear to have been viewed as a multipurpose animal that were generally kept at least until the end of their working lives in most instances. It must be remembered that these animals more than likely shared the homes, in separate but joined pens, and therefore to some extent the living environment, of their keepers. Aside from providing the more obvious secondary products of traction and dairy produce, their dung was used for fuel and the warmth generated from their bodies was potentially an important heat source during colder weather. These less apparent (archaeologically speaking) secondary products as well as the closer proximity that these animals potentially shared with their owners is likely to have had profound implications for the way in which they were viewed and perceived within the farmer's mind, and in the wider community.

This viewpoint potentially indicates a far greater level of significance attributed to cattle than if the animal was raised and kept predominately for meat. Animals kept primarily for meat are likely to feature less in ritual activity, as the act of their sacrifice arguably has only slightly more significance than if they are being slaughtered for meat on a routine basis. Sacrifice of a larger animal and one that has a broader range of uses makes the act of sacrifice, and consequent perception associated with that act, far more significant. In short, while it is axiomatic that meat was a very important resource from cattle, the fact that the cow was also of such importance for other purposes is likely to have given it special significance. To reinforce this, one need only look at the way this species appears in iconography and in religious / cult settings on a wider geographic basis to appreciate not only how important cattle were, but also how valued socio-culturally they must have been.

What must also be remembered is that the functions and potential attitudes implied from the Neolithic onwards through faunal research, are arguably far more fluid than we are able to establish from the assemblages studied. It is likely that fluctuations noted from period to period are in fact a function of discreet advances in land use and progressive land expansion. However, the general view of the animal changes little as its overall functionality has not altered considerably, of course this only remains true until something dramatic happens to shift this balance.

Focusing on the evidence from the Romano-British period, in particular the research that points to a highly systematic means of meat processing, there would appear to have been a distinct divergence that potentially impacted on the population as a whole. The view of the cow seems to have shifted from being seen as a multipurpose, symbolically significant animal (the Romans had a strong sacrificial association with cattle; for example, white animals were sacrificed to 'celestial deities' and black cattle reserved for 'infernal deities (Urquhart 1983: 82)) to one with more importance as a source of meat protein. Certainly it would appear that not enough is made of the changes in cattle size. While the social developments of the Romano-British and subsequent periods appear to indicate a need for greater work potential, initiating improvements in size, it is not out of the question that the reversal in diminution in size may indicate a desire to increase size rapidly for slaughter. Drawing on modern parallels the size of cattle, and indeed the other major domesticates, have been increased considerably in most cases purely for increases in meat production.

This is not to imply that cattle were not seen as animals of ritual significance, more that they were progressively needed to meet an increase in demand for meat. Consequently their main significance moves from one associated with a range of activities to one based on meat production and procurement. If the rationale that perception is linked to functionality is adhered too, then the economically visible shift in use, based on increased numbers of animals seen in urban Romano-British sites (Maltby 1981; 1994), systematic butchery and trade specific implements, should be indicative of a subtle shift in perceptions.

From the various strands of evidence available, and in particular the tangible indications elucidated from the cut mark analysis, it can be suggested that certainly from urban Romano-British sites, cattle are no longer afforded the same level of socio-cultural importance and are in fact seen as far more of a 'commodity'. The move in terms of importance is arguably balanced by a complimentary shift in their economic value, at the expense of ritual / symbolic significance. While impossible to qualify without further research, the butchery from the Romano-British period brings to mind the highly organised, 'commercial practices' of the modern meat industry, of which the author has personal experience. This should not be taken to imply that the Romano-British meat processors were dealing with carcasses in the same dispassionate manner in which modern abattoirs function; rather that if the meat processing of animals in general (not just cattle) had become orchestrated into stages of slaughter and dismemberment for greater efficiency, then potentially the individuals involved in animal husbandry were not involved in the slaughter and dismemberment process. It is likely that animals were brought to urban enclaves on the hoof in order to meet the demand that was apparently being generated (Maltby 1989); this in itself would point to a compartmentalisation of the meat procurement process resulting in less contact by urban inhabitants with the animals they consumed. This may not have been the case for the smaller domesticates such as pig and sheep, but it is probable that the larger cattle were raised away from the urban setting. This may have potentially led to a similar, if not quite so pronounced, detachment by the urban populations with the rural environment and related experiences that are apparent in modern industrialised societies. With the establishment of urban enclaves it is likely that a certain disconnection may have already occurred with wild animals; as the above demonstrates it is probable that this extended to include associated domestic animals as they no longer formed part of the urban faunal 'menagerie'.

Furthermore, it is potentially the case that the horse became more important for traction, horses being more efficient beasts of burden then cattle. Conversely cattle are a more efficient ruminant and therefore are better at converting plant material into protein. This combination of factors would ultimately reduce their importance for traction and increase their value for meat production. These issues, pooled with a potentially new attitude to animals as a whole brought in with the invading peoples, would certainly seem to support the notion that cattle in the Romano-British period were effectively starting to be seen as a strictly economic 'commodity', a pattern that potentially continued and was reinforced in the ensuing periods.

Conclusion

Humans are exploitative; this is an undeniable truth regarding our attitude to the environment and the animals within it. We envelop our exploitation in a mantle of culture that permits our utilization to continue. This point effectively outlines why it is of paramount importance to incorporate broader interpretations of animal perceptions into the types of information zooarchaeological research can divulge. In effect, whether we are interested in the economic / subsistence strategies or perceptions of animals it is clear that each impact on the other.

It can be argued that although many perceptions of animals relate to species that have limited 'economic' value to the society in question, there is still an element of 'functionality impacting on symbolism' that would certainly be of importance in attempting to evaluate the representational perception of the main domesticates. Using cattle to illustrate this point it is clear that to many societies across the globe, this domesticate is perhaps one of the most economically significant species; key to this broad economic value is the multifunctional manner in which this species is exploited. In tandem, there are few animals that have commanded the same ritual / cult and symbolic associations both spatially and chronologically as cattle have. It is evident that the sheer presence of a lion, for example, commands a considerable sense of awe; however associations of courage, vigour and strength are derived from the animal's hunting ability and defence of its pride / territory; the wolf is both revered and persecuted because of adeptness at hunting; the fox is considered guile and wily because of its adaptability; all of these perceptions are as much based on the way the animal functions within its environment as they are on physical presence and appearance. Thus, while there have certainly been considerable changes in the appearance and stature of cattle, we must not forget the impacts function and perceived role in the environment and society have on associated perceptions.

Therefore, we need to be aware that changes in the use of the animal are likely to be coupled with a change in the perception of the animal. These changes are frequently interpreted as a series of individual / discreet stages when in fact the whole process is likely to have been far more fluid; perceptions of animals are dynamic and reflect the attitudes of the people as the animal itself evolves within their environment. The conceptualisations / perceptions that are attributed to an animal surely echo something of the value the animal has; be that as a commodity or otherwise. Attitudes towards animals are ultimately based on how they may have been perceived due to the benefits they conferred because of the advances they allowed early humans and subsequent populations to make. These cultural attributes and attitudes need not be beyond the remit of zooarchaeologists. We must remember that many of the figurines and statues of any given society that are studied in depth by other branches of archaeology, will invariably have their naissance in the animals that zooarchaeologists study on a day-to-day basis. Therefore, we should attempt to move beyond purely economic interpretations from the bone material studied and not wait for these factors to be highlighted from the study of other artefacts. To reinforce this point, I would add to our list of secondary products non-economic factors such as the place of animals within our society / the symbolic and cult representations that they personify and the fluctuating cultural perceptions dependent on our uses and modes of exploitation.

Acknowledgements

I would like to take this opportunity to express my sincere thanks to Mark Maltby, who directed my initial enquiries towards this line of research and Dr Preston Miracle for his continued and invaluable support and advice. Special thanks to the editor, Dr Aleks Pluskowski, for his time, patience and advice not just with this particular paper, but countless other projects; and finally Peterhouse, Cambridge for providing the essential financial assistance that has allowed me to continue this line of research.

References

Allen, T. (1990). *An Iron Age and Romano-British Enclosed Settlement at Watkins Farm, Northmoor, Oxon*, Oxford University Commission for Archaeology, Oxford.

Barker, G. (1985). *Prehistoric Farming in Europe*, Cambridge, Cambridge University Press.

Bartosiewicz, L., Van Neer, W. and Lentacker, A. (1997). *Draught Cattle: their Osteological Identification and History*, Tervuren, Annales Science Zoologique.

Bowman, J. (1977). *Animals for Man*, London, Edward Arnold Ltd.

Charles, M. Halsted, P., and Jones, G. (1998). 'The archaeology of fodder', *Environmental Archaeology*, 1, 1-15.

Clutton-Brock, J. (1981). *Domesticated Animals from Early Times*, London, Heinmann.

Davis, P. and Dent, A. (1966). *Animals that Changed the World*, London, Phoenix House.

De Cupere, B., Lentacker, A., Van Neer, W., Waelkens, M., and Verslype, L. (2000). 'Osteological evidence for the draught use of cattle: first application of a new methodology', *International Journal of Osteoarchaeology*, 10, 254-67.

Done, G. (1986). 'The animal bones from areas A & B', in, M. Millett and D. Graham (eds.), *Excavations in the Romano-British Small Town at Neatham, Hampshire 1969-79*, Hampshire, Hampshire Field Club.

Fries, R. and Ruvinsky, A. (eds.) (1999). *The Genetics of Cattle*, Oxon, CABI Publishing.

Grant, A. (1975). 'The animal bones', in B. Cunliffe (ed.), *Excavations at Porchester Castle – Roman*, London, Society of Antiquaries.

Grant, A. (1984). 'Animal husbandry in Wessex and the Thames Valley', in B. Cunliffe and D. Miles (eds), *Aspects of Iron Age in Central Southern Britain*, Oxford, University of Oxford Committee for Archaeology.

Grant, A. (1991). 'Animal bones', in, B. Cunliffe and C. Poole (ed.), *Danebury: an Iron Age Hillfort in Hampshire. Vol 5: the Excavations 1979-88: the Finds*, London, Council for British Archaeology.

Hambleton, E. (1999). *Animal Husbandry Regimes in Iron Age Britain*, Oxford, BAR British Series 282.

Jackson, W. (1943). 'Animal bones', in R. Wheeler (ed.), *Maiden Castle, Dorset*, London, The Society of Antiquaries.

Jope, M. and Grigson, C. (1965). 'Faunal remains', in A. Keiller (ed.), *Windmill Hill and Avebury – 1925-39*, Oxford, Clarendon Press.

King, A. (1984). 'Animal bones and the dietary identity of military and civilian groups in Roman Britain, Germany and Gaul', in T. Blagg and A. King (eds.), *Military and Civilian in Roman Britain: Cultural Relationships in a Frontier Province*, Oxford, BAR British Series 136.

Leary, R. (1998). *Excavations at the Romano-British Settlement at Pasture Lodge Farm, Long Bennington, Lincolnshire, 1975-77 by H. M. Wheeler*, Lincoln, Trent & Peak Archaeology Trust.

Legge, A. (1981). 'The agricultural economy', in R. Mercer (ed.), *Grimes Graves, Norfolk, Excavations 1971-2: Vol 1*, London, HMSO.

Maltby, M. (1981). 'Iron Age, Romano-British and Anglo-Saxon animal husbandry – a review of the faunal evidence', in M. Jones and G. Dimbleby (eds.), *The Environment of Man: the Iron Age to the Anglo-Saxon Period*, Oxford, BAR British Series 87.

Maltby, J. M. (1984). 'Animal bones and the Romano-British economy', in C. Grigson and J. Clutton-Brock (eds.), *Animals and Archaeology 4: Husbandry in Europe*, Oxford, BAR International Series 227.

Maltby, J. M. (1989). 'Urban and rural variation in the butchery of cattle in Romano-British Hampshire', in D. Serjeantson and T. Waldron (eds.), *Diets and Crafts in Towns*, Oxford, BAR British Series 199.

Maltby, M. (1990). 'The exploitation of animals in the Stonehenge environs in the Neolithic and Bronze Age', in J. Richards (ed.), *The Stonehenge Environs Project*, London, English Heritage.

Maltby, M. (1993). 'Animal bones', in P. Woodward, J. Davies and A. Graham (eds.), *Excavations at the Old Methodist Chapel and Greyhound Yard, Dorchester, 1981-1984*, Dorchester, Dorset Natural History and Archaeological Society.

Maltby, M. (1994). 'The meat supply of Roman Dorchester and Winchester', in A. Hall and H.

Kenward (eds.), *Urban-Rural Connexions: Perspectives from Environmental Archaeology*, Oxford, Oxbow.

McCormick, F. (1992). 'Early faunal evidence for dairying', *Oxford Journal of Archaeology*, 11, 2, 201-9.

Milisaukas, S. and Kruk, J. (1991). 'Utilization of cattle fro traction during the later Neolithic in southeastern Poland', *Antiquity*, 65, 562-6.

Murphy, P. Albarella, U. Germany, M. and Lock, A. (2000). 'Production, imports and status: biological remains from a Late Roman farm at Great Holts Farm, Boreham, Essex, UK', *Environmental Archaeology*, 5, 35-48.

Nodcle, A. (2000). 'Large vertebrate remains', in E. Price (ed.), *Frocester: A Romano-British Settlement, its Antecedents and Successors*, Stonehouse, Gloucester and District Archaeological Research Group.

Seetah, K. (2004). 'Multidisciplinary approach to Romano-British cattle butchery', in M. Maltby (ed.), *Intergrating Zooarchaeology*, Oxford, Oxbow.

Seetah, K. in prep. 'Romano-British butchery practice: new light on an old trade'.

Serjeantson, D. (1995). 'Animal bones', in R. Cleal, K. Walker and R. Montague (eds.), *Stonehenge in its Landscape: Twentieth-century Excavations*, London, English Heritage.

Sherratt, A. (1981). 'Plough and pastoralism', in I. Hodder, G. Issacs and N. Hammond (eds.), *Patterns of the Past*, Cambridge, Cambridge University Press.

Sherratt, A. (1983). 'The secondary exploitation of animals in the old world', *World Archaeology*, 15, 1, 90-103.

Urquhart, J. (1983). *Animals on the Farm*, London, MacDonald & Co.

Zimmerman Holt, J. (1996). 'Beyond optimisation: alternative ways of examining animal exploitation', *World Archaeology*, 28, 1, 89-109.

Red Deer's Role in Social Expression on the Isles of Scotland

James, T. Morris

Introduction

This paper is part of an ongoing project examining the relationships between humans and red deer on the isles of Scotland. The aim of this project is to take a broad chronological view of the economic and social significance of red deer to the inhabitants of these isles. The research area consists of the four main island groups that are located off Scotland's north and western coasts: Orkney, Shetland, the Inner Hebrides and the Outer Hebrides (*Figure 2.1*).

This research was carried out using published and where available, unpublished faunal reports. Studies by Hambleton (1999) and King (1978, 1984, 1999) have shown it is possible to create a synthesis using published data. This study differs slightly in that it concentrates on one species over a large chronological span (Mesolithic to modern day). Syntheses of this nature are and will become increasingly important in zooarchaeology as developer-led archaeology is now resulting in a large number of site-specific reports, where the time and monetary resources are not always available to place the faunal data within a regional or chronological framework.

The literature search for this project revealed hundreds of excavation reports, but unfortunately many did not contain faunal data. The quantifiable faunal data found were entered into a database and split into separate entries per time period. The literature search resulted in ninety-nine entries from sixty sites, with sixteen of the sites being multi-period. Some faunal reports were found from early 20th century publications that are discussed in the text but were not included in the database as the faunal data was not quantified. The majority of the faunal data came from the Outer Hebrides and Orkney (*Table 2.1*).

Shetland produced the smallest amount of faunal data, mostly consisting of antler rather than skeletal material. In the faunal reports examined, red deer were represented by three bones; two from the late Neolithic site of Scord of Brouster, a metacarpal and navicular-cuboid, were only tentative identifications, as the material was too eroded for the author to be sure (Noddle 1986), whilst the red deer bone from the broch at Scalloway (Sullivan 1998) was a skull fragment which may have been transported in with antler. None of the antler documented in the reports was unshed. The available published faunal data indicates that red deer may not have been present on Shetland, and that the antler present on some sites could have been imported from Orkney, mainland Scotland or Norway.

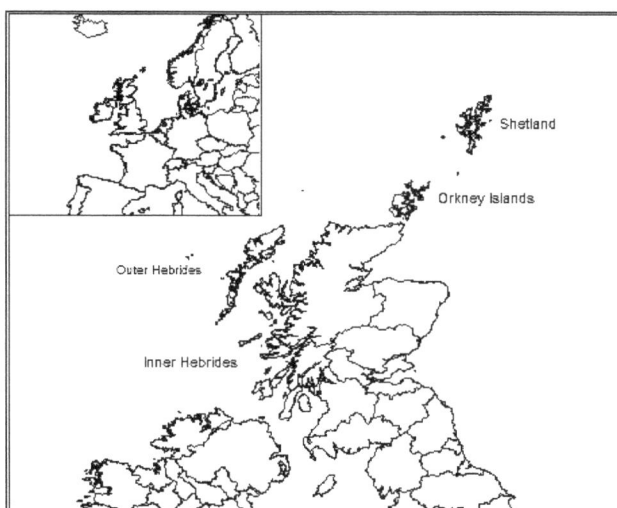

Figure 2.1: Map showing the location of the island groups

Period \ Island group	Outer Hebrides (21)	Inner Hebrides (14)	Orkney (18)	Shetland (6)
Mesolithic (8500- 4000BC)		4		
Neolithic (4000-1500BC)	3		10	1
Bronze Age (1500-700BC)	6	2	3	
Iron Age (700BC - AD400)	28	7	6	4
Pictish/Norse (AD 400-1100)	7	2	5	
Medieval (AD 1100-1500)	2	1	4	
Post-Medieval (AD 1500-1700)	1			1
Multi-period	2	2	2	
Total	49	14	30	6

Table 2.1: Number of entries for each time period, per island group. The number in brackets indicates the number of sites.

The study indicated that red deer were an important source of food to the inhabitants of the other island groups from the Mesolithic to the Iron Age. There appears to be a decline in the exploitation of red deer on some islands from the Iron Age, with red deer possibly becoming extinct on some islands at this time. On Orkney, red deer are not found in published medieval contexts, and possibly became extinct from the island group at this time. Red deer do continue to inhabit the Inner and Outer Hebrides in the medieval period and remain an important food source on some islands.

During the study it became clear that red deer where not only important as a source of food, but were possibly treated and viewed in a different way to other animals – both wild and domestic – by the islands' inhabitants, as demonstrated by the number of special deposits. This paper aims to explore this aspect of the study.

Red deer: a liminal creature

At the Neolithic settlement of Links of Noltland on the Isle of Westray, Orkney, a burial deposit of at least fifteen red deer was discovered during excavation. The deer were deposited together in an area that covered approximately 3.5m by 3m, and it also appeared that they had all been deposited in one episode (Sharples 2000). The analysis by Armour-Chelu (1992) using Lowe's (1967) methodology, suggested that the group consisted of eleven deer of fourteen months of age, two aged two years, and two aged five years. It was also possible to sex some of the deer, the results of which indicated that the majority of the younger deer were female, and two of the five-year-old deer were male (Armour-Chelu 1992:267). There were also a number of other notable features about the deposit; a large set of antlers, a large cod and two bird wings were also deposited along with the deer. Furthermore, the deer, with one exception, were all laid on their left side (Sharples 2000).

It is possible the remains were from a feast, but the report clearly notes that many of the bones were articulated, and Armour-Chelu; stresses that no butchery marks were found (1992:266). It therefore seems likely that the meat from the deer may not have been consumed. Why then should such a valuable economic resource be wasted in this way? One plausible functional explanation could be that the remains are of deer that were feeding upon the crops growing around the settlement and were therefore slaughtered (Armour-Chelu 1992:267). However this does not explain why the deer were not processed for consumption. Also contemporary studies of red deer indicate that they occupy a set territory, and that the males and females live in separate groups, except when rutting, (Clutton-Brock *et al* 1982:191-197). If all the deer were deposited at the same time, then humans could have purposely gone out to hunt both the female and male groups, or they were hunted when the deer were rutting in September to November, at which time the majority of crops would have been harvested.

If we look at the type of contexts that red deer are found in during the Neolithic in Orkney, we find that they occur in both mortuary and settlement contexts. In some mortuary contexts, deer appear to be the dominant mammal. The Knowe of Yarso, a long stalled cairn on the isle of Rousay, contained a number of semi-articulated / unarticulated red deer remains, with a MNI (Minimum Number of Individuals) of 34 animals (Platt 1935). The type of methodology used by the author for the calculation of MNI is unknown. The deer were found in all parts of the chamber, but the majority came from the inner chamber 3B, which produced a MNI of 10. The entrance to chamber 3B is only 2 to 3 feet high (*Figure 2.2*), and therefore it is unlikely that the bones were introduced by natural means, as suggested by Barber (1988). Red deer would simply have been too large to get down the passageway and therefore would have to have been brought in by humans.

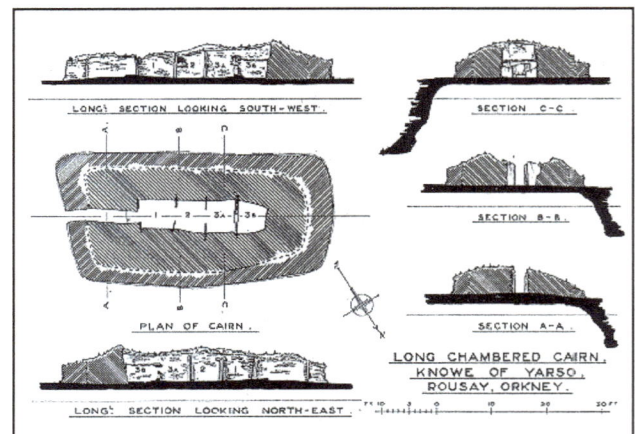

Figure 2.2: Plan and sections of the chambered carin of Yarso (Callander and Walter 1935).

A number of theories have been put forward to explain the deposition of animal remains within chambered tombs, ranging from sacrificial offerings (Clutton-Brock 1979), funerary feasting (Renfrew 1979) through to totemic practices (Hedges 1983, Jones 1998).

Jones views the animals deposited within the cairns as being representative of the social use of the landscape surrounding the location of the cairn. Therefore the high numbers of red deer present at Yarso can be attributed to its position high up a hillside, often inhabited by red deer (Jones 1998). If this is the case, then the cairns which are near to Yarso in a similar landscape, may well have a high proportion of red deer in their faunal assemblages.

The Knowe of Ramsay, a chambered cairn very close to Yarso, (*Figure 2.3*), is also dominated by red deer remains, with a MNI of 14 (Platt 1936). However, the nearby chambered cairn of Blackhammer, which contained a few fragments of red deer in its faunal assemblage, was dominated by sheep and cattle (Platt 1937a). Further along the coast, the chambered cairn at Midhowe contained only two fragments of red deer bone (Platt 1934), and this cairn is at a significantly lower altitude than Yarso. Studies of red deer have indicated that separate groups often keep to the same range (Clutton-Brock et al 1982:191-197), which could mean that people may have associated particular places with red deer. There is a strong case for a possible form of totemic practice associated with the area of Yarso, although other nearby cairns would require examination to confirm this theory.

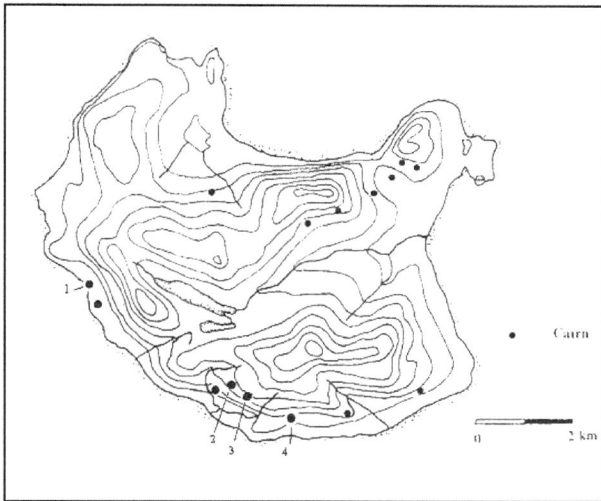

Figure 2.3: The distribution of chambered cairns on Rousay. 1:Midhowe; 2:Ramsay; 3:Yarso; 4:Blackhammer (after Renfrew 1979:14, altered by author).

Of the chambered cairns excavated, Yarso and Ramsay are the only ones in Orkney where red deer elements are common within the chambers. They may not be abundant, but along with cattle and sheep, red deer are the only other animal to be recovered from the majority of chambered cairns, (Barker 1983). In all the published reports of chambered cairns from Orkney examined for this study, red deer remains are always found within the chamber, (Baker 1983, Clutton-Brock 1979, Halpin 1997, Platt 1934, 1935, 1936, 1937a, 1937b, Smith et al 1994). Many of the domestic animal elements recovered are often from outside the chamber, possibly representing evidence of feasting similar to that found in the vicinity of Bronze Age barrows in southern England (Allen et al 1995).

The majority of wild fauna are found inside the chambered cairns, and in some cases only certain parts are represented. Where birds are deposited in chambered cairns, the remains predominantly consist of the wings, head and feet only. These elements are often missing from settlement midden deposits (Jones 1998). Included within red deer burials / deposits at the Links of Noltland were two bird wings, perhaps indicating that the deposit

was viewed in the same way as chambered cairn deposits. At the Bay of Skaill on the Isle Mainland, Orkney, there is a deposit of four red deer. The similarity between this deposit and that of the Links of Noltland is that they are both next to boundary walls (Sharples 2000). Perhaps these burials represented displays of power and control of an important animal. The lack of butchery marks on the deer from the Links of Noltland has been taken to indicate that the red deer were not defleshed (Sharples 2000), and therefore could have been symbolic of control as well as the capability to waste an economic resource, through conspicuous non-consumption.

It appears that during the Neolithic of Orkney, red deer were deposited in specific places. Ross (1967) brings together evidence suggesting that deer in the Iron Age were considered capable of shape shifting, forming a liminal category (a state of transition / existence where a being or object is between two types of social definition, see Van Gennep 1909 and Turner 1967, 1969) between the living and supernatural worlds. The areas where red deer were deposited can also be considered to be liminal in nature; the boundaries that circled settlements were a means of symbolically and functionally dividing the world; betwixt and between worlds, they were neither in one world or the other (Huntington and Metcalf 1991:30). Therefore the boundaries may represent areas in which objects of a liminal nature were deposited (Hill 1995:82). The same is true for chambered cairns that could represent a boundary between the dead and living worlds.

Other, possibly ritual deposits of red deer are also found in areas which could be considered liminal. At the Outer Hebrides Bronze Age site of Cladh Hallen, antlers were often found buried within postholes and pits after they have gone out of use. Antlers are often deposited in monuments in the south of England in such a way. At the late Neolithic site of Durrington Walls 440 antler picks were recovered in total, 80% from the southern circle where almost every posthole had a pick placed in the packing (Wainwright and Longworth 1971:354). There also appears to be a pattern to the distribution of antler and deer bones within the nearby contemporary site of Woodhenge (Pollard 1995)

Special red deer deposits were also found at A'Cheardach Bheag, an Iron Age wheelhouse situated on South Uist, Outer Hebrides (Fairhurst 1971), where a red deer jaw kerb was discovered (*Figure 2.4*). It ran in an arc 2 feet 6 inches out from the centre of the hearth, consisting of half a red deer mandible, with the ascending ramus thrust into the ground, teeth downward, and each overlapping at least one, and frequently two, of the adjacent bones (Fairhurst 1971). The bones were not burnt so we can therefore assume that the hearth was no longer in use at the time of deposition. Perhaps they were deposited when the hearth went out of use. The middle Iron Age broch at Howe, Orkney also contained a special deposit of red deer. Within a well on the edge of the settlement, a deposit of a MNI of 6 red deer was discovered. Many of the bones recovered were burnt and derived from younger animals, leading to suggestions that these represented roasted whole carcasses of young deer (Smith *et al* 1994:149). The report does not mention the other 428 red deer bones from this phase being deposited in the same way. Perhaps the deer remains from the well are the remnants of a feast, or some other event. What is certain is that red deer were an important animal to the people of Howe during the middle Iron Age, and would have provided over half of the meat consumed by the occupants of the settlement (Smith *et al* 1994:148). The well may have been considered a special feature, and was no longer in use when the deer were deposited. Therefore these animals may have been an offering. It is unknown if they were butchered and consumed in a normal way, but they were certainly deposited differently.

Figure 2.4: Photo of the red deer jaw kerb from A'Cheardach Bheag, (Fairhurst 1971).

The deposits at Howe, Clad Hallen and A'Cheardach Bheag are in features that may have gone out of use. The lack of burning on the mandible at A'Cheardach Bheag, certainly indicates that the hearth would no longer have been in use. Tilley (1996:63-64) believes that the social behaviour of the deer, and the gender and fertility symbolism of antler growth made deer a symbolic resource, offering rich metaphorical and metonymic possibilities for drawing and creating allusions and analogies. Therefore the seasonal re-growth of antler may have led prehistoric people to see them as a powerful symbol for the renewal of life. Red deer remains could have been placed in postholes and other features as an offering to thank the spirit world, similar to the interpretation of offerings in Iron Age pits in the south of England (Cunliffe 1992).

It would appear that red deer were perceived in a special way during the Neolithic and the Iron Age on both Orkney and the Outer Hebrides. Unfortunately, we have little evidence from the Inner Hebrides indicating any special relationship during prehistory. Red deer were probably viewed as liminal creatures, possibly due to their re-growth of antler. Red deer were also neither fully wild or domestic, but appear to have been managed and even transported to the Islands in the Neolithic (Serjeantson 1990). In terms of possible ritual deposits they were treated differently to domestic animals. For example at the Iron Age wheelhouse at Sollas, on North Uist, Outer Hebrides, neither red deer nor any other wild animal were included in the animal burials that are found within the house (Finlay 1991). Red deer were not treated in the same way as other fauna – both domestic and wild – and possibly had an ambiguous status between the two. During the Orcadian Neolithic they were deposited in places of a possible liminal nature. Due to the lack of Neolithic faunal assemblages, it is unknown whether they were treated in such a way in the Outer and Inner Hebrides. Red deer could also have been used as displays of power. The deposit at Links of Noltland may have been a message by the community, to others that they had economic power and control to dispose of a great number of red deer. It is possible the deer jaw kerb at A'Cheardach Bheag was constructed as a sign of power, of control over a powerful and ritually important animal. In the Iron Age midden at Northton, Outer Hebrides (Finlay 1984), and the Bronze Age middens at Point of Buckquoy, Orkney, (Rackham 1989), are deposits that contain large amounts of red deer bones. These could also be displays of power, expressing 'look how much red deer we can hunt, consume and therefore have power over'.

What is certain is that red deer were viewed in a special way. At the Iron Age Kilpheder wheelhouse on South Uist, red deer motifs were scratched into some of the pottery; these are the only examples of animal depictions on pottery from the isles of Scotland (Lethbridge 1952). It appears that to the prehistoric populations of Orkney and the Outer Hebrides red deer were an ambiguous animal, neither wild nor domestic, and possibly a powerful symbol for the renewal of life.

Red deer: a creature of status

The available evidence indicates that red deer were exploited for a number of economic and social reasons from the Neolithic to the Iron Age, in Orkney, the Outer Hebrides and the Inner Hebrides. Although most of the evidence for the use of deer as a symbolic tool comes from Neolithic Orkney, they continued to be important in the Iron Age both symbolically (see above) and as a source of meat, as shown at Howe (Smith *et al* 1994) and Warebeth Broch (Sellar 1989) on Orkney, Dun Ardtreck (Mackie 1965), Dun Mor Vaul (Noddle 1974), Dun Bhuirg (Noddle 1981) and Dun Cul Bhuirg (Noddle 1978-80) in the Inner Hebrides, and Northton (Finlay

1984), Bostadh, Berie and Cnip (Mulville and Thoms *in prep*) in the Outer Hebrides.

It would therefore appear that venison was more important for the Iron Age communities of the Inner Hebrides and Outer Hebrides than Orkney. But there is little Iron Age faunal data published for Orkney and more work is needed before a meaningful conclusion can be reached. In the Outer Hebrides, the Isles of Lewis and Harris seem to be the main areas of exploitation. This is possibly due to the islands size, which could of help limit competition with domestic species. On the Inner Hebrides red deer remained an important supply of meat, and a form of stock management may even have been taking place as suggested by the ageing data from Dun Mor Vaul (Noddle 1974).

By the end of the Iron Age red deer appear to have been in decline. At Howe on Orkney (Smith *et al* 1994), the percentage of red deer in the faunal assemblages peaks in the fourth and first centuries BC and starts to decline from that point, and from the fourth to eighth century AD only 5% of the NISP assemblages consist of red deer bones. On South Uist, Outer Hebrides, the percentage of red deer also drops at the end of the Iron Age, but not to the same extent as Orkney, whilst the Viking sites of Bornish (Mulville 1999) and A'Cheardach Bheag (Finlay 1984) still contain around 10% red deer in their assemblages. There is also a decline in the amount of red deer in the Pictish assemblage from Dun Mor Vaul, Tiree, in the Inner Hebrides (Noddle 1974). It would therefore appear that during the late Iron Age and Pictish periods there is a drop in the utilisation of red deer, which continues in the Viking periods.

Unfortunately the limited amount of data on late Iron Age and Pictish faunal assemblages from the nearby mainland of Scotland prevents us from seeing if the drop in the utilisation of red deer occurred there as well. On the Outer Hebrides the use of red deer does not significantly decrease until the late Viking period. This may therefore indicate that the decline in exploitation of red deer on the Outer Hebrides was driven by cultural factors, a pattern which continues into the medieval period. On Orkney, deer are not found in early medieval contexts, and it would appear that they became extinct from the islands around this time. The evidence from the Outer Hebrides seems to indicate that red deer did continue to be utilised into the medieval period, as both Udal North on North Uist and A'Cheardach Mhor on South Uist still have red deer remains present, albeit in very small quantities (Finlay 1984).

The collected faunal data indicate that there is a drop in the utilisation of red deer from the Iron Age onwards. Special deposits are also no longer found, although Pictish iconography indicates that the red deer was still viewed as an important animal. Engravings of red deer are found on some of the earliest (Class I) Pictish stones and are sometimes found in close association with representations of dogs (Gordon 1964-66), indicating that the hunting of red deer may have been culturally important. The meanings of the Pictish stone symbols are thought to date back to the Iron Age and possibly beyond. The five mammals displayed on Pictish Class I stones – deer, dog, ox, pig and horse – are the same group of 'holy animals' mentioned by Celtic writers (*Ibid*), with the stag representing a spirit of the forest important in the hunt as well as a symbol of prosperity and fertility (Ritchie 1989). With the conversion of the Pictish kingdoms to Christianity in the 8th and 9th centuries, the engravings on the stones change to elaborate Christian iconography, categorised as Class II. Red deer are still represented on these stones, with some displaying both Christian symbols and hunting scenes with stags. It is possible that such hunting scenes alluded to the Christian soul in pursuit of Christ (the deer) and salvation (Foster 1996:95). The Class II stones are thought to have fulfilled three functions: to act as testimonies to the Church's claims to the land, to evoke high status and ritual authority of their secular patrons, and to reinforce a sense of Pictish identity through the use of symbols from Class I stones (*Ibid*). Therefore the inclusion of hunting scenes with deer may have displayed ecclesiastical and aristocratic territorial rights, the hunt and the status that comes with the right to hunt. These motifs may also have expressed their control over an animal that could still have been considered mystical.

Although there is an overall drop in the utilisation of red deer, they remain important on some sites. At the Columbian and later Benedictine medieval monastery on Iona, Inner Hebrides, 38% of the faunal assemblage from a long established midden dating from the 9th to the 13th centuries consisted of red deer (Noddle 1981). The faunal data indicates that the utilisation of red deer at the monastery may have changed over time with high amounts of astragali, calcanea and metatarsals being found in the lower layers of the midden and a greater diversity of elements being found towards the top (Noddle 1981). The high amount of back foot bones could indicate that hind limbs are being brought to the site, rather than the whole carcass; red deer haunches form a fairly convenient load for carrying over the shoulder. Also the island of Iona is probably too small to support a red deer population. The island has a land area of 7.76 km², which modern studies of red deer ranges suggest could only support a couple of animals, hardly a viable population (Clutton-Brock *et al* 1982). It is therefore likely that the red deer originated from the nearby larger Isle of Mull.

One of the reasons why so many red deer were brought to the monastery on Iona may be related to the prestigious status of the animals. A comparable pattern exists between the red deer MNE (Minimum Number of Elements) from the Iona monastery and the fallow deer MNE from Launceston Castle (Albarella and Davis 1996) in Cornwall, dating to the medieval period (*Figure 2.5*). Launceston Castle also has a high number of hind limb bones and it is thought that for every whole fallow deer

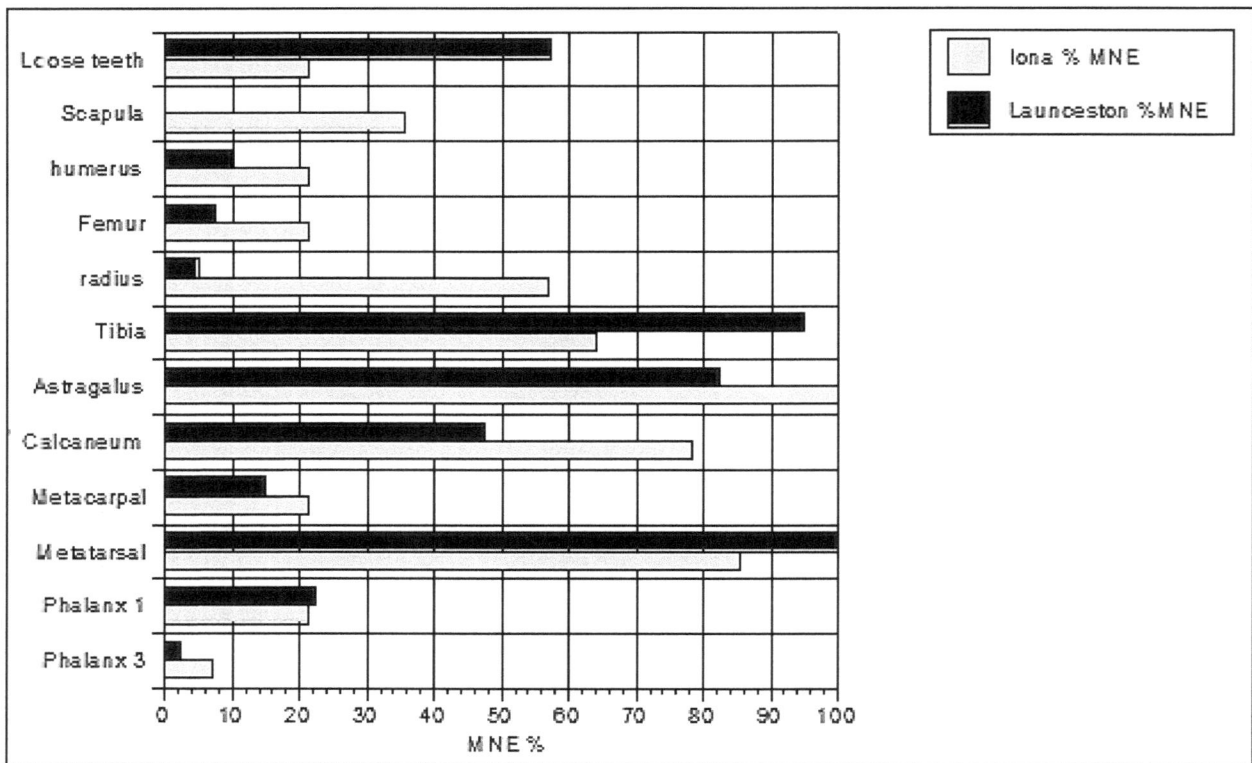

Figure 2.5: Percentage of Red deer MNE elements from Iona and Lauceston Castle.

carcass brought to the castle, some eight to ten haunches were brought in. The same pattern also occurs at Barnard Castle (Jones et al 1985) and Okehampton (Maltby 1982). In these cases the deer are being brought in as a high status food, and perhaps the same process is taking place at the Iona monastery, although not to the same degree, as analysis of element data from Iona does indicate that more whole deer were being brought in than at Launceston.

Although after the Iron Age the use of red deer in potential ritual deposits does not appear to continue, red deer may still be used in a symbolic manner. From the Anglo-Saxon period onwards in England, deer hunting became more popular amongst the elite and after the Norman Conquest many deer parks were established. Hunting by the 'common' people became outlawed and hunting deer was predominantly a sport of the elite, although poaching did take place. In the medieval period it appears that the nature of the inter-relation that existed between man and animals was dependent on the social position held (Grant 1988). The faunal data from Iona could suggest that red deer are being used in a similar way, as also indicated by the Pictish class II stones. Benedictine monastic houses in southern Britain also had access to venison and it is estimated that monastic corporations owned eight to nine percent of the deer parks in south-western Britain (Bond 1994). It seems that although hunting itself was forbidden by canon law, the consumption of venison was still undertaken, perhaps to reflect the status of the house, as accounts show that

venison was normally served when nobility were being entertained (Bond 2001).

Conclusion

Evidence of special red deer deposits from Orkney and the Outer Hebrides indicates that the species may have been used in a number of ritualistic ways. The deposits of red deer within chambered tombs indicate that on Orkney, it may have been conceptualised as a totemic animal used to identify with the landscape. It may also have been viewed as a liminal animal, possibly due to the yearly cycle of antler re-growth, and possibly used for displays of wealth and power through conspicuous non-consumption. On the island groups, with the exception of Shetland, red deer was also an important source of meat up to the late Iron Age. In this respect the island groups appear to differ from the mainland, where the utilisation of red deer as a meat source was minimal from the Neolithic onwards. Antler may have remained important symbolically but the majority of the evidence for this comes from the south of England.

From the Iron Age onwards the symbolic use of red deer seems to have changed. Red deer are no longer an important source of meat and there is a steady decline from the middle Iron Age onwards, although Pictish iconography indicates that the hunt may have become socially important. Evidence from Iona indicates that red deer were still being exploited for meat but possibly only as an indication of a group's status. On the mainland and in England, hunting of deer also become more important with the activity restricted to the aristocracy and elite. The hunting and consumption of deer become a symbolic means of expressing and maintaining one's position within society. Red deer may have been used in a similar way in the Inner Hebrides. If that is the case then one theme that is continuously present from the Neolithic to the medieval period in relation to the symbolic use of red deer is power. Red deer may have been used as symbols of power through conspicuous non-consumption in the Neolithic, whilst in the medieval period they may have been used as symbols of power through consumption.

Acknowledgments

My greatest debt is to the numerous authors listed in the bibliography, without their work, synthesis of this type would not be possible. Mark Maltby, Jacqui Mulville and Mike Parker-Pearson were of great help during the project that resulted in this article. I am grateful to Alek Pluskowski for inviting me to submit a paper and for his patience, to Krish Seeth for his comments on the first draft of this paper and Sarah-Jane Hathaway for her comments and continuing support.

References of Sites used in the project

Orkney

Armour-Chelu, J. M. (1992). *Vertebrate Resource Exploitation, Ecology, and Taphonomy in Neolithic Britain, with Special Reference to the Sites of Links of Noltland, Etton, and Maiden Castle*, unpublished PhD., UCL, Institute of Archaeology and British Museum.

Barker, G. (1983). 'The animal bones', in J. W. Hedges (ed.), *Isbister. A chambered Tomb in Orkney*, BAR British Series 115.

Clutton-Brock, J. (1979). 'Report of the mammalian remains other than rodents from Quanterness', in C. Renfrew (ed.), *Investigations in Orkney*, London, The Society of Antiquaries.

Hodgson, G. W. I, and Jones, A. (1982). 'The animal bone', in N. A. McGavin (ed.), Excavations at Kirkwall 1978, *Proceeding of the Society of Antiquaries of Scotland*, 112, 392-436.

MacCormick, F. (1984). 'Large mammal bone', in N. Sharples (ed.), 'Excavations at Pierowall Quarry, Westray, Orkney', *Proceedings of the Society of Antiquaries of Scotland*, 114, 75-125; Fiche 2, D10.

Noddle, B. A. (1983). 'Animal bones from Knap of Howar', in A. Ritchie (ed.), 'Excavation of a Neolithic farmstead at Knap of Howar, Papa Westray Orkney', *Proceedings of the Society of Antiquaries of Scotland*, 113, 40-121.

Noddle, B. (1976-77). 'The animal bones from Buckquoy, Orkney', in A. Ritchie (ed.), 'Excavations of Pictish and Viking-age farmsteads at Buckquoy, Orkney', *Proceeding of the Society of Antiquaries of Scotland*, 108, 174-227.

Paterson, L. (1998). 'Faunal remains', in E. McB, Cox, O. Owen and Pringle, D. (eds.), 'The discovery of medieval deposits beneath the Earl's Palace, Kirkwell, Orkney', *Proceedings of the Society of Antiquaries of Scotland*, 128, 567-580.

Rackham, J. D. (1986). 'An analysis of the animal remains', in C. D. Morris and N. Emey (eds.), 'The chapel and enclosure on the Brough of Deerness, Orkney:Survey and Excavation, 1975-1977', *Proceedings of the Society of Antiquaries of Scotland*, 116, 301-374.

Rackham, J. D. (1989). 'Area 6: the biological assemblage', in C. D. Morris (ed.), *The Birsay Bay Project, Volume 1*, Durham, University of Durham, Department of Archaeology.

Rackham, J. D. (1989). 'Excavations beside the brough road: The biological assemblage', in C. D. Morris (ed.), *The Birsay Bay Project, Volume 1*, Durham, University of Durham, Department of Archaeology.

Rackham, J. D. (1989). 'Excavation 1960: The biological assemblage', in C. D. Morris (ed.), *The Birsay Bay Project, Volume 1*, Durham, University of Durham, Department of Archaeology.

Rackham, J. D. Bramwell, D. Donaldson, A. M. Limbrey, S. Penelope, S. and Wheeler, A. (1989). 'Cutting 5 and 6: the biological assemblage and soil sample', in C. D. Morris (ed.), *The Birsay Bay Project, Volume 1*, Durham, University of Durham, Department of Archaeology.

Seller, T. J. (1989). 'Bone report', in B. Bell and C. Dickson (eds.), 'Excavations at Warebeth (Stromness cemetery) Broch, Orkney', *Proceedings of the Society of Antiquaries of Scotland*, 119, 101-131; Fiche C1- G2.

Seller, T. J. (1982). 'Bone material', in C. L. Curle (ed.), *Pictish and Norse Finds from the Brough of Birsay 1934-74*, Edinburgh, Society of Antiquaries of Scotland.

Smith, C. with the late Hodgson, G, W, I, Armitage, P, Clutton-Brock, J, Dickson, C, Holden, T. and Smith, B. B. (1994). 'Animal bone report', in B. B. Smith (ed.), *Howe: Four Millennia of Orkney Prehistory*, Edinburgh, Society of Antiquaries of Scotland Monograph.

Shetland

Halpin, E. (1995). 'Mammal bone', in S. P. Carter, R. P. J. McCullagh and A. MacSween (eds.), 'The Iron Age in Shetland: Excavations at five sites threatened by coastal erosion', *Proceedings of the Society of Antiquaries of Scotland*, 125, 429-482; Fiche 2, c7-c14

Halpin, E. (1996). 'Animal bone', in S. Carter and D. Fraser (eds.), 'The sands of Breckon, Yell, Shetland: Archaeological survey and excavation in an area of eroding windblown sand', *Proceedings of the Society of Antiquaries of Scotland*, 126, 271-301.

Noddle, B. (1986). 'Animal bones', in A. Whittle, M. Keith-Lucas, A. Milles, B. Noddle, S. Rees and J. C. C. Romans (eds.), *Scord of Brouster. An Early*

Agricultural Settlement on Shetland, Oxford, Oxford University Committee for Archaeology.

Smith, C. and Hodgson, G. W. (1983). 'Report on the animal remains', in D. Hall and W. J. Lindsay (eds.), 'Excavations at Scalloway Castle 1979 and 1980', *Proceedings of the Society of Antiquaries of Scotland*, 113, 554-593.

Sullivan, T. O'. (1998). 'The mammal bone', in N. Sharples (ed.), *Scalloway. A Broch, Late Iron Age settlement and Medieval Cemetery in Shetland*, Oxford, Oxbow.

Inner Hebrides

Grigson, C. and Mellars, P. (1987). 'The mammalian remains from the Middens', in P. Mellars (ed.), *Excavations on Oransay*, Edinburgh, Edinburgh University Press.

Harman, M. (1981). 'Animal remains from Machrins, Colonsay', in J. N. G. Ritchie (ed.), 'Excavations at Machrins, Colonsay', *Proceedings of the Society of Antiquaries of Scotland*, 111, 263-281.

Harman, M. (1983). 'Animal remains from Ardnave, Islay', in J. N. G. Ritchie and H. Welfare (eds.), 'Excavations at Ardnave, Islay', *Proceedings of the Society of Antiquaries of Scotland*, 113, 302-366.

Mackie, E. W. (1965). *Excavations on Two Gallered Dun's on Skye in 1964 and 1965. Interim Report*, Glasgow, Glasgow University.

McCormick, F. (1981). 'The animal bones from Ditch 1', in J. Barber (ed.), 'Excavations in Iona', *Proceedings of the Society of Antiquaries of Scotland*, 111, 282-380.

Mercer, J. (1978). 'The investigation of the King's cave, Isle of Jura, Argyll', *Glasgow Archaeological Journal*, 5, 44-70.

Noddle, B. (1981). 'A comparison of Mammalian Bones found in the Midden Deposit with others from the Iron age site of Dun Bhuirg', in R. Reece (ed.), *Excavations in Iona 1964 to 1974*, London, Institute of Archaeology.

Noddle, B. (1974). 'Report on the animal bones found at Dun Mor Vaul', in e. W. Mackie (ed.), *Dun Mor Vaul. An Iron Age Broch on Tiree.* Glasgow, University of Glasgow Press.

Noddle, B. (1978-80). 'Animal bones from Dun Cul Bhuirg, Iona', in J. N. G. Ritchie, and A. M. Lane (eds.), 'Dun Cul Bhuirg, Iona, Argyll', *Proceedings of the Society of Antiquaries of Scotland*, 110, 209-2.

Outer Hebrides

Finlay, J. (1984). *Faunal Evidence for Prehistoric Economy and Settlement in the Outer Hebrides to 400AD.* Unpublished Ph.D., Edinburgh.

Finlay, J. (1991). 'Animal bones', in E. Campbell (ed.), 'Excavations of a wheelhouse and other Iron Age structures at Sollas, North Uist, by R J C Atkinson in 1957', *Proceedings of the Society of Antiquaries of Scotland*, 121, 117-173; Fiche 1, D1-3, F10.

Haq ul, S. (1989). *Remains of Mammalian Fauna from Kildonan, South Uist Outer Hebrides*, unpublished MSc dissertation, Sheffield University.

Hamshaw-Thomas, J. F. (1991). *Fildonan South Uist Faunal Analysis, Interim Report on the 1991 Sample*, unpublished report.

Mulville, J. (2000). 'The faunal remains', in P. Foster and J. Pouncett (eds.), 'Excavations on Pabbay, 1996-1998: Dunan Ruadh (PY10) and the Bagh Ban Earth House (PY56)', in K. Branigan and P. Foster (eds.), *From Barra to Berneray*, Sheffield, Sheffield Acadmeic Press.

Mulville, J. (2000). 'The faunal remains', in P. Foster and J. Pouncett (eds.), 'Sampling excavations on Sandray and Mingulay, 1995-1996', in K. Branigan and P. Foster (eds.), *From Barra to Berneray*, Sheffield, Sheffield Acadmeic Press.

Mulville, J. and Thoms, J. in prep. *Animals and Ambiguity in the Iron Age of the Western Isles.*

Mulville, J. (1999). *The Faunal Remains from Bornish, South Uist.* Available from

http://www.cf.ac.uk/hisar/archaeology/reports/hebrides99/TheFaunalRemains.html [Accessed 20th June 2001]

Mulville, J. (1999). 'The faunal remains', in M. Parker Pearson and N. Sharples (eds.), *Between Land and Sea. Excavations at Dun Vulan, South Uist*, Sheffield, Sheffield Academic Press.

Serjeantson, D. (nd). *Mammal, Bird and Fish Remains from the Udal (north), N. Uist, Interim Report*, unpublished report.

Additional references

Allen, M. J. Morris, M. and Clark, R. H. (1995). 'Food for the living: a reassessment of a Bronze Age barrow at Buckskin, Basingstoke, Hampshire', *Proceedings of the Prehistoric Society*, 61, 157-189.

Armour-Chelu, J. M. (1992). Vertebrate Resource Exploitation, Ecology, and Taphonomy in Neolithic Britain, with Special Reference to the Sites of Links of Noltland, Etton, and Maiden Castle, unpublished Ph.D, UCL, Institute of Archaeology and British Museum.

Albarella, U. and Davis, S. J. M. (1996). 'Mammals and birds from Launceston Castle, Cornwall: decline in status and the rise of agriculture', *Circaea*, 12, 1, 1-156.

Barber, J. (1988). 'Isbister, Quanterness and the Point of Cott: The formation and testing of some middle range theories', in J. C. Barrett and I. A. Kinnes (eds.), *The Archaeology of Context in the Neolithic and Bronze Age*, Sheffield, Sheffield Academic Press.

Barker, G. (1983). 'The animal bones', in J. W. Hedges (ed.), *Isbister. A Chambered Tomb in Orkney*, BAR British Series 115.

Bond, C. J. (1994). 'Forests, chases, warrens and parks in medieval Wessex', in M. Aston and C. Lewis (eds.),

The Medieval Landscape of Wessex, Oxford, Oxbow Monograph.

Bond, J. (2001). 'Production and consumption of food and drink in the Mediaeval Monastery', in G. Kevill, M. Aston and T. Hall (eds.), *Monastic Archaeology*, Oxford, Oxbow.

Callander, G. J. and Walter, G. G. (eds.) (1935). 'A long, stalled cairn, The Knowe of Yarso, in Rousay, Orkney', *Proceeding of the Society of Antiquaries of Scotland*, 10, 325-351.

Clutton-Brock, J. (1979). 'Report of the mammalian remains other than rodents from Quanterness', in A. C. Renfrew (ed.), *Investigations in Orkney*, London, Society of Antiquaries.

Clutton-Brock, J. Guinness, F. E. Albon, S. D. (1982). *Red Deer. Behavior and Ecology of Two Sexes*, Edinburgh, Edinburgh University Press.

Cunliffe, B. (1992). 'Pits, preconceptions and propitiation in British Iron Age', *Oxford Journal of Archaeology*, 11, 1, 69-83.

Fairhurst, H. (1971). 'The Wheelhouse site A' Cheadach Bheag on Drimore Machair,

South Uist', *Glasgow Archaeological Journal*, 2, 72-106.

Foster, S. M. (1996). *Picts, Gaels and Scots*, London, Historic Scotland/Batsford.

Finlay, J. I. (1984). *Faunal Evidence for Prehistoric Economy and Settlement in the Outer Hebrides to 400AD*, unpublished Ph.D., Edinburgh University.

Finlay, J. I. (1991) 'Animal bones', in E. Campbell (ed.), 'Excavations of a wheelhouse and other Iron Age structures at Sollas, North Uist, by R J C Atkinson in 1957', *Proceedings of the Society of Antiquaries of Scotland*, 121, 117-173; Fiche 1, D1-3, F10.

Grant, A. (1988.) 'Animal resources', in G. Astill and A. Grant (eds.), *The Countryside of Medieval England*, Oxford, Blackwell.

Gordon, C. A. (1964-66). 'The Pictish animals observed', *Proceeding of the Society of Antiquaries of Scotland*, 118, 215-220.

Halpin, E. (1997). 'Animal, bird and fish bone', in J. Barber (ed.), *The Excavation of a Stalled Cairn at Point of Cott Westray, Orkney*, Edinburgh, Scottish Trust for Archaeological Research.

Hambleton, E. (1999). *Animal Husbandry Regimes in Iron Age Britain*, Oxford, BAR British Series 282.

Hedges, J. W. (ed.) (1983). *Isbister. A Chambered Tomb in Orkney*, Oxford, BAR British Series 115.

Hill, J. D. (1995). *Ritual and Rubbish in the Iron Age of Wessex*, Oxford, BAR British Series 242.

Huntington, R. and Metcalf, P. (1991). *Celebrations of Death. The Anthropology of Mortuary Ritual*, Cambridge, Cambridge University Press, 2nd edition.

Jones, A. (1998). 'Where eagles dare. Landscape, animals and the Neolithic of Orkney', *Journal of Material Culture*, 3, 3, 301-324.

Jones, R. T. Sly, J. Simpson, D. Rackham, J. and Locker, A. (1985). 'The terrestrial vertebrate remains from the Castle, Barnard Castle', *Ancient Monuments Laboratory Report*, 7/85.

King, A. C. (1978). 'A comparative survey of bone assemblages from Roman sites in Britain', *Bulletin of the Institute of Archaeology, London*, 15, 207-32.

King, A. C. (1984). 'Animal bones and the dietary identity of military and civilian groups in Roman Britain, Germany and Gaul', in T. Blagg and A. C. King (eds.), *Military and Civilian in Roman Britain*, Oxford, BAR British series 137.

King, A. C. (1999). 'Diet in the Roman world: a regional inter-site comparison of the mammal bones', *Journal of Roman Archaeology*, 12, 117-202.

Lethbridge, T. C. (1952). 'Excavations at Kilpheder, South Uist, and the problem of brochs and wheel-houses', *Proceedings of the Prehistoric Society*, 18, 184-203.

Lowe, V. P. W. (1967). 'Teeth as indicators of age with special reference to red deer (*Cervus elaphus*) of known age from Rhum', *Journal of Zoology*, 152, 137-153.

Noddle, B. (1974). 'Report on the animal bones found at Dun Mor Vaul', in Mackie, E. W. (ed.), *Dun Mor Vaul. An Iron Age Broch on Tiree*, Glasgow, University of Glasgow Press.

Noddle, B. (1978-80). 'Animal bones from Dun Cul Bhuirg, Iona', in J. N. G. Ritchie, and A. M. Lane (eds.), 'Dun Cul Bhuirg, Iona, Argyll', *Proceeding of the Society of Antiquaries of Scotland*, 110, 209-29.

Noddle, B. (1981). 'A comparison of Mammalian Bones found in the Midden Deposit with others from the Iron age site of Dun Bhuirg', in R. Reece (ed.), *Excavations in Iona 1964 to 1974*, London, Institute of Archaeology.

Noddle, B. (1986). 'Animal bones', in A. Whittle, M. Keith-Lucas, A. Milles, B. Noddle, S. Rees and J. C. C. Romans (eds.), *Scord of Brouster. An Early Agricultural Settlement on Shetland*, Oxford, Oxford University Committee for Archaeology.

Mackie, E. W. (ed.) (1965). *Excavations on Two Gallered Dun's on Skye in 1964 and 1965*, Glasgow, Interim Report Glasgow University.

Maltby, M. (1982). 'Animal and bird bones', in R. A. Higham (ed.), 'Excavations at Okehampton Castle, Devon. Part 2 – The Bailey', *Proceedings of the Devon Archaeological Society*, 40, 114-35.

Mulville, J. (1999). *The faunal remains from Bornish, South Uist*, available from http://www.cf.ac.uk/hisar/archaeology/reports/hebrides99/TheFaunalRemains.html [Accessed 20th June 2001]

Mulville, J. and Thoms, J. in prep. *Animals and Ambiguity in the Iron Age of the Western Isles*.

Platt, M. I. (1934). 'Report on the animal bones', in G. J. Callander and G. G. Walter, (eds.), 'A long stalled chambered cairn or mausoleum (Rousay type) near Midhowe, Rousay, Orkney', *Proceeding of the Society of Antiquaries of Scotland*, 10, 321-349.

Platt, M. I. (1935). 'Report on the animal bones', in G. J. Callander and G. G. Walter, (eds.), A Long, Stalled cairn, The Knowe of Yarso, in Rousay, Orkney.

Proceedings of the Society of Antiquaries of Scotland, 10, 325-351.

Platt, M. I. (1936). 'Report on the animal bones found in the Chamberd cairn, Knowe of Ramsay, Rousay, Orkney', in G. J. Callander and G. G. Walter (eds.), 'A Stalled Chambered cairn, the Knowe of Ramsay, at Hullion, Rousay, Orkney', *Proceedings of the Society of Antiquaries of Scotland,* 11, 407-419.

Platt, M. I. (1937a). 'Report on the animal bones', in G. J. Callander and G. G. Walter (eds.), 'Long stalled cairn at Blackhammer, Rousay, Orkney', *Proceedings of the Society of Antiquaries of Scotland*, 11, 297-308.

Platt, M. I. (1937b). 'Report on the animal bone', in C. Calder (ed.), 'A Neolithic double-chambered cairn of the stalled type and later structures on the Calf of Eday, Orkney', *Proceedings of the Society of Antiquaries of Scotland,* 11, 115-154.

Pollard, J. (1995). 'Inscribing space: formal deposition at the Late Neolithic monument of Woodhenge, Wiltshire', *Proceedings of the Prehistoric Society*, 61, 137-56.

Rackham, J. D. (1986). 'An analysis of the animal remains', in C. D. Morris and N. Emey (eds.), 'The chapel and enclosure on the Brough of Deerness, Orkney: Survey and excavation, 1975-1977', *Proceedings of the Society of Antiquaries of Scotland,* 116, 301-374.

Renfrew, A. C. (1979). *Investigations in Orkney*, London, Society of Antiquaries.

Ritchie, A. (1989). *Picts*, Edinburgh, HMSO.

Ross, P. (1967). *Pagan Celtic Culture*, London, Routledge.

Serjeantson, D. (1990). ' The introduction of mammals to the Outer Hebrides and the role of boats in stock management. *Anthropozoologica.* 13. 7-18

Sharples, N. M. (2000). 'Antlers and Orcadian rituals: an ambiguous role for red deer in the Neolithic', in A. Ritchie (ed.), *Neolithic Orkney in its European Context*, Cambridge, McDonald Institute for Archaeological Research.

Smith, C. with the late Hodgson, G, W, I, Armitage, P, Clutton-Brock, J, Dickson, C. Holden,T. and Smith, B. B. (1994). 'Animal bone report', in B. B. Smith (ed.), *Howe: Four Millennia of Orkney Prehistory*. Edinburgh, Society of Antiquaries of Scotland.

Sellar, T. J. (1989). 'Bone report', in B. Bell and C. Dickson (eds.), Excavations of a Warebeth (Stromness cemetery) Broch, Orkney, *Proceeding of the Society of Antiquaries of Scotland,* 119, 101-131; Fiche C1- G2.

Sullivan, T O'. (1998). 'The mammal bone', in N. Sharples (ed.), *Scalloway. A Broch, Late Iron Age settlement and Medieval Cemetery in Shetland*, Oxford, Oxbow.

Tilley, C. (1996). *An Ethnography of the Neolithic: Early Prehistoric Societies in Southern Scandinavia*, Cambridge, Cambridge University Press.

Turner, V. (1967). *The Forest of Symbols*, Ithaca, Cornell University Press.

Turner, V. (1969). *The Ritual Process*, Chicago, Aldine.

Van Gennep, A. (1909). *Les rites de passage*, Paris, Emile Nourry.

Wainwright, G. J. and Longworth, I. H. (1971). *Durrington Walls: Excavations 1966-1968*, London, Society of Antiquaries.

Animals, Ashes & Ancestors

Howard Williams

Introduction

Cemetery excavations and osteological studies have revealed the widespread practice of animal sacrifice in the early Anglo-Saxon cremation rituals of eastern England (Bond, 1993; 1994; 1996; McKinley, 1993; 1994; Wells, 1960; Wilkinson, 1980). Food offerings (i.e. joints of meat, usually pig or sheep/goat) and sometimes the severed heads of horses or intact horses and dogs are buried in early Anglo-Saxon inhumation graves but only rarely, (Crabtree, 1995; Filmer-Sankey & Pestell, 2001; Fern, forthcoming; Vierck, 1971; Wilson, 1992). In stark contrast, it appears that almost half of the cremation graves that are recovered intact and systematically-examined contain evidence of animal sacrifice (Bond, 1996; see also Richards, 1987). Even if animals were sacrificed during inhumation funerals they were rarely interred in graves, so there appears to have been a close connection between animal sacrifice and the cremation process. Moreover, the frequency of species, dominated by horse and sheep/goat, contrasts with animal bone recovered from contemporary settlements where sheep/goat and cattle dominate assemblages (Crabtree, 1995). It is therefore possible that animals were selected, perhaps bred specifically, for sacrifice, consumption and conflagration in funerals.

Previous interpretations of this phenomenon have identified the importance of animal sacrifice as possible evidence for pagan afterlife beliefs and evidence of the Germanic cultural origins of groups practising the rite (Filmer-Sankey & Pestell, 2001; Hills, 1998; Wilson, 1992). Social explanations have also been sought. The extra expenditure of labour in collecting the pyre-fuel and building a large enough pyre to cremate both animals and humans, together with the material wealth that animals reflected suggests that the rite may have been a means of demonstrating the status and wealth of mourners or the deceased (Hills, 1998). Animals may have been important symbols of identity and allegiance, of equal significance to the portable artefacts usually considered in this light (Bond, 1996). Consequently, recognised variations in the provision of animals in relation to the provision of grave goods, urn form and decoration, and the age and sex of the human remains combine to suggest links between animal sacrifice and the expression of social structure and the symbolic grammar of mortuary display (Ravn, 1999; 2003; Richards, 1987; 1992). In addition, ongoing research by Chris Fern is exploring the significance of horse burial in particular, illustrating the distinctive roles of these animals between inhumation and cremation rites (Fern, forthcoming).

In a recent paper this author attempted to add to this debate. The roles and significance of animals in early Anglo-Saxon cremation rituals was interpreted with the support of analogies from ethnographies and medieval literature illustrating some of the shamanistic themes of transformation that might have linked animal sacrifice and cremation. It was argued that early Anglo-Saxon animal sacrifice in cremation rituals was not concerned simply with the display of the identities of the living or with the afterlife destination of the deceased. Cremation and animal sacrifice instead mediated the transformation of the dead person between social, cosmological and ontological states, forming part of an 'ideology of transformation' in early Anglo-Saxon society (Williams, 2001).

This paper aims to build upon these themes by exploring the evidence for animals both *on* and *in* early Anglo-Saxon cinerary urns in greater detail. This analysis suggests the association of animals upon and within cinerary urns emphasised themes of ambiguity and transformation in the post-cremation ritual. This formed part of a wider 'ideology of transformation' seen in the depiction of animals in a fragmented and ambiguous form on contemporary Style I metalwork (Dickinson 2002; Leigh 1984). In the mortuary context, the emphasis on transformation and ambiguity may have allowed animals to have an agency affecting the commemoration of the dead. As enhancers of social memory, animals connected the living with the dead and the supernatural. They may have been perceived as guides on the journey of the dead to the afterlife and could even have been regarded as integral elements of the social person in death. In a sense, animals were good to eat, good to think, but also good to remember with.

Ashes & Ancestors

To appreciate the close relationship between cremation and animal sacrifice, we must first understand how cremation operated as a means of commemoration in past societies. Cremation is not the process of destruction often caricatured by archaeologists. Cremation is a 'catch-all' phrase that encompasses many separate but sequential ritual acts. These might include the preparation of corpses, animals and materials upon a pyre, the display of this image of death, followed by the spectacle of its dissolution. However, the conflagration of the pyre rarely marks the end of the funeral. In early Anglo-Saxon England (as in many societies past and present) mourners appear to have returned to examine the ashes once the pyre was cool enough to approach. They then appear to have endeavoured to retrieve, sort, wash, transport, inter and distribute artefacts and ashes (McKinley 1994). Cross-culturally, the significance of these acts can vary considerably (Williams, 2004). Yet a common theme in many societies is the use of the ashes as a material means of constituting the new and transformed identity of the deceased as a member of the community of the dead or as an ancestor. One means of emphasising the new status the dead receive in the post-cremation rite is to collect the ashes into a new physical and corporeal form: a 'second body' (Serematakis 1991: 177-212). In some societies this 'second body' can take the form of statues, effigies that represent the deceased or made from the ashes, while in others, it is simply enough to secure a new material and spatial location for the dead. In early Anglo-Saxon cremation rituals, the 'second body' can be seen as provided by the burial deposit. This usually consisted of a decorated ceramic urn containing pyre goods, grave goods and the ashes themselves. These rites can be seen as means of constituting new identities for the dead following the cremation. Therefore, cremation was a 'technology of remembrance' (Jones 2003); serving in the selective remembering and forgetting of the deceased by transforming and then rebuilding the social, cosmological and ontological identity of the dead (Williams 2001; 2003; forthcoming).

Against this background, animal sacrifice takes on a central significance in the pre-cremation rites, the cremation itself, and subsequent post-cremation rituals. We can imagine that animals contributed in many ways to the memorable spectacle created by the funeral as they were ridden, driven, used to bear the body and materials to the pyre site, exchanged, killed, butchered, cooked and eaten. Moreover, those animals selected for sacrifice and placed on the pyre served to create a memorable 'scene' in which animals and the dead person were closely connected and then transformed by fire together. The role of animals continued in the post-cremation rituals, as their remains were collected, transported and placed in ceramic urns with the human remains and artefacts. This enmeshed relationship of animals and people with each other suggests an explicit parity in, and ambiguity between, the way that cremation rituals transformed both human and animal remains. Cremation in early Anglo-Saxon society incorporated both animals and the cadaver into a new ancestral identity. In order to develop this argument, this paper will explore two ways in which animals contributed to the identities of the early Anglo-Saxon cremated dead, first discussing the zoomorphic decoration of urns, and second the animal-derived artefacts and animal remains found within urns.

Animals on cinerary urns

Although there are a proportion of vessels from the cremation cemeteries from eastern England that are undecorated, the vast majority (c. 80%) were decorated in some way. Indeed, it has been suggested that many of the undecorated vessels were accessory vessels (perhaps containing food or liquid) accompanying decorated cinerary urns, making the overall proportion of decorated *cinerary* urns much higher still (Hills 1999). The decoration displays a bewildering variety (e.g. *Figure 3.1*). Incised decoration included horizontal lines around the pot, separating fields of decoration that exhibited vertical and diagonal lines, chevrons, (standing) arches

and swags (hanging arches). Plastic decoration is also found, usually comprising of round or vertical bosses either consisting of clay additions to the outer surface or forms created by pushing out the clay from within. Stamped decoration is also recovered from many urns, consisting of a range of dots and stamped designs impressed into the surface of the vessel, usually in horizontal, vertical, diagonal or chevron patterns. These three decorative forms are often used in combination. As a general rule, the decoration is abstract in character, forming patterns that adorn the upper half of the vessel (Richards 1992; Hills 1999). Despite attempts to classify the decoration into a typology and some successful attempts to identify 'workshops' and 'potters' (Myres 1969; 1977a), the overall impression is of complex variability with no one pot resembling another. Given the contrast with domestic assemblages that are rarely decorated, it is possible that many of the pots may have been made especially as funerary containers, or at least selected especially from the most valued domestic urns as appropriate for the burial context (Richards 1987).

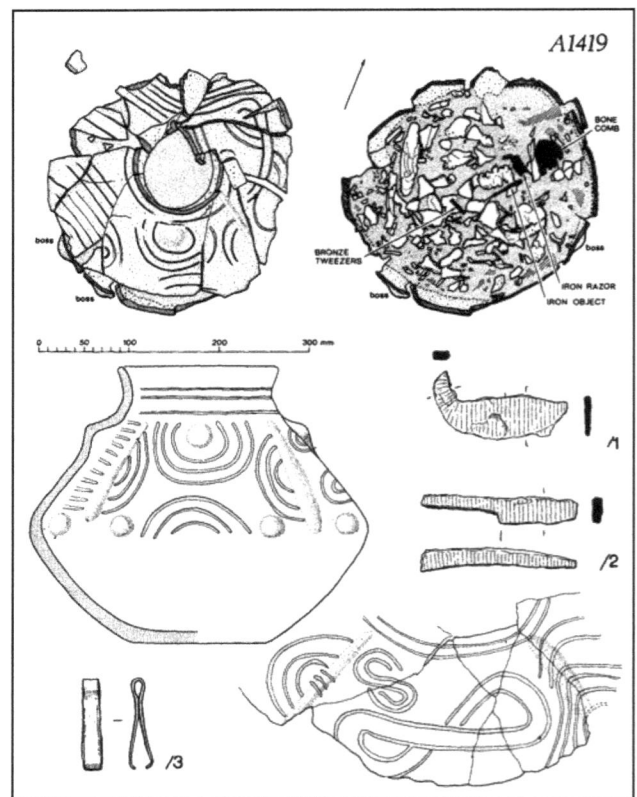

Figure 3.1: Burial A1419 from the Sancton cemetery, East Yorkshire (after Timby 1993: 342). Reproduced from the Archaeological Journal with the kind permission of the Royal Archaeological Institute.
Animals Stamped on Cinerary Urns

Animal stamps (Briscoe's type K3; Briscoe, 1982: 18; 1983: 69) are a rare element of the repertoire of stamps found in early Anglo-Saxon cremation cemeteries in the East Midlands and East Anglia (*Figure 3.2*). In the most recent study of these stamps by Bruce Eagles and Diana Briscoe, they were able to identify thirty six examples from among the thousands of stamped urns known from eastern England (Eagles & Briscoe, 1999; Hills, 1983; Myres, 1977a 350-1; figs. 358-9). For example, at Spong Hill, a small number of urns include stamps of deer (burial 1021, Hills, 1977: 148; burial 2937, Hills et. al., 1994: 159), sheep (burial 1265, Hills, 1977: 148), horses (burial 3114, Hills, et. al. 1994: 159; burial 2443, Hills, et. al. 1987: 133) and birds (burial 2642A, Hills, et. al. 1987: 133). Similar animal stamps are found on a tiny number of urns from other cremation cemeteries such as Caistor-by-Norwich (Myres & Green, 1973), Lackford (Lethbridge, 1951) and Newark (Kinsley, 1989; see Eagles & Briscoe 1999). Eagles & Briscoe regard horses as the most commonly depicted animal, mirroring their high frequency as animal sacrifices, (see below; Eagles & Briscoe, 1999; 101) although it is notable that the proportion of 'wild' animals in this admittedly small sample is higher than their frequency as sacrifices within cremation urns. In most cases, the animals are depicted side-on, either facing left or right, although in some cases there are 'backward-facing' animals, usually thought to represent horses (*Figure 3.3*). Most of the stamps depict the animals in a 'procession' around the pot in one or more zones of decoration (see below). In other cases, the animal stamps 'inhabit' the zones created by diagonal and chevron patterns of incised and stamped decoration (*Figure 3.2*). Concerning their cultural affiliation, Catherine Hills (1983; 1999) notes similarities with the animals depicted upon C-series gold bracteates (particularly in the back-facing animal on urn 2443 from Spong Hill: Hills et. al., 1987: 133) rather than with Style 1 animal art, hinting towards possible links with southern Scandinavia for the inspiration for these designs. In terms of their date, Myres (1977a) assigned them to the latest phase of decorated funerary pottery (i.e. later sixth century AD), although more recently Eagles & Briscoe (1999) are able to show that these stamps date to the late fifth and early sixth-centuries AD when associated dateable artefacts can be found. Animal stamps are closely associated with other motifs such as swastikas and 'wyrm' stamps (see below). These appear in turn to be associated with certain male-gendered and high-status objects suggesting that animal stamps were restricted to particular elite families who used the unusual naturalistic depictions of animals to distinguish their status and identity from others and perhaps also their ideological and mythical status (Hicks, 1983; Hills, 1998; Ravn, 1999; 2003).

In contrast, the majority of early Anglo-Saxon pottery stamps, including the most commonly occurring stamps, are abstract designs (e.g. crosses, stars, grids etc.) although there are some stamp motifs that *might* represent animals albeit in an ambiguous and abstracted manner. Briscoe's (1982; 1983) type K1a & b 'insects', 'maggots' and K2 'snails' are possible representations of animals but appear unconvincing to this writer. Equally ambiguous but potential animal stamps include Briscoe's

type G crescent stamps, many of which resemble a horse's hoof (Fern, forthcoming).

Meanwhile Briscoe's types H 'S-shaped' stamps could be seen as serpentine and are often referred to as 'wyrm' stamps (Briscoe, 1982; 1983; Myres, 1977a). A third possibility is Briscoe's type K2 'Planta Pedis' motif (Briscoe, 1982: 18; 1983; 69) which could be seen as either representations of human or animal footprints (*Figure 3.3*). However, the zoomorphic nature of these stamps is by no means explicit (contra. Briscoe 1982; 1983; Myres 1969: 137-9; Myres, 1977a: 62). Are these deliberately ambiguous allusions to animals (analogous to those of Style 1 animal art: Leigh 1984; Dickinson 2002), or should they be considered simply as abstract designs? Interestingly, the animal stamps and wyrms often 'process' around the pots in comparable ways to animal stamps (e.g. Spong Hill burial 2107; Hills & Penn, 1981: 195). As noted above, the rare instances of naturalistic animal stamps from Spong Hill (stamp groups 44 and 45) are often accompanied with 'wyrm' and swastika designs (Briscoe & Eagles 1999: 101; Hills et. al., 1994: 9 & 11), while an even rarer example of a freestyle hunting scene from Spong Hill burial 2594 is also adorned with horseshoe stamps (Hills et. al., 1987: 153. See below).

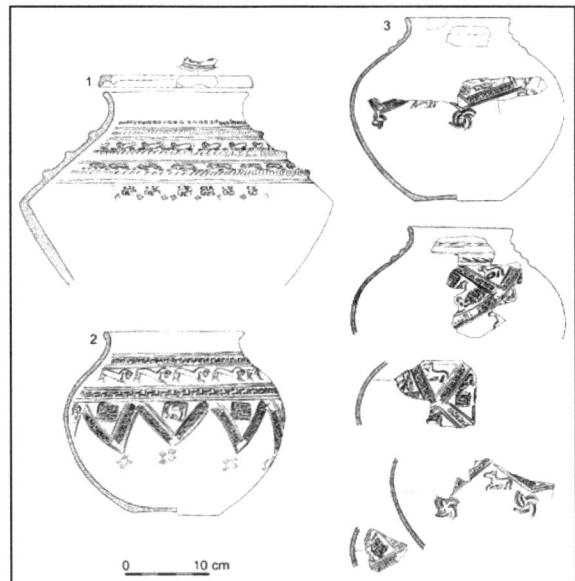

Figure 3.2: Urns from three burials from Spong Hill adorned with animal stamps: 1 – grave 2443, 2 – 2642A (both after Hills et. al. 1987: 133), 3 – grave 3114 (Hills et. al. 1994: 159). Reproduced with the kind permission of Norfolk Landscape Archaeology.

To explore these patterns further, the frequency of each commonly occurring stamp motif was assessed in relation to the presence or absence of animal remains generally and horse remains in particular (*Figures 3.4 & 3.5*). It appears that stamped urns overall were slightly more likely to receive animal remains, particularly those with chevron, grid and feet/maggot stamps (*Figure 3.4*). No clear pattern can be seen with the provision of horses (the most commonly sacrificed animal species, see below), although again it appears that stamp decorated urns are slightly more likely to receive horse sacrifice than unstamped urns. In summary, it appears that stamping, whether abstract or zoomorphic, may have a general association with animal sacrifice, although there appears no specific association between zoomorphic stamps and the presence of animal remains.

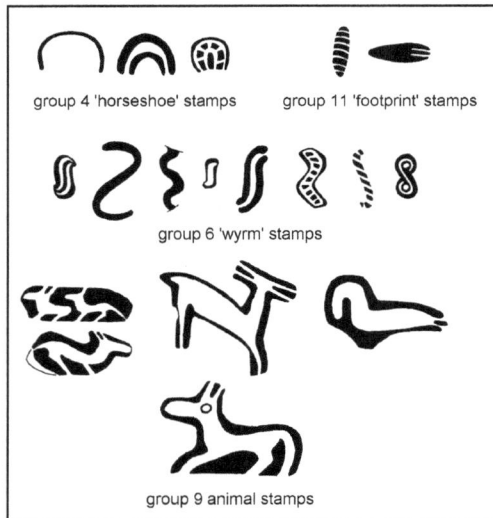

Figure 3.3: Examples of animal stamps, and possible 'zoomorphic' stamps (horseshoes, 'wyrms' and 'feet') from Spong Hill (redrawn after Hills. et. al. 1994).

If these motifs are accepted as holding animal significance, then the overall number of pots associated with animal designs increases substantially but remains a minority in relation to the total number of stamped urns in any given early Anglo-Saxon cremation cemetery. Furthermore, the fact that stamps encircle urns in processions equivalent to lines of animals and that they are more commonly associated with animal sacrifice does seem to hint that the very act of stamping (abstract or zoomorphic) may have some animal-related significance.

Animals Incised and Moulded onto Cinerary Urns

The rarity of naturalistic depictions of animals in the stamp-decorated pottery finds a parallel in the small number of instances where incised and plastic decoration incorporates animal motifs. For example, horses or deer are incised on two pots from Lackford in Suffolk (Lethbridge, 1951: 30; figure 6). Furthermore, unusual examples of hunting scenes are found on urn 2594 from Spong Hill (Hills et. al 1987: 60; 153) and one unprovenanced urn (Myres, 1977a: 354, fig.364). These can be interpreted as copies of designs on Roman and contemporary Byzantine bronze vessels (Hicks 1993). There is also a freestyle depiction of a dog or wolf from Caistor-by-Norwich burial R9/10; interpreted as representing Loki's wolf-son Fenrir from the Norse

apocalypse Ragnarok (Myres & Green, 1973: 118; fig. 44). The connection to Norse mythology remains questionable, as is Myres' (1977a: 65) assertion that it is the only instance of a 'realistically drawn pictorial scene', but the animal representation is unambiguous. Another equally unique and enigmatic vessel comes from grave 67 at the Newark cemetery (Kinsley, 1989: 41; 118). The pot is adorned with incised lines, stamps and hollow bosses in a variety of unusual shapes. Two of the bosses represent four-limbed beasts viewed from above and with arms splayed out on either side of their bodies. The muzzles and brow-ridge are distinguished and their eyes, noses and spine are marked out by stamps (*Figure 3.7*). One interpretation is that they represent bears' pelts, a view that gains some support from rare instances of bear claws found in cremation burials from Elsham, Sancton and Spong Hill (Kinsley, 1989: 12). Whether intended to represent bears, they could represent stretched-out animal skins rather than living animals (Eagles & Briscoe 1999: 100). Alternately, they may depict the animal in a 'split representation' (showing both sides at once) similar to Style 1 animal art (Kristoffersen 1995). These instances at least show that naturalistic representations *could* be employed on cinerary urns, but their rarity suggests that this was not of common significance for the cremation rite. Equally notable is that many appear to represent wild animals as opposed to the domestic species found within urns.

As with the stamped decoration we are left with the quandary of either seeing the rare instances of naturalistic animal representations upon urns as aberrations or as only being unusual in the explicit clarity with which the animal images are rendered. The use of abstract stamp designs adorning the 'bear-skin' animals from Newark shows that stamps are used to mark out the eyes and other features of the animals (Kinsley, 1989: 118). This leads us to examine some of the many supposedly 'zoomorphic' motifs identified by J.N.L. Myres (1977b), formed individually or in combination by incised, stamped and plastic motifs, with greater sympathy than would otherwise be the case if viewed in isolation. The most convincing of which include urn 285 from St John's Cambridge in which the bosses are clearly zoomorphic with animal faces (Myres, 1977a: fig. 243; 1977b). Similarly, Sancton pot 2580 has sharp projecting bosses with beak-like heads (Myres & Southern, 1973: 96 & 97; Myres, 1977a: 343, fig. 346). In other cases, bosses are provided with 'eyes' on a number of vessels including urns from Thurmaston (Myres, 1977a: 282; fig 250), Kingston-on-Soar (Myres, 1977a: 343, fig. 346) and a pot from Castle Acre (Myres, 1977a: 215, fig. 155). Another urn from Thurmaston (Leicestershire) grave number 88 sported bosses with 'fur' created by lines projecting from a 'spine' as well as 'eyes formed by two stamps (Myres, 1977a: 247; fig. 200; P. Williams, 1983: 54, *Figure 3.8*).

In further cases, the bosses resemble insects with incised lines forming their legs running off the edge of the boss (Myres, 1977a: 240; fig. 190 & Myres, 1977a: 282; fig. 249).

Stamp Decoration in Burials with Animal Remains

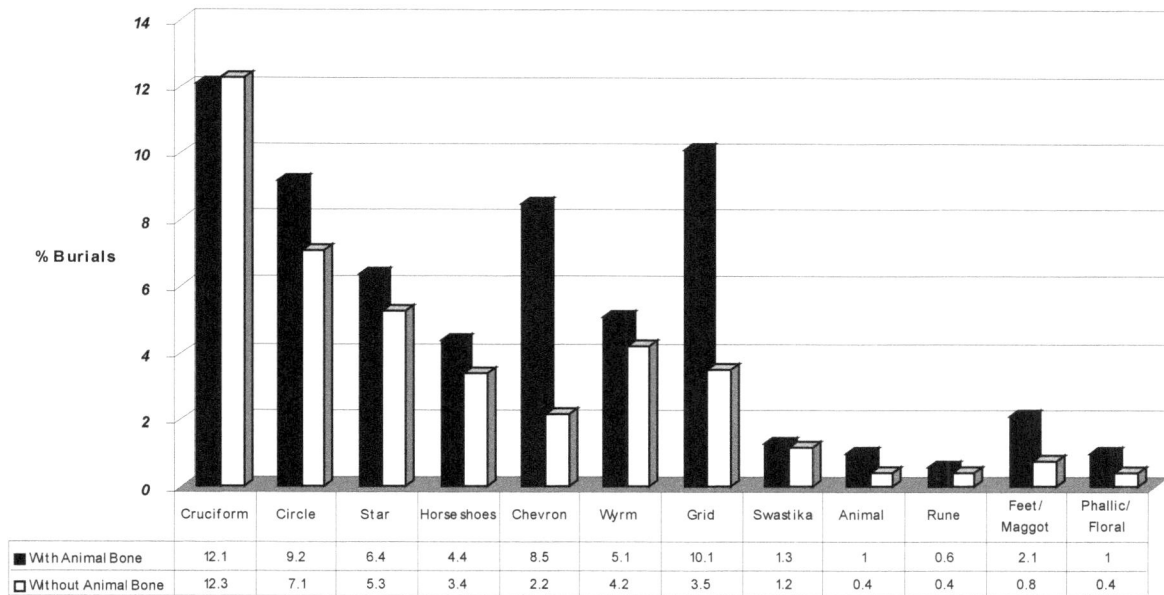

	Cruciform	Circle	Star	Horseshoes	Chevron	Wyrm	Grid	Swastika	Animal	Rune	Feet/ Maggot	Phallic/ Floral
■ With Animal Bone	12.1	9.2	6.4	4.4	8.5	5.1	10.1	1.3	1	0.6	2.1	1
□ Without Animal Bone	12.3	7.1	5.3	3.4	2.2	4.2	3.5	1.2	0.4	0.4	0.8	0.4

Figure 3.4: Stamped decoration in cremation burials with and without animal remains at Spong Hill.

Stamp Decoration with and without Horse Remains

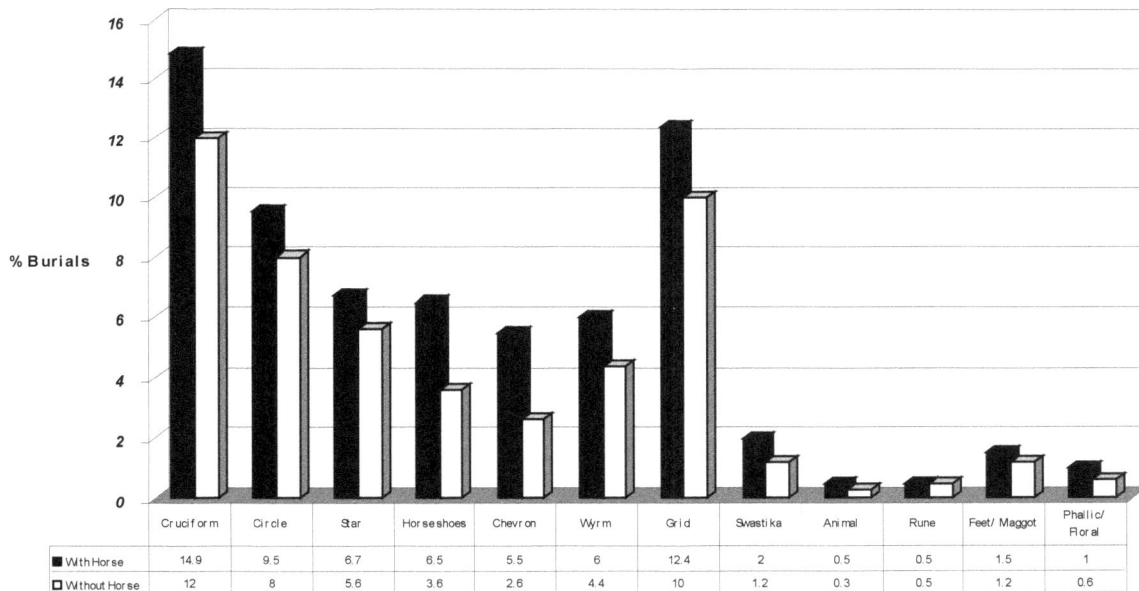

	Cruciform	Circle	Star	Horseshoes	Chevron	Wyrm	Grid	Swastika	Animal	Rune	Feet/ Maggot	Phallic/ Floral
■ With Horse	14.9	9.5	6.7	6.5	5.5	6	12.4	2	0.5	0.5	1.5	1
□ Without Horse	12	8	5.6	3.6	2.6	4.4	10	1.2	0.3	0.5	1.2	0.6

Figure 3.5: Stamped decoration in cremation burials with and without horse remains at Spong Hill.

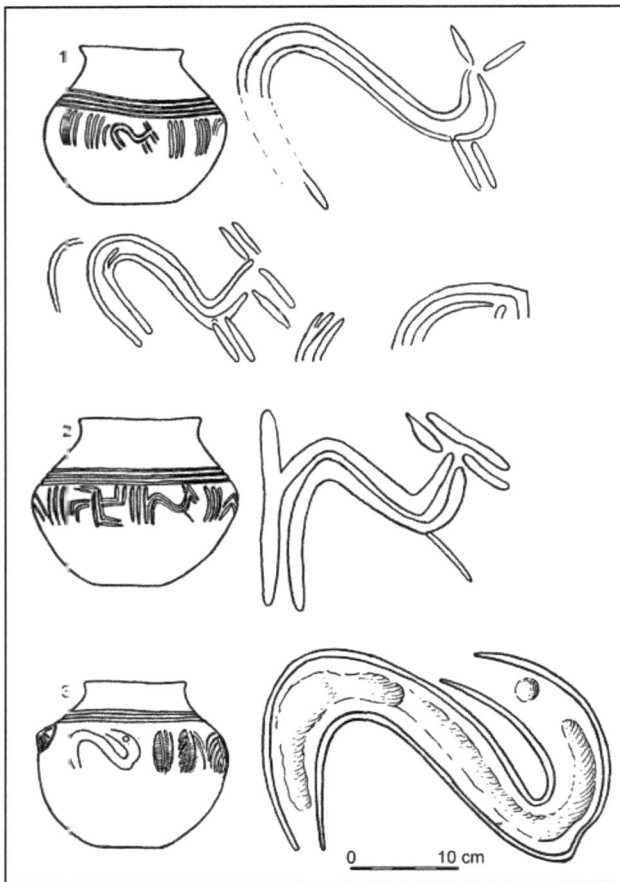

Figure 3.6: Incised motifs of quadrupeds and a 'wyrm' from Lackford (after Lethbridge 1951: 30 & 50).

Among the cases that Myres discusses are pots that depict S-shaped 'wyrm' freehand designs and attributed with a ritual significance as a protective device (Myres, 1977a: 66). The most convincing example is from Lackford pot 48 (Lethbridge, 1951: 50; Myres corpus no: 2473; Myres, 1977a: 66; *Figure 3.6*). Similar but abstract S-shaped and figure-of-eight motifs that have no explicit animal features might, by analogy, be seen as zoomorphic (e.g. Myres, 1977a: 244; fig. 196 & Spong Hill urn 2196: Hills & Penn, 1981: 124; figure 1). Given the use of horses' foot stamps on many pots, it is equally possible that incised or plastic hanging and standing arches were also intended to represent hoof prints and therefore allude to animals as part of pot decoration (e.g. Myres, 1977a; 240; fig. 191). A common theme linking all of these elements is that they do not represent animals *per se*. If they represent animals at all, they are in an ambiguous, abstracted and abbreviated manner comparable in theme (if not appearance) to the ambiguity found on Style I animal art in England (Leigh 1984; Dickinson 2002).

A final unique instance of animal representation comes from a now-lost lid of a cinerary urn from the Newark cemetery (Kinsley, 1989: 179; Milner, 1853; *Figure 3.9*). The nineteenth-century illustration of the urn shows two birds perched upon it facing in the same direction. This

fascinating instance opens a further possibility in animal representations in cremation rites. Were animals frequently placed over, rather than on, cinerary urns? Is this illustration unique or rare only because the animals were rendered in clay rather than other, less durable substances? A similar problem surrounds the interpretation of the Spong Hill 'chairperson'; a cinerary urn lid depicting a seated human figure (Hills, 1980; Hills et. al., 1987: 80; 162). It remains tempting to suggest that while lids depicting animals and humans were rare, representations of beasts and persons made of perishable material were frequently placed upon above-ground monuments. Unfortunately given the disturbed nature of most graves, proving this speculation is unlikely to be straightforward.

Encircling the Ashes & Animating Urns

There are further ways in which animals may have symbolically contributed to the decoration of cinerary urns. As we have seen, few of the stamps, plastic and incised decoration *resemble* animals, yet many of the designs will have been made from tools made *from* animals. Catherine Hills (1977: 13), following J.N.L. Myres (1969) has noted how few pottery and metal stamps are found from early Anglo-Saxon contexts; most stamps that are retrieved are made of antler or bone. More recently, Eagles & Briscoe suggest that some animal stamp designs are so sharp as to be best explained as produced by metal dies (Eagles & Briscoe, 1999; 101), however their absence from archaeological contexts remains intriguing. The possibility that most dies were made from bone or antler may simply reflect the practicality and availability of these materials for making stamps. Yet this may have been another recognised way in which the identities of animals were instrumental in constructing early Anglo-Saxon cinerary urns, and in turn, perhaps also the identities of those interred within. Furthermore, it is notable that horse-teeth have been found used as stamps, as on one pot from Lackford (50, 68B, Lethbridge, 1951: 49; Myres, 1977a: 205; fig 143; Briscoe ,1982: 19; 1983: 69). A further piece of evidence comes from the occasional use of the feet of brooches and wrist clasps as stamps since these are often themselves adorned with animal art (Briscoe, 1982: 19; 1983: 69; Briscoe, 1985; Eagles & Briscoe 1999). Even combs, themselves made of bone or antler, are used to decorate pots (Myres 1977a: 64-5). Therefore, the very *act* of stamping and (more generally) decorating pots, may have been seen as adorning the dead with animal elements even if animals are not clearly depicted.

There remain two further related ways in which animal qualities may be embodied upon cinerary urns. Both concern the overall use of decorative schemes rather than individual motifs. First, as noted above, pots are sometimes 'encircled' with decoration. Both Julian Richards (1992) and Catherine Hills (1999) have noted that the grammar of early Anglo-Saxon cinerary urn decoration focuses upon the upper surface (see *Figure 3.1*).

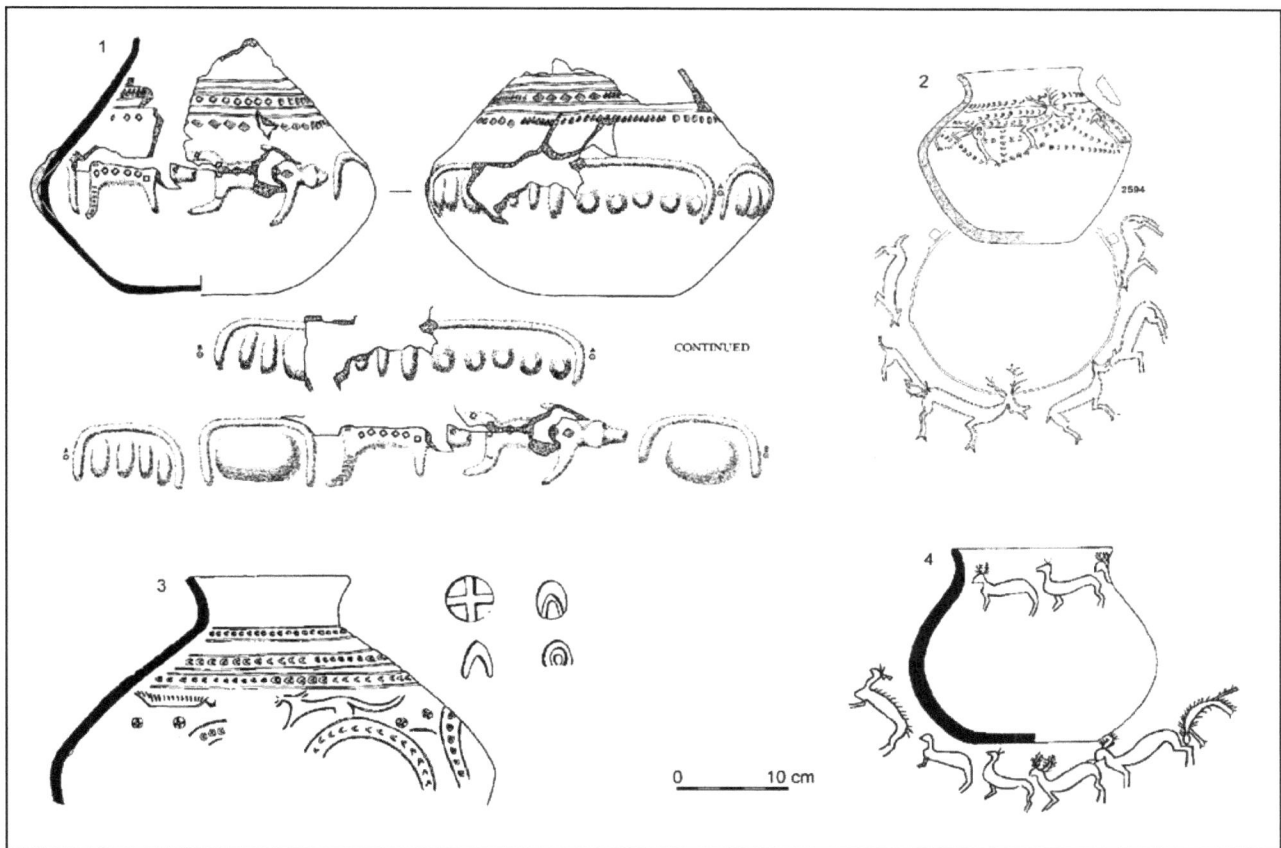

Figure 3.7: Incised and plastic animals on early Anglo-Saxon pottery from: 1 - Newark grave 67 (Kinsley 1989: 118), 2 - Spong Hill grave 2594 (after Hills et. al. 1987: 153), 3 - Caistor-by-Norwich grave R9/10 (after Myres 1977a: fig. 364), 4 - an unprovenanced find (after Myres 1977a: fig. 364). Reproduced with the kind permission of English Heritage; Norfolk Landscape Archaeology & Cambridge University Press.

This suggests that urns were intended to be seen from above, both during the funeral and during the burial ritual. When viewed in this way, the incised, plastic and stamped decoration often appears differently to its appearance side-on as in archaeological illustrations. From above, the decoration creates an encircling series of concentric designs, 'framing' the cremated remains

These Migration-Period Scandinavian renditions of Roman imperial coins are often seen as symbols of political and sacred authority depicting horses, birds and human figures, often appearing to merge and transform into each other. This imagery has often been linked to the psychopompic and shape-shifting attributes of shamans and the Norse god Odin in particular (e.g. Hedeager 1997; 1999). Indeed, the role of abstract decoration in adorning surfaces, thresholds and liminal zones is widely found in many late Antique and early medieval artefacts, art and architecture (Hawkes, 1997). This has some specific implications for the funerary context of the cinerary urns, for just as the pot physically contains the ashes, so the decoration creates a symbolic boundary, 'framing' the cremated remains of humans and animals.

Indeed, this may have mirrored the 'framing' of the

within the pot (*Figure 3.1*). While Richards (1992) noted that the designs show similarities to contemporary annular brooches, Hills has observed how both the motifs employed and the 'framing' of animal and human cremated material by the decorated cinerary urns, resemble the same relationship identified on the punch-marked surrounds of gold bracteates (Hills, 1999; 23-4). cadaver as it was dressed and placed on the pyre surrounded by sacrificed animals earlier in the funerary process. In this sense, the very act of decoration enhanced the remembrance of animals and people in association in death through the different stages of the funeral.

A related quality of the decorative schemes employed on cinerary urns is their processional and continuous character. This allowed the 'framing' effect of the decoration to appear 'animated' (e.g. *Figure 3.1*). When viewed from above, the designs create a striking, continuous and vibrant surface comparable to the procession of beasts created by zoomorphic stamps. This enclosing and 'moving' layer of decoration around the urn brings to mind the use of abstract art in other cultures as a 'technology of enchantment': a means of creating a complex and alluring pattern to 'trap' the eye, giving the decoration an 'agency' over the viewer (see Gell, 1992;

1998). If this point is accepted, it suggests a slightly different view of the decoration of cinerary urns beyond the potential individual significance of particular motifs. Rather than 'merely decorative' (Speake, 1980), 'iconic' (Hawkes, 1997) or 'symbolic' of social identity (Richards, 1992), the encircling and animating character of these designs may have given them apotropaic and mnemonic qualities. By this it is meant that, despite the precise 'meanings' of the art, the act of decorating, and choosing such vessels to contain the ashes, may have been connected mnemonic choices. Whether resembling animals or made *by* animals, the decoration served to protect and distinguish the boundary between the living and the dead (see also Myres 1969: 138-9). Moreover, the theme of decorating pottery as an active choice, and a means of creating a homology between pots and bodies has been widely discussed in ethnography and archaeology (e.g. David et. al. 1988). Therefore, the use of animal motifs in pot decoration may have been linked not only with the creation of an apotropaic barrier, but also to the concept of the urn as a second body and its surface as a second 'skin', a protective layer holding together the fragmented and distorted vestiges of the person retrieved from the cremation pyre. In terms of the mourner's experience, this decorated upper surface would be the last image of the deceased before their concealment in the grave. Although the precise details would have not been long remembered, the striking patterns may have been intended to be recalled and evoked at the next funeral, the brief display of decoration serving to impact on the senses and in turn to create memory (see Küchler 2002). Implicit, and (more rarely) explicit, animal forms may have contributed to this use of the urn as a second body and as a protective and mnemonic surface.

Animals within cinerary urns

Having explored the possible significance of animals upon urns, let us now look at the contribution of animals to the contents of cinerary urns of the fifth and sixth centuries AD. The discussion here focuses on the evidence from the Spong Hill cemetery that provides our largest sample of well-excavated and well-published cremation burials, incorporating data courteously provided in electronic form by Catherine Hills. References are also made to the data from the Sancton cemetery that provides a smaller, but equally valuable source of data for this study.

Animal Artefacts in Cinerary Urns

Although bone and antler artefacts have long been recognised from cremation graves, only with the examination of the cremated material from Spong Hill and Sancton by an animal bone specialist has their full range and frequency been recognised (Bond, 1996). This appears to contrast with inhumation graves where bone is rarely found, although this might largely be the result of differential preservation: burnt bone and antler is more likely to survive than unburnt objects, and the cinerary urns offer protection from acidic soils meaning that they are more likely to survive in cremation contexts (Hills, 2001). Yet it is worth entertaining the possibility that the materiality of these objects gave them a particular significance with the cremation rite in which animal sacrifice seems to have had such an important role.

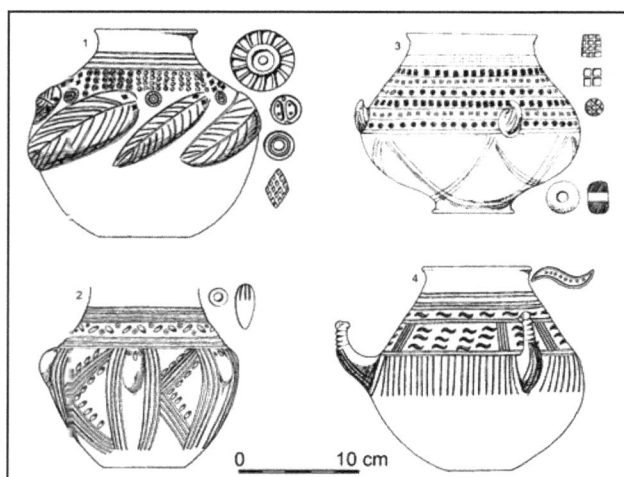

Figure 3.8: Possible zoomorphic bosses from: 1 – Thurmaston (after Myres 1977a: fig. 200); 2 – Castle Acre (after Myres 1977a: fig. 155); 3 – Sancton (after Myres 1977a: fig. 346); 4 – Cambridge St. John's (after Myres 1977a: fig. 243). Reproduced with the kind permission of Cambridge University Press.

Figure 3.9: Birds from Newark (after Milner 1853).

% Animal Species Buried Singly (i.e. with no other animal species identified)

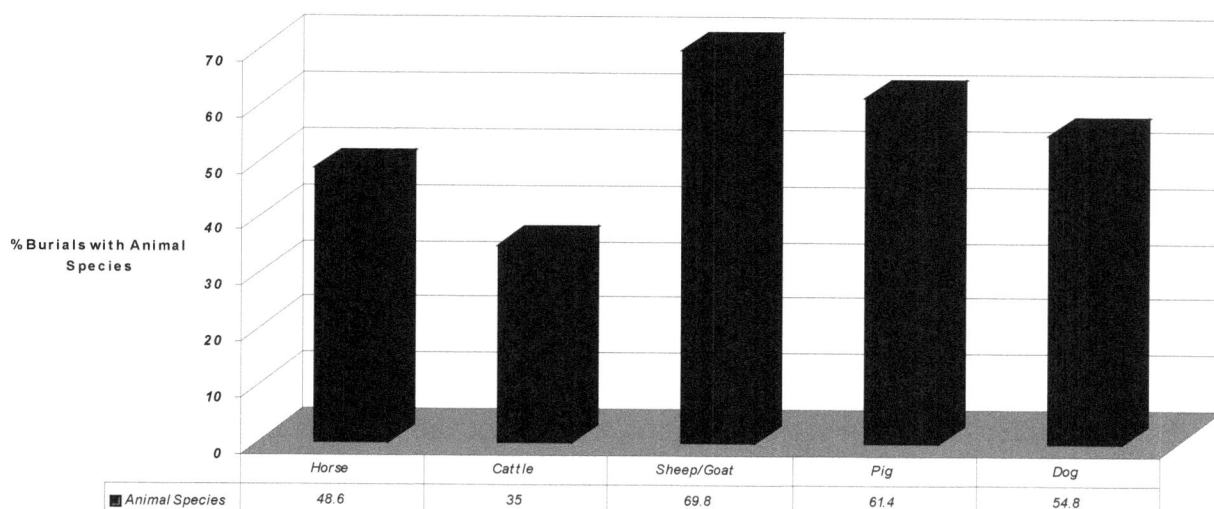

Animal Species	Horse	Cattle	Sheep/Goat	Pig	Dog
	48.6	35	69.8	61.4	54.8

Figure 3.10: Single animal species buried with the dead at Spong Hill.

The most common intact artefacts found in cremation bones are combs, items usually constructed from deer antlers (MacGregor, 1985). Elsewhere I have explored further the potential significance of combs as artefacts closely connected with the management of hair and the body's surface. It is possible that combs had a symbolic and mnemonic role; serving to articulate the building of a new 'body' for the dead in the post-cremation rituals. They may have also emphasised a conceptual connection between the heads of persons and those of the deer from whence the materials used to make combs were originally derived (Williams, 2003).

Other items made of bone, antler and ivory were specifically connected with male and female gendered identities. Surprisingly many include the ivory bag rings that are clearly evidence of female clothing placed on the pyre; these were prestige items acquired through exchange with the Continent (Hills, 2001). Bone and antler rings that have been suggested as having a potential amuletic significance (Meaney, 1981) are also frequently found in cinerary urns as are spindle whorls made of bone and antler. Male-gendered items frequently interred in cinerary urns include bone beads (perhaps sword beads (Hills, 1977), and playing pieces made of worked bone and antler (e.g. Myres & Green, 1973).

While practical and taphonomic factors may be enough to explain the high proportion of artefacts made from animal remains in cremation burials when compared with inhumation graves, it is tempting to suggest that their animal associations resonated with the importance of animal sacrifice and the act of inscribing, stamping and moulding elements of animals onto the surfaces of cinerary urns. For instance, burial 2594 from Spong Hill

(see above) was not only adorned with a hunting scene overlain by horseshoe stamps, the urn also contained a comb that was possibly made from antler (Hills et. al., 1987: 60).

Animal Remains in Cinerary Urns

Let us now return our attention to the widespread practice of sacrificing animals followed by the inclusion of their cremated remains in the cinerary urns (see Bond, 1996; Hills, 1998; McKinley, 1994; Timby 1993). Just under half of the undisturbed cremation burials at Spong Hill contained cremated animal bone (McKinley, 1994). Because of their burnt, distorted and fragmented nature, the vast majority of animal remains identified from cremation burials could not be assigned to any particular species. When they were recognised, horse and 'large ungulates' (most likely horses) outnumber sheep/goat, followed in frequency by cattle, pig and dog. Wild mammals, birds and fish were only rarely found (Bond, 1993; 1994; 1996; McKinley, 1993; 1994).

Burials could contain the remains of one animal species or a combination of different species (*Figures 3.10 & 3.11*). A more detailed study of the Spong Hill evidence suggests that sheep/goat, pig and dog are most commonly found on their own, whereas horses are as likely to be found with or without other animals. Meanwhile cattle are twice as likely to be accompanied by other animals rather than being found in isolation (*Figure 3.10*). The most common combinations are unsurprisingly, given their high frequencies, burials with horse and sheep/goat (*Figure 3.11*). All other combinations are equally represented (horse and pig, horse and cattle, sheep/goat and cattle, sheep/goat and pig, cattle and pig).

Meanwhile, the only repeatedly occurring combination of three animals is horse, sheep/goat and cattle. This evidence appears to suggest that horse and sheep/goat had important and overlapping, but distinct, roles in the cremation ritual; horses tend to require other animal sacrifices of joints of meat, whereas joints of meat do not always require whole animal sacrifices. Meanwhile, it appears that offerings of pork were associated with distinct individuals, usually found without other animal remains. In contrast cattle were rarely found on their own and can perhaps be considered as an additional animal used in funerals of higher expenditure (perhaps reflecting high status mourners or individuals) augmenting the more common sacrifice of horses and sheep/goat (*Figure 3.11*).

Animal Species Combinations

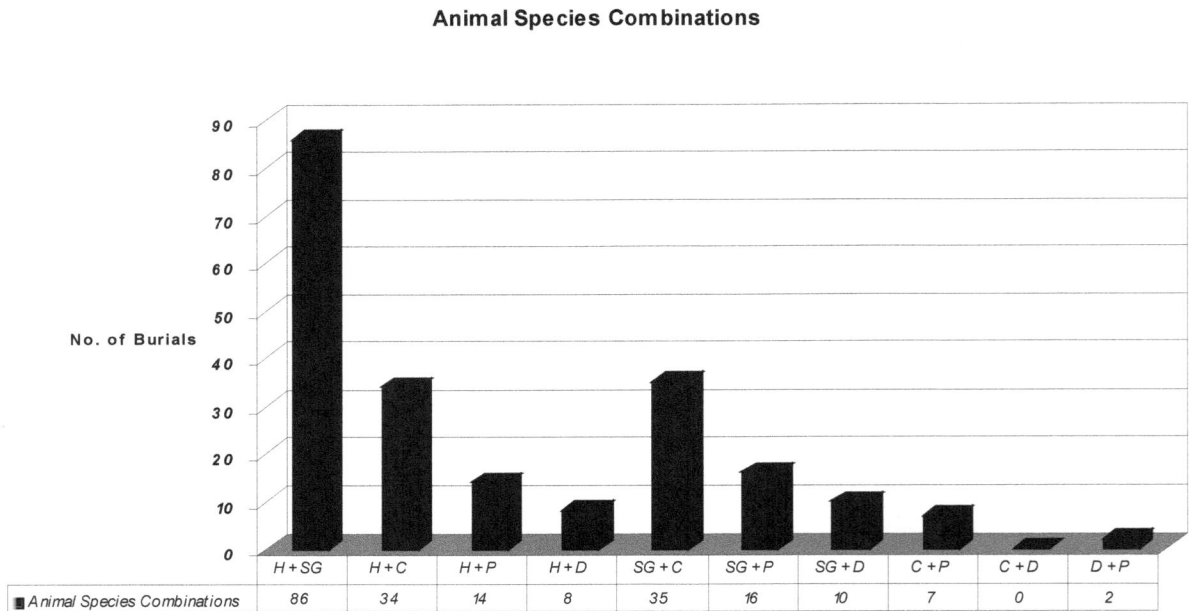

■ Animal Species Combinations	H + SG	H + C	H + P	H + D	SG + C	SG + P	SG + D	C + P	C + D	D + P
	86	34	14	8	35	16	10	7	0	2

Figure 3.11: Combinations of animal species buried with the dead at Spong Hill

Male-gendered Artefacts with Animal Remains

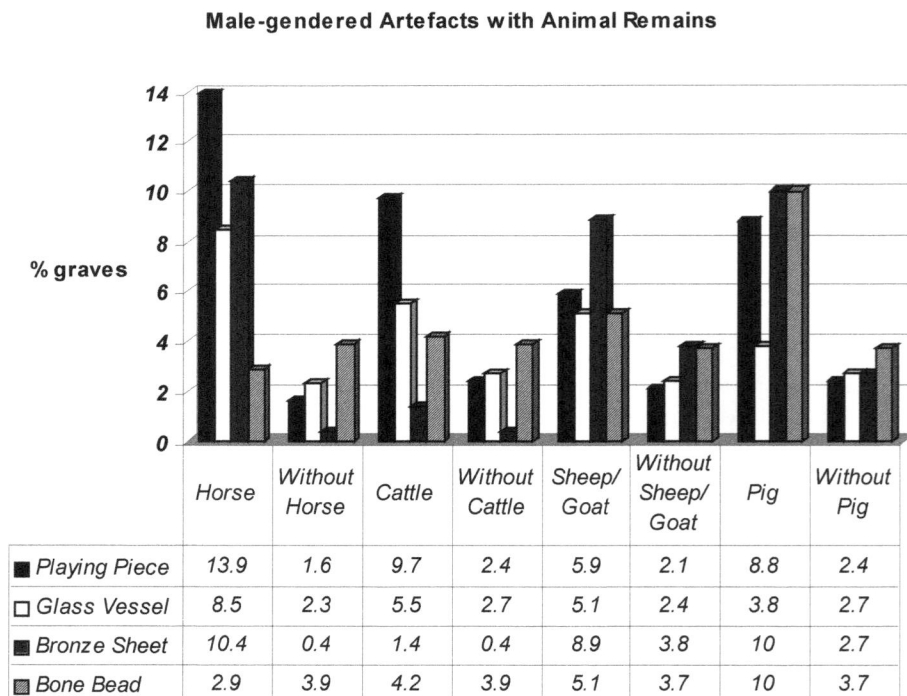

	Horse	Without Horse	Cattle	Without Cattle	Sheep/ Goat	Without Sheep/ Goat	Pig	Without Pig
■ Playing Piece	13.9	1.6	9.7	2.4	5.9	2.1	8.8	2.4
□ Glass Vessel	8.5	2.3	5.5	2.7	5.1	2.4	3.8	2.7
■ Bronze Sheet	10.4	0.4	1.4	0.4	8.9	3.8	10	2.7
▨ Bone Bead	2.9	3.9	4.2	3.9	5.1	3.7	10	3.7

Figure 3.12: Correlations between male-gendered artefacts and animal remains at Spong Hill.

The sacrificed animals in urns fall into two types, those present as whole animals, and those that were cremated as joints of meat. As Bond (1996) notes, it is not always possible to clearly decide between these two. However, as a rule it appears that horse, dog and cattle tended to be placed on the pyre as whole animals while sheep/goat and pig were present as joints of meat (i.e. food offerings). However, the distinction cannot be simply seen in terms of animals as sacrifices and animals as 'food offerings'; both were sacrifices and both involved a ritual display of the killing of the animal and both were transformed by fire in a comparable way to the corpse(s). Both may also represent a 'share' of the deceased's wealth or that inherited by kin, or alternately gifts from those attending the funeral. Each category might equally have been perceived as shared by, or exchanged between, the living and the dead. Even whole animals may have been partly consumed by mourners prior to cremation. Moreover, joints and whole animals may have been perceived as being 'consumed' by the fire and by the deceased.

Yet the distinction between the provision of whole animals and joints of meat does appear to have some significance, for it appears that animals that were cremated whole were those associated with transportation (horse and cattle) while dogs appear in many cultures to have a unique connection to people in daily life and in ritual. Interestingly, these are the animals most commonly viewed as shamans' familiars and used as psychopomps to guide the dead to the afterlife in societies with shamanistic conceptions of necrogeography (Eliade, 1954; Vitebsky, 1995; Williams, 2001). As we shall see, this was a distinction that affected who and how the remains were interred.

Grave Goods & Animal Remains

There are two ways that we can discuss the provision of animal remains in relation to mortuary variability: by identifying patterns in the provision of animal remains in relation to the biological sex discerned for the human remains, and the provision of pyre- and grave-goods. Patterns are limited by the potential destructive biases of the cremation which both make the identification of biological information from human remains and the identification of fragmented and distorted artefacts problematic. However, some broad trends can be identified through a systematic analysis of the Spong Hill cemetery data. Catherine Hills (1998) and Mads Ravn (1999; 2003) have already noted patterns in the provision of horse remains and male-gendered artefacts with high-status associations including rare instances of weapons found in urns, glass and bronze vessels, buckets, playing pieces and large collections of artefacts (Hills, 1998: 152). This suggests that horses *could* be one sign of an elite group burying their dead in the cemetery, who, (as seen above) also employed animal stamps (see also Ravn 2003). However, although patterns exist, they are rarely clear-cut and exclusive relationships between any artefacts and the provision of animal remains. This suggests that while animal remains were deployed in different ways in relation to the social identity of the deceased and mourners, animal sacrifice had a broader significance that was not restricted to a small elite.

A selection of male and female-gendered artefacts (by analogy with broadly contemporary inhumation rites (see Stoodley, 1999) and their correlation with sexed graves at Spong Hill) were tabulated against the provision of animal remains (*Figures 3.12 & 3.13*). Male-gendered artefacts are more difficult to identify in cremation burials due to the absence of weaponry. However, certain items are usually associated with the wealthier male inhumation graves including playing pieces, glass vessels, bronze sheet (often suggesting the burial of bronze vessels) and bone beads (some of which may have been sword-beads). In comparison with the frequency of animal remains in the rest of the Spong Hill cemetery, it is clear that animal remains are over-represented in graves with all four of these male-gendered artefacts (*Figure 3.12*). Playing pieces, glass vessels and bronze vessels are over-represented with all animal species, but particularly in association with horse remains. Bone beads in contrast show little direct correlation with horse, cattle or sheep, but are frequently associated with pig.

Female-gendered artefacts reveal a contrasting pattern, being under-represented in association with horse and (to a lesser extent) cattle (*Figure 3.13*). There appear to be no differences in the provision of female-gendered artefacts with and without sheep/goat remains. Meanwhile, all female-gendered artefacts are more commonly found with pig remains and they are under-represented in association with horse remains.

Two further sets of artefact types were selected; items found with both sexes but seemingly having an important role in the post-cremation ritual as 'grave goods' (either added unburned to the cinerary urn or selectively retrieved from the pyre debris for internment). These are toilet implements (including tweezers, shears and razors) and bone and antler combs (including double-sided, single-sided and miniature forms) (*Figure 3.14*). It was noticed that combs are over-represented with sheep/goat and pig, under-represented with cattle and found in similar numbers with and without horse remains in comparison with the rest of the cemetery population. Tweezers and shears were over-represented with all animal species while razors demonstrate no clear patterns other than being more common with cattle remains than without. Since cattle have been identified as a species added to the wealthier graves and usually found with other animal species, razors may have had a similar function as adjuncts to the more commonly buried tweezers and shears. These patterns suggest that items associated with the management of the external surface of the body in life, and perhaps interred to articulate the building of a new body in death (see Williams, 2003), were closely linked to the internment of animal remains.

Female-gendered Artefacts with Animal Remains

	Horse	Without Horse	Cattle	Without Cattle	Sheep/Goat	Without Sheep/Goat	Pig	Without Pig
■ Brooch	3	4.9	2.8	4.9	6.8	4.5	6.3	4.7
□ Glass Beads	13.3	22.1	15.3	21.6	20.3	20.8	31.3	21.1
▨ Spindlewhorl	4.5	2.5	1.4	2.7	3.1	2.6	8.2	2.5
▨ Bone & Antler Rings	0.5	1.5	0	1.5	1.7	1.4	3.8	1.4
■ Ivory Rings	3.5	8.8	8.3	8.4	12.3	7.7	16.3	13.8

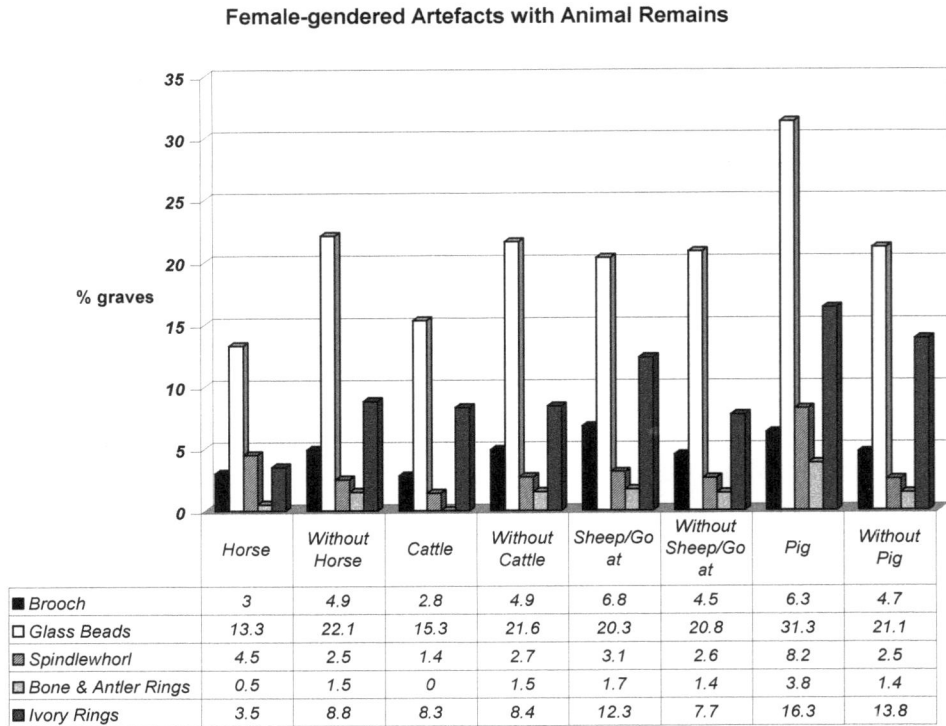

Figure 3.13: Correlations between female-gendered artefacts and animal remains at Spong Hill.

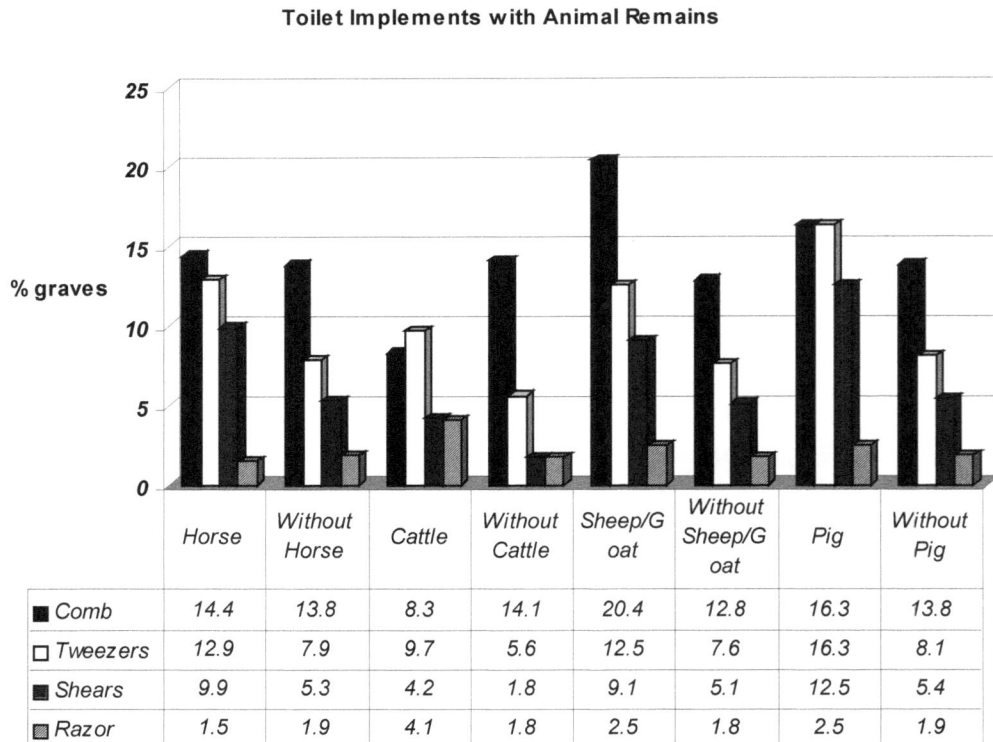

Toilet Implements with Animal Remains

	Horse	Without Horse	Cattle	Without Cattle	Sheep/Goat	Without Sheep/Goat	Pig	Without Pig
■ Comb	14.4	13.8	8.3	14.1	20.4	12.8	16.3	13.8
□ Tweezers	12.9	7.9	9.7	5.6	12.5	7.6	16.3	8.1
■ Shears	9.9	5.3	4.2	1.8	9.1	5.1	12.5	5.4
▨ Razor	1.5	1.9	4.1	1.8	2.5	1.8	2.5	1.9

Figure 3.14: Correlations between combs, toilet implements and animal remains at Spong Hill.

Number of Artefacts with Animal Remains

Number of Artefacts in Grave	1	2	3	4	5	6	7	8
■ All Graves %	39.7	25.4	15.9	10.6	5	2.2	0.5	0.5
□ Horse %	7.7	8.7	11.3	12.4	11	12.5	25	25
■ Cattle %	2.6	2.7	1.7	2.6	2.7	12.5	0	0
▨ Sheep/Goat %	33.1	24.5	15.7	12.1	8.6	4.7	1.9	1.2
■ Pig %	3.8	3.8	4.8	6.5	3.9	9.4	12.5	0

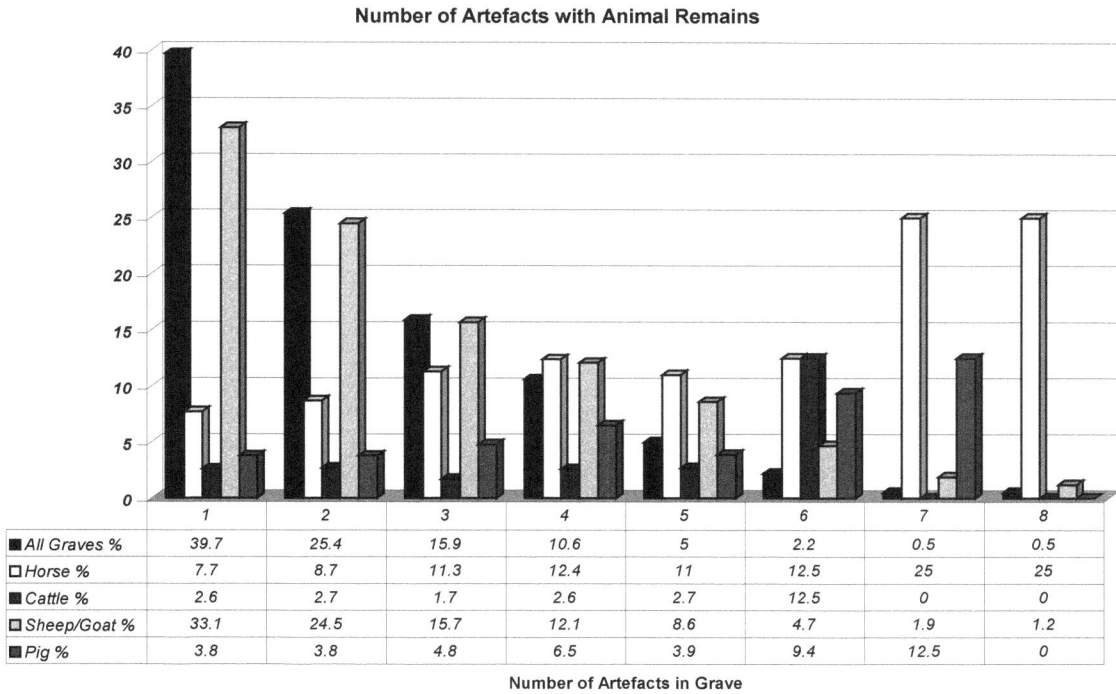

Figure 3.15: Correlations between burial wealth (measured in terms of the numbers of artefacts in graves) and animal remains at Spong Hill.

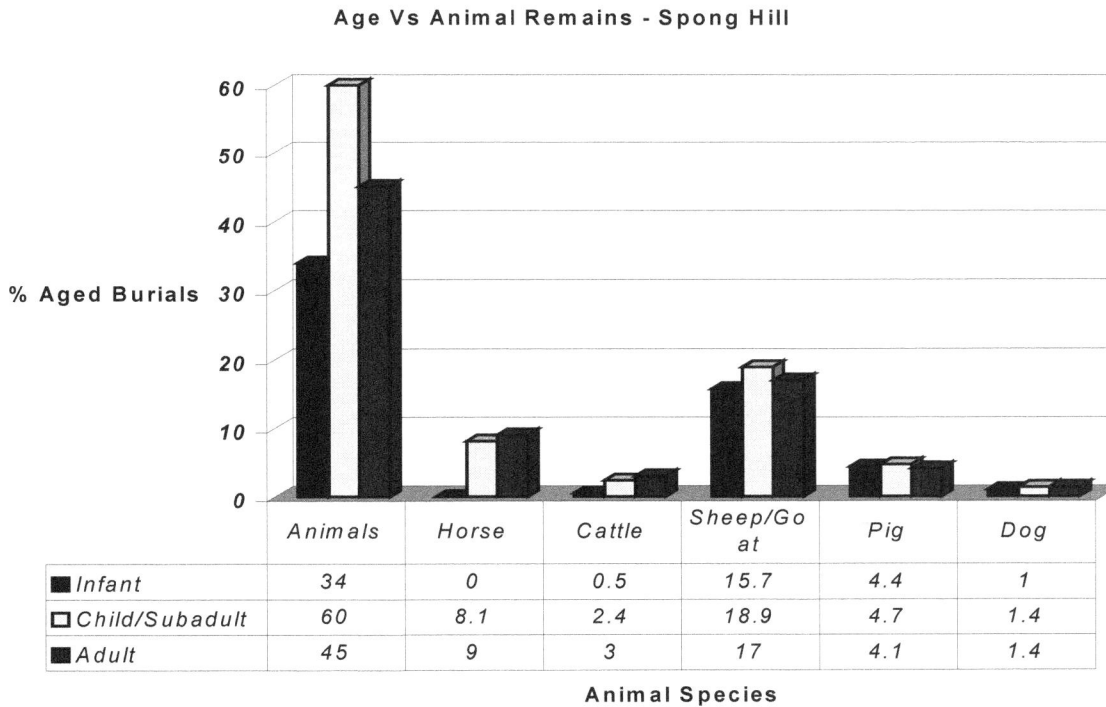

Age Vs Animal Remains - Spong Hill

Animal Species	Animals	Horse	Cattle	Sheep/Goat	Pig	Dog
■ Infant	34	0	0.5	15.7	4.4	1
□ Child/Subadult	60	8.1	2.4	18.9	4.7	1.4
■ Adult	45	9	3	17	4.1	1.4

Figure 3.16: Correlations between biological age at death & animal remains for Spong Hill.

31

Finally, the number of artefact types placed in graves was correlated against the provision of animal remains (*Figure 3.15*). This illuminates some clear patterns. The provision of sheep/goat follows closely with the overall numbers of graves in each category, showing no clear pattern in provision with poorer or wealthier graves. In contrast, cattle and pig, but especially horse, are more common than would be expected in wealthier graves, suggesting that they were more likely to be interred during funerals with a greater expenditure on artefacts.

In summary, it appears that while animal remains were a ubiquitous and non-exclusive practice within early Anglo-Saxon cremation rituals, different species were association with the provision of different types of artefact connected to the gendered identity, age and social status of the deceased as perceived by mourners.

Human & Animal Remains

Patterns between the osteological sex and age of the cremated human remains and the provision of animal remains for the Spong Hill and Sancton cemeteries allow us to build upon this picture (*Figures 3.16, 3.17, 3.18 & 3.19*). The age categories of the dead can only be broadly identified given the fact that the osteological evidence is often poor and fragmented. In this study, the evidence is combined into three very broad age categories (infant, child/subadult & adult). Similarly sexing cremated human remains is a challenge, and the categories of '?male' and '?female' encompass McKinley's (1994) 'possible' and 'probable' categories, and 'male' and 'female' reflecting the more 'certain' sexing categories. Some of the patterns noted here have already been recognised by McKinley (1993; 1994), Hills (1998) and Ravn (1999; 2003).

In terms of the presence of animal remains at Spong Hill and Sancton, children and subadults tend to have more animal remains interred with them than adults, who in turn, have more than infant graves (*Figures 3.16 & 3.18*). A more detailed break-down of the age patterns suggests that animal remains are most often placed with subadults and young adults (aged 13 – 25: Williams 2001). These were individuals of an age where they may have ridden horses during travel, hunting and warfare and may dealt regularly with domestic animals in daily life, but had yet to reach their potential as fully fledged members of their communities (see Härke, 1997). It is possible therefore that the provision of animals reflects elements of the deceased's identity in life, but also an aspired identity yet to be reached. Such aspirations to status may have been less important in either the funerals of very young, or mature individuals. Consequently, it is tempting to see commemoration through animal sacrifice as a 'prospective' rite promoting a new identity for the dead rather than a direct reflection of the social identity enjoyed in life. In terms of the sex of those interred with animals (*Figures. 3.17 & 3.19*), both sexes are frequently associated with animals, but there is a bias towards a higher frequency of male graves containing animal remains at both Spong Hill and Sancton. In summary, this evidence suggests that although animal sacrifice was a widespread rite and not exclusive to any single age or gender group, more younger males were afforded animal sacrifices than other groups.

Patterns can be identified in the provision of individual species with those graves that have been aged and sexed and these build upon the patterns identified in the provision of grave goods. Age is correlated with the provision of different species (*Figures 3.16 & 3.18*). Horse is absent from infant graves at both cemeteries. They are equally found among children, subadults and adults at Spong Hill, but more common among children and subadults at Sancton. Cattle also tend to be associated with adults at both cemeteries. In contrast, sheep/goat and pig are common with all ages at Spong Hill and (to a lesser extent) at Sancton. In contrast, the sex of the deceased shows little consistent correlation with the provision of animal remains. Sheep/goat at Spong Hill and pig and horse at Sancton are more common in male graves. Meanwhile in female-sexed graves, pig was more common at Spong Hill (supporting the pattern identified above in the association of female-gendered grave goods with pig remains), while in contrast cattle and sheep/goat are more common at Sancton (although this pattern is exacerbated by the few graves assigned as 'certain' males in the Sancton sample: *Figures 3.17 & 3.19*).

The mortuary practices at the two cemeteries appear to have varied, warning us against relying too heavily on the Spong Hill data as 'typical' for all early Anglo-Saxon cremation cemeteries (see also Richards 1987; Ravn 2003). Yet the evidence shows how in different ways, animals at both sites were used to contrast the distinctive identities of particular social categories in death. It also provides further support that whole animals (mainly horse) were closely linked to the social identity of the deceased in death (reflected in their absence from infant graves and tendency to be associated with child, subadult and younger individuals). Meanwhile, the addition of joints of meat as food offerings was more ubiquitous and less restricted. One explanation might be that sheep/goat and pig were less prized as symbols of identity but represented funerary exchanges of livestock and feasting activities commonly held during funerals. These may have been gifts from the mourners and important means of commemorating the dead, but were less connected to the particular identity of the dead person and their transformation in the funerary ritual.

Animal Accessory Urns

An infrequent but significant ritual practice identified at Spong Hill was the provision of 'animal accessory' urns. These can be defined as second urns placed with the cinerary urn that, while sometimes containing human cremated material, primarily consist of animal remains (McKinley, 1994: 93). In other cases, the majority of animal bone was deposited in a pit around, under or to one side of the cinerary urn. At Spong Hill, at least forty-seven 'animal accessory' vessels were identified, although most instances are 'possible' and 'probable' given the fragmented nature of the evidence. These account for 1.3% of the cremation burials from Spong Hill (McKinley, 1994: 93) although further examples may have been overlooked. The practice has been identified at other cemeteries such as Sancton, Newark, Loveden Hill and Baston (McKinley, 1994: 93; Wilkinson, 1980).

A review of the Spong Hill evidence provides an indication of how the animal remains were treated in comparison with the typical cinerary urns (*Figure 3.20*). First, a much higher proportion of accessory vessels were plain compared with a much smaller proportion of the overall burial assemblage. This demonstrates that there existed a clear distinction made in terms of the types of decoration seen as appropriate for animal accessory vessels. It has been argued by Chris Fern that this trend is particularly apparent for urns containing horse remains (Fern, forthcoming).

The kind of decoration on animal accessory vessels is also different from the cinerary urns they accompany and the cemetery assemblage as a whole (*Figure 3.20*). In the general assemblage, incised decoration is most common, followed by stamped decoration and plastic decoration. This is broadly reflected in those urns containing human remains associated with animal accessory vessels although plastic decoration is more common than might be expected from the overall cemetery trend. In contrast, the vast majority of the decoration upon the possible animal accessory vessels is incised decoration while stamped decoration is rare and plastic decoration identified in only one instance. This evidence shows that, when buried together during the funeral, different decorative schemes were considered appropriate for the main cinerary urn and the animal accessory vessel. The latter were not afforded those motifs most commonly used to mark out the division between the living and the dead (Richards 1987; see above).

What of the animal remains placed in cinerary urns and their animal accessories compared with the general cemetery assemblage? (*Figure 3.21*). It is clear that horse, large ungulates (probably horse), sheep/goat, (and to a lesser extent) cattle are particularly over-represented in urns with animal accessories compared with the general population. Equally notable is the low numbers of pig remains associated with graves with animal accessory urns. It appears that accessory vessels tend to receive the remains of the larger, whole, sacrificed species of horse and cattle while more of the joints of meat of sheep/goat are placed with the human remains. The prosaic explanation for this pattern is that whole cremated large animals including horse and cattle are more likely to need an extra urn to inter the ashes. Alternately, those funerals in which greater effort is expended on cremating the dead

with large animals might also pay greater attention to the collection and burial of the cremated remains. Yet, as mentioned before, it might also be the case that horses and cattle were different categories of sacrifice to the pig and sheep/goat, attributed a distinctive status and afforded a treatment in death that partially contrasted with, but was generally comparable to, the disposal of human remains (see above; Williams, 2001; Fern forthcoming).

There were some patterns in the provision of grave goods and the age and the sex of the human remains provided with animal accessory vessels (*Figures 3.22 & 3.23*). While all age and sex groups are represented in the small sample, it is notable that there was only one infant and no 'certain' female burials associated with animal accessory urns. It is also worth noting that there were no brooches (the most diagnostic female-gendered artefact type) found associated with animal accessory vessels (see also Hills 1998).

In summary, animal accessory vessels are difficult to securely identify in the archaeological record and the rite was only an occasional practice at Spong Hill. In those cases where animal accessories are found, it tends to be an adult and male rite. This appears to support the importance of decoration in association with graves in which human and animal remains were mixed. The evidence also shows that animal accessory vessels were interred to contain the ashes of large ungulates (usually horses) that had been cremated as whole animals on the pyre. Horses were afforded a distinctive treatment from joints of mutton and pork: animals that not only could be eaten, but acted as traction and transportation in life, and perhaps also in death.

Mixing Animals and Humans

In most cases, human and animal cremated remains were mixed together in the same cinerary urns for burial. This is unlikely to have been by accident. Despite the destruction and distortion caused to the corpses of humans and animals, it is likely that bones of people and sacrificed beasts would remain clearly visible and distinct. Although the pyre might collapse in such a way as to mix human and animal remains, experimental and ethnographic studies show that often anatomic positions and the locations of separate corpses are broadly maintained in the pyre debris below where the bodies were placed on the pyre prior to conflagration. In other words, if cremated remains were picked out of the ashes, it would be apparent which elements were those of humans and which belonged to the sacrificed animals. Consequently, if the intention had been to separate and maintain the distinction between the deceased person and sacrificed beasts then this would usually have been possible in the post-cremation ritual (Williams, 2004,). Not only would animal and human bone remain distinctive in its form, but in many societies, the careful handling and examination of cremated bone is than a

Sex Vs Animal Remains - Spong Hill

	Animals	Horse	Cattle	Sheep/Goat	Pig	Dog
■ Male	69	8.2	8.2	29.5	4.9	1.6
□ Male?	42	9.8	3.5	13.9	2.9	1.2
■ Female?	48	7.7	1.9	20.8	5	0.8
▨ Female	51	6.1	8.5	17.1	8.5	2.4

% Sexed Burials (y-axis: 0, 10, 20, 30, 40, 50, 60, 70)

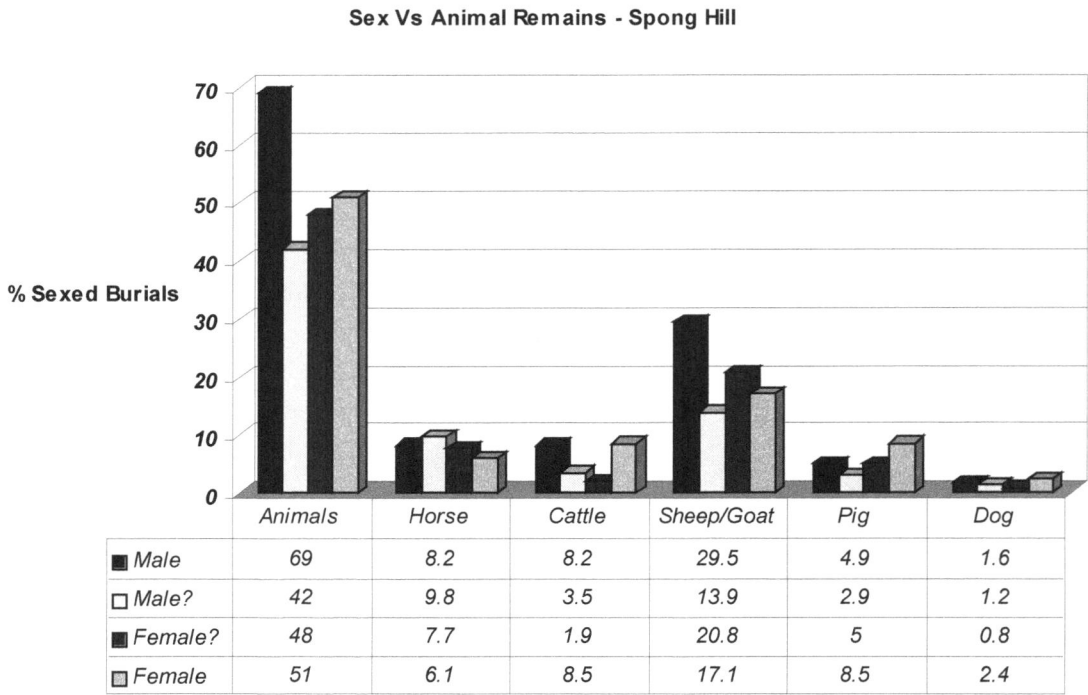

Figure 3.17: Correlations between biological sex & animal remains for Spong Hill.

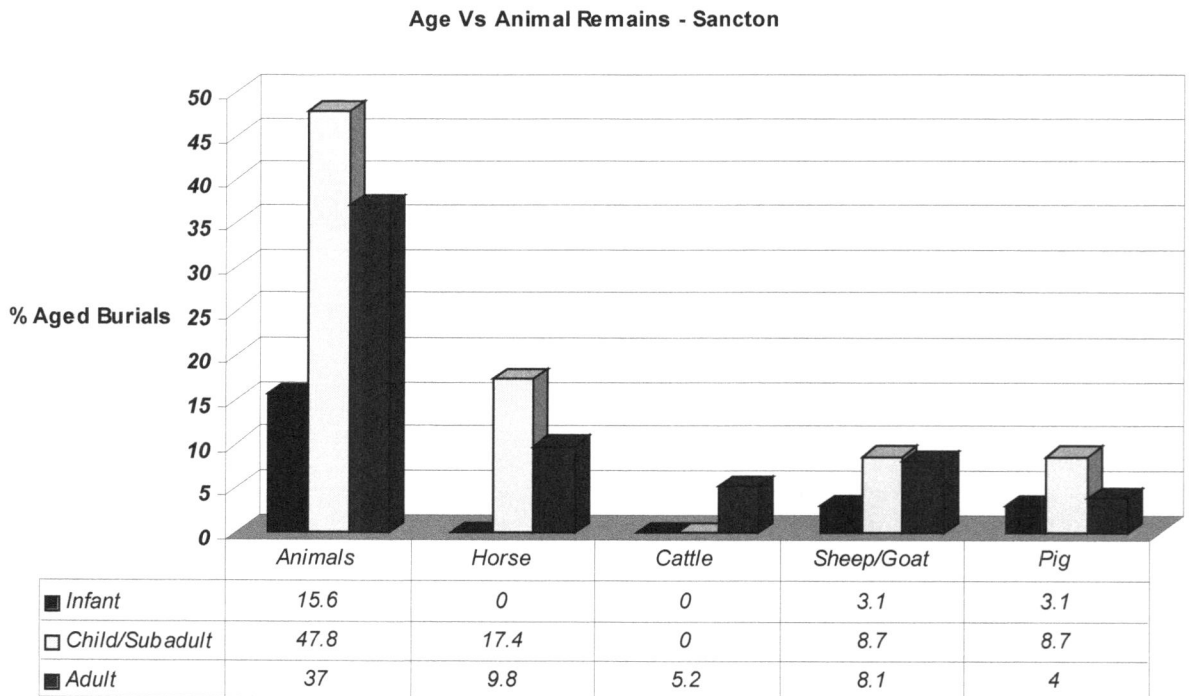

Age Vs Animal Remains - Sancton

	Animals	Horse	Cattle	Sheep/Goat	Pig
■ Infant	15.6	0	0	3.1	3.1
□ Child/Subadult	47.8	17.4	0	8.7	8.7
■ Adult	37	9.8	5.2	8.1	4

% Aged Burials (y-axis: 0, 5, 10, 15, 20, 25, 30, 35, 40, 45, 50)

Figure 3.18: Correlations between biological age at death & animal remains for Sancton.

34

Sex Vs Animal Remains - Sancton

	Animals	Horse	Cattle	Sheep/Goat	Pig
■ Male	50	16.7	0	0	0
□ ?Male	53.5	13.9	0	7	11.6
■ ?Female	39.6	11.3	5.7	9.4	3.8
□ Female	28.6	4.8	7.1	9.5	2.4

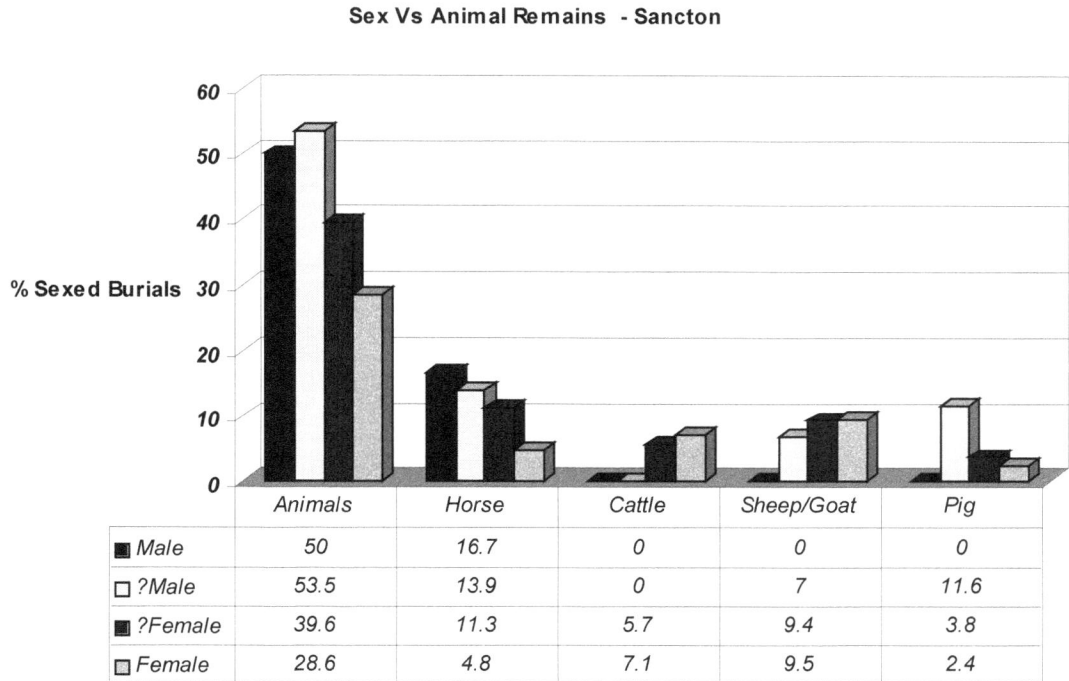

Figure 3.19: Correlations between biological sex & animal remains for Sancton.

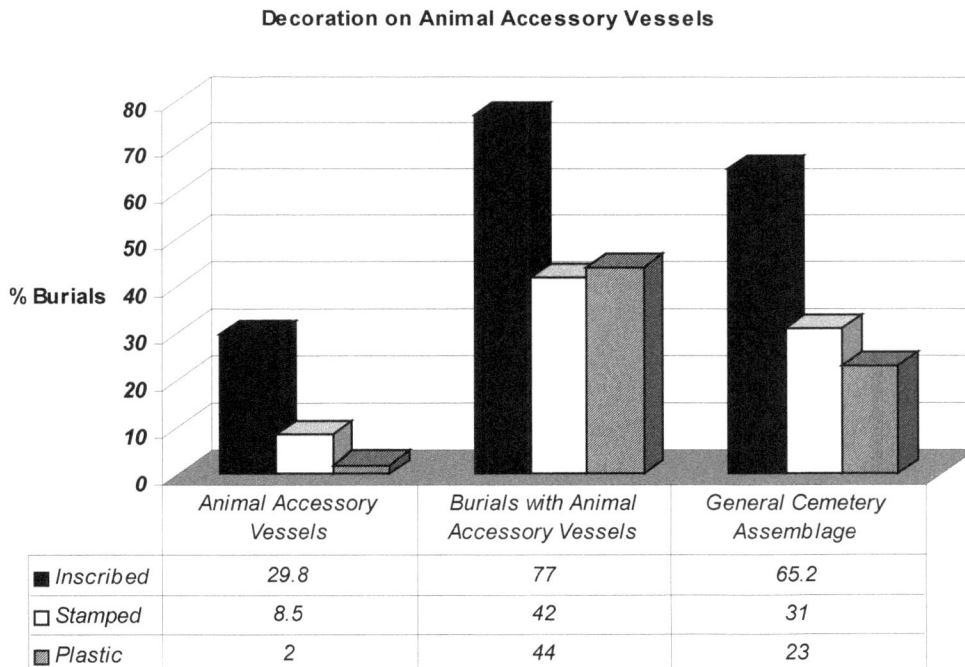

Decoration on Animal Accessory Vessels

	Animal Accessory Vessels	Burials with Animal Accessory Vessels	General Cemetery Assemblage
■ Inscribed	29.8	77	65.2
□ Stamped	8.5	42	31
▦ Plastic	2	44	23

Figure 3.20: A comparison of the types of decoration adorning animal accessory vessels with those found on the cinerary urns associated with them, and the general cemetery population at Spong Hill.

Aged Burials with Animal Accessories

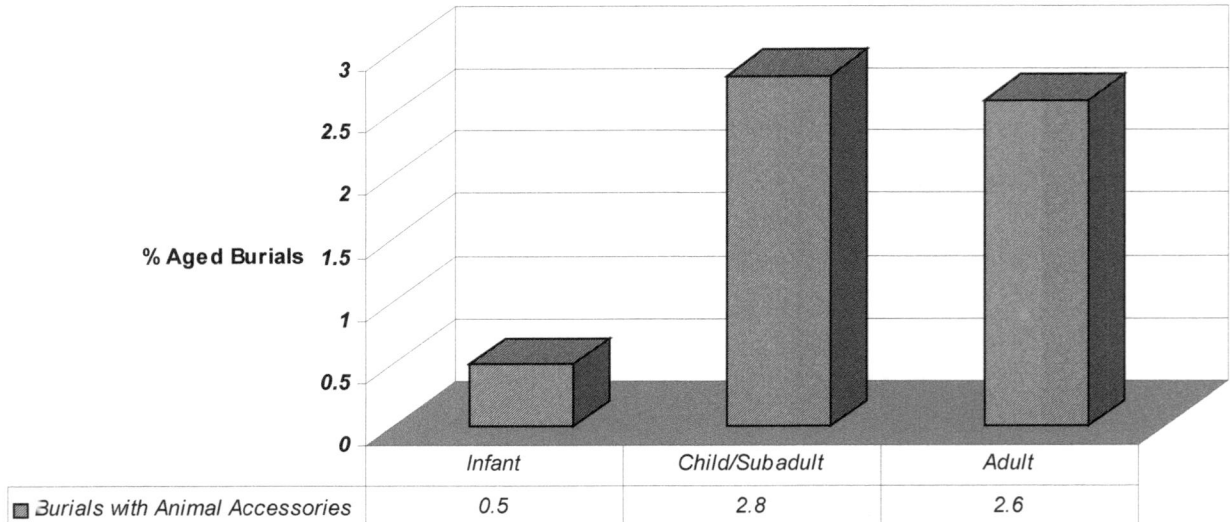

	Infant	Child/Subadult	Adult
▣ Burials with Animal Accessories	0.5	2.8	2.6

Figure 3.21: The biological age at death of individuals interred with animal accessory vessels at Spong Hill.

Sexed Burials with Animal Accessories

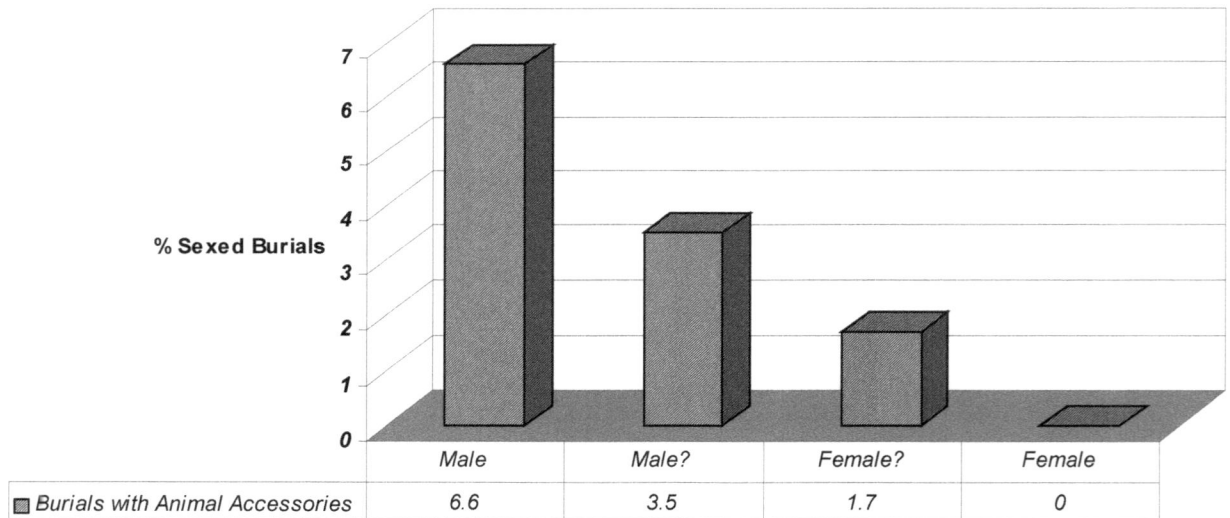

	Male	Male?	Female?	Female
▣ Burials with Animal Accessories	6.6	3.5	1.7	0

Figure 3.22: The biological sex of individuals interred with animal accessory vessels at Spong Hill

% Frequencies of Animals from Animal Accessories and Burials with Animal Accessories

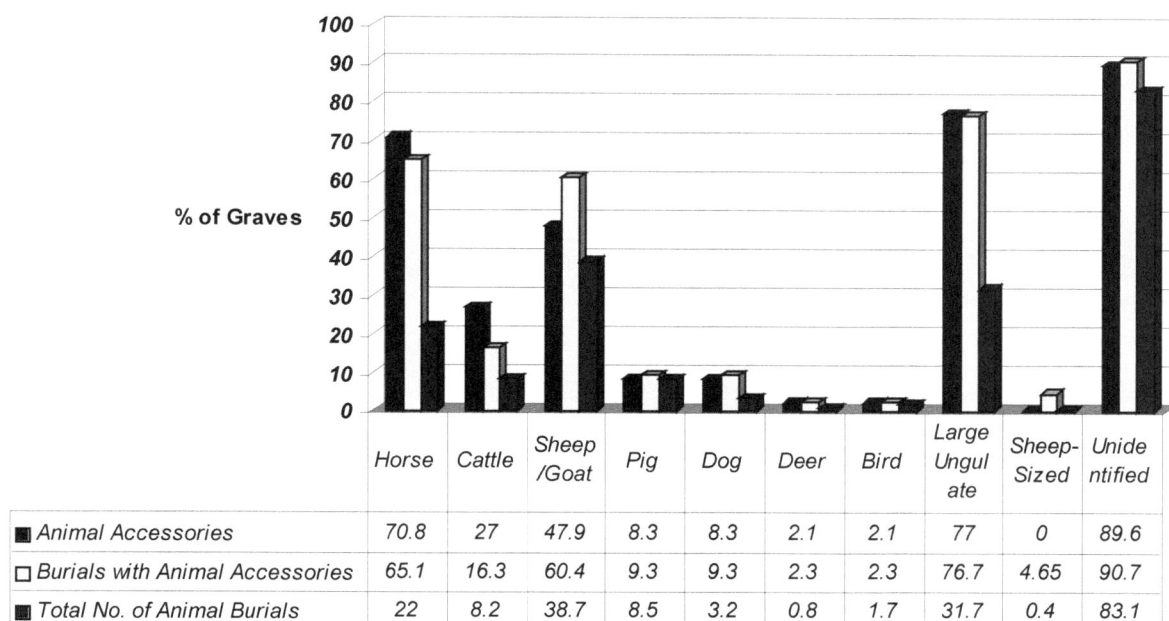

	Horse	Cattle	Sheep /Goat	Pig	Dog	Deer	Bird	Large Ungul ate	Sheep- Sized	Unide ntified
■ Animal Accessories	70.8	27	47.9	8.3	8.3	2.1	2.1	77	0	89.6
□ Burials with Animal Accessories	65.1	16.3	60.4	9.3	9.3	2.3	2.3	76.7	4.65	90.7
■ Total No. of Animal Burials	22	8.2	38.7	8.5	3.2	0.8	1.7	31.7	0.4	83.1

Figure 3.23 The proportion of animal species in animal accessory vessels and burials accompanied by animal accessory urns.

casual process, as with secondary burial rites, the remains can be carefully examined, handled and sometimes used in divination (Williams, 2004).

Therefore, the very act of collecting and including animal remains within the cinerary urns selected to the burial of the ashes needs to be considered as an active and deliberate statement about the changing identities and relationships between animals and people; in most cases both were cremated and both were consigned to the earth in cinerary urns.

Discussion – an ideology of transformation in early Anglo-Saxon England

The evidence presented here builds upon a range of recent studies showing the potential complexity of animal-human relations in medieval times (e.g. papers in Plusowski, 2002; Salisbury 1994; papers in this volume). Although largely archaeological in its focus, this paper draws upon a range of ideas from anthropology and history concerning animals, death and social memory as well as an attempt to interpret and integrate more theoretical approaches with the results of osteological analyses of human and animal bone from cremation burials. In this way, the paper follows Plusowski's lead in arguing to the necessity for multi-disciplinary approaches to the study of human-animal relations in the Middle Ages (Plusowski, 2002; 154, 163-8). From such a perspective, animals can be seen as important resources, companions, symbols and metaphors for medieval people. Furthermore, animals were material resources for

commemorating the dead, but perhaps also 'mnemonic agents' that affected agents' that affected how social identities were transformed and how memories were configured through their sacrifice and associated with the dead (see also Williams, 2004).

This evidence combines to suggest that animals were sacrificed and cremated as a means of promoting a rich display of death and destruction to enhance the memorable nature of the funeral prior to and upon the pyre. Such sacrifices may be linked to symbolism of regeneration and rebounding violence found in funerals across cultures, where the act of killing and subsequent releasing of vitality is seen as a form of victory over death and a restoration of the social order (Bloch & Parry 1982). In terms of social memory, animal sacrifice and display of animal remains on the pyre created a powerful 'image' that was visible for only a short period as part of a unique display before being consigned to oblivion. Hence the intensity of funerary display, combined with its brevity, may have combined to ensure the efficacy of animal sacrifice and cremation as mnemonic practices (see also Küchler, 2002). Moreover, animals were subsequently employed in the post-cremation rituals in the creation of a new identity, memory and physical body for the deceased as an ancestor. The ancestors created from the ashes were not simply composed of the physical remains of the dead person; the 'second bodies' of the dead were composed of pots, artefacts and human and animal remains and may have encapsulated the biographies and identities of each of these elements. Social memory: relations between the living, the dead and the ancestors, was probably a central theme in these transformations and ambiguities (Williams, 2003; forthcoming). Memory was constructed through the technological process of cremation more than the building of a permanent memorial to the dead. Consequently, the sacrifice of animals created a memorable event, but also facilitated in the selective remembrance of the deceased in their transformation from living person to ancestor. The repeated employment of these rituals over time would have contributed to the emergence of ritual traditions linked to ancestral memories made of animals and humans. Cremation and animal sacrifice created mythological and social memories. They may have also driven traditions of ritual behaviour over decades and centuries as funerals repeatedly employed animals to commemorate the dead at successive funerals. Rather than the single funerary events, it is through the repeated expectation that animal sacrifice was necessary as a means of conceiving of, and selectively remembering and forgetting the deceased's identity, that made animals integral to social memory.

Yet what was the precise meaning of animal-person relations in the early Anglo-Saxon mortuary context? We cannot know precisely how the 'rebuilding' of the body was understood in early Anglo-Saxon eastern England, and how animals contributed to social identity. Archaeologists and anthropologists are familiar with the complex roles of animals within funerals in many cultures (e.g. Huntingdon & Metcalf 1991). Animals, and different animal species can constitute different social identities in a direct, totemic way (Richards 1992), or they can relate to genealogies and cosmology in more complex senses (e.g. Tilley 1999: 51-2). Animals can be part of material resources amassed and exchanged at funerals, but also their images can be connected to the dead, in both ways they can serve in the constitution of personhood and in remembering and forgetting the dead (e.g. Küchler, 2002). Human-animal relations can be related to ideas of 'dividual' personhood, in which elements of humans and animals become inter-changeable among the ancestors and in which the exchange and sacrifice of animals articulate the changing identities of persons living and dead (see Barraud et. al. 1994). Moreover, animals can transform the dead, and become integral elements of the identity of ancestors (Chamberlain & Parker Pearson, 2001: 88-96; Jones 1998; Parker Pearson, 1999; 61-67).

But why was the emphasis placed upon human-animal ambiguities and the transformation of animals and people in early Anglo-Saxon cremation rituals? In many cultures, animals can also have specific shamanistic associations, acting as 'agents' that transform the identities of the shaman or the dead during rituals. In other instances, animals can represent shamans in their altered state of Being, and animal-spirits can act as 'familiars' of shamans and the dead, guiding them between worlds (e.g. Lewis-Williams, 2001). These themes may be applicable to the early medieval world.

Certainly animals as psychopomps appear to have held an integral part of northern pagan mythology from what little archaeological and written sources appear to tell us (Eliade 1954; Glosecki 1989; Price 2000). Indeed, metamorphosis was a common theme in both classical and medieval thought (Salisbury 1994). These ideas have been explored in relation to the fifth and sixth centuries concerning the representations of animals and people upon gold bracteates (see above; e.g. Hedeager, 1997; 1999), gold figurines (Back-Danielson, 2002) and Style I animal art (Dickinson, 2002; Kristoffersen 1995; Leigh, 1984; Lindström & Kristoffersen 2001). Concerning mortuary practices in particular, metaphors of journeying have been discussed in relation to Gotlandic picture stones (Andrén 1993), while Neil Price has made an explicit shamanistic interpretation of Scandinavian burial rites in the later first millennium AD (Price, 2002). Against this broader background, it may be possible to suggest that the emphasis upon human-animal relations in early Anglo-Saxon cremation rituals and animal art may both be connected to shamanistic concepts of transformation of the soul between worlds. However, a specifically shamanistic interpretation and a 'literal' reading of the blurring of animal-human identities in death is only one perspective. Whether the early Anglo-Saxons actually believed in mutability between animals and persons in death or this was merely a means of metaphorically dealing with and celebrating the social, cosmological and ontological changes that death initiated, it seems that an 'ideology of transformation' connected much of the art and mortuary practices of the North Sea world in the fifth and sixth centuries, of which early Anglo-Saxon England was part. This theme in mortuary practices as an 'ideology of transformation' helps us to consider the roles of cremation as a means of constituting early Anglo-Saxon social memories and, in turn, social identities.

Acknowledgements

I would like to thank Catherine Hills for originally providing the Spong Hill data in an electronic format that I adapted for use in this study. Thanks to the editor Aleks Pluskowski to his comments on an earlier draft of this paper and thanks also to Chris Fern for allowing me to reference his forthcoming research. All errors remain my responsibility.

References

Back Danielsson, I-M. (2002), '(Un)masking gender — gold foil (dis)embodiments in late Iron Age Scandinavia', in Y. Hamilakis, M. Pluciennik and S. Tarlow (eds.), *Thinking through the Body. Archaeologies of Corporeality*, New York, Kluwer/Plenum.

Barraud, C, de Coppett, D., Iteanu, A. & Jamous, R. (1994). *Of Relations and the Dead,* Oxford, Berg.

Bloch, M. and Parry, J. (1982). 'Introduction: death and the regeneration of life', in M. Bloch and J. Parry (eds.), *Death and the Regeneration of Life*, Cambridge, Cambridge University Press.

Bond, J. M. (1993). 'Cremated animal bone', in J. Timby (ed.), 'Sancton I Anglo-Saxon cemetery. Excavations carried out between 1976 and 1980', *Archaeological Journal*, 150, 243-365.

Bond, J. M. (1994). 'Appendix 1: the cremated animal bone', in J. McKinley, *Spong Hill. Part VIII The Cremations,* East Anglian Archaeology 69, Dereham, Norfolk Museum Service.

Bond, J. M. (1996). 'Burnt offerings: animal bone in Anglo-Saxon cremations', *World Archaeology* 28, 1, 76-88.

Briscoe, T. (1982). 'Anglo-Saxon pot stamps', in D. Brown, S. C. Hawkes and J. Graham-Campbell (eds.), *Anglo-Saxon Studies in Archaeology and History*, 2, Oxford, BAR British Series.

Briscoe, T. (1983). 'A classification of Anglo-Saxon pot stamp motifs and proposed terminology', *Studien zur Sachsenforchung*, 4, 57-71.

Briscoe, T. (1985). 'The use of brooches and other jewellery as dies on pagan Anglo-Saxon pottery', *Medieval Archaeology*, 29, 136-141.

Chamberlain, A. and Parker Pearson, M. (2001). *Earthly Remains: The History and Science of Preserved Human Bodies,* London, British Museum.

Crabtree, P. (1995). 'The symbolic role of animals in Anglo-Saxon England: evidence from burials and cremations', in K. Ryan and P. Crabtree (eds.), *The Symbolic Role of Animals in Archaeology,*

Philadelphia, MASCA, University of Pennsylvania Museum of Archaeology and Anthropology.

David, N. Sterner, J. and Gavua, K. (1988). 'Why pots and decorated', *Current Anthropology*, 29, 3, 365-89.

Dickinson, T. (2002). 'Translating animal art. Salin's Style I and Anglo-Saxon cast saucer brooches', *Hikuin*, 29, 163-86.

Eagles, B. and Briscoe, D. (1999). 'Animal and bird stamps on early Anglo-Saxon pottery', *Studien zur Sachsenforschung*, 13, 99-112.

Eliade, M. (1954). *Shamanism – Archaic Techniques of Ecstasy,* Harmondsworth, Penguin.

Fern, C. (forthcoming). 'The horse in early Anglo-Saxon mortuary contexts, c.450-700', in S. Semple and H. Williams (eds.) *Anglo-Saxon Studies in Archaeology & History,* 13.

Filmer-Sankey, W. and Pestell, T. (2001). *Snape Anglo-Saxon Cemetery: Excavations and Surveys 1824-1992,* Bury St Edmunds, East Anglian Archaeology 95.

Gell, A. (1992). 'The technology of enchantment and the enchantment of technology', in J. Coote and A. Shelton (eds.), *Anthropology: Art and Aesthetics*, Oxford, Clarendon.

Gell, A. (1998). *Art and Agency*, Oxford, Oxford University Press.

Glosecki, S. O. (1989). *Shamanism and Old English Literature*, London, Garland.

Härke, H. (1997). 'Early Anglo-Saxon social structure', in J. Hines (ed.), *The Anglo-Saxons from the Migration Period to the Eighth Century: An Ethnographic Perspective*, Woodbridge, Boydell.

Hawkes, J. (1997). 'Symbolic lives: the visual evidence', in J. Hines (ed.), *The Anglo-Saxons from the Migration Period to the Eighth Century*, Woodbridge, Boydell.

Hedeager, L. (1997). 'Odins offer. Skygger af en shamanistisk tradition i nordisk folkevandringstid, *Tor,* 29, 265-78.

Hedeager, L. (1999) 'Myth and art: a passport to political authority in Scandinavia during the Migration Period', in T. Dickinson & D. Griffiths (eds.), *The Making of Kingdoms. Anglo-Saxon Studies in Archaeology and History* 10, Oxford, Oxbow.

Hicks, C. (1993). *Animals in Early Medieval Art*, Edinburgh, Edinburgh University Press.

Hills, C. (1977). *The Anglo-Saxon Cemetery at Spong Hill, North Elmham. Part I: Catalogue of cremations*, East Anglian Archaeology 6, Dereham, Norfolk Archaeological Unit.

Hills, C. (1980). 'Anglo-Saxon chairperson', *Antiquity*, 54, 210, 52-4.

Hills, C. (1983). 'Animal stamps on Anglo-Saxon pottery in East Anglia', *Studien zur Sachsenforchung*, 4, 93-110.

Hills, C. (1998). 'Did the people of Spong Hill come from Schleswig-Holstein?', *Studien zur Sachsenforchung* 11, 145-54.

Hills, C. (1999). 'Spong Hill and the Adventus Saxonum', in C. Karkov, K. Wickham-Crowley and B. Young (eds.), *Spaces of the Living and the Dead: An Archaeological Dialogue*, Oxford, Oxbow.

Hills, C. (2001). 'From Isidore to Isotopes: ivory rings in early medieval graves', in H. Hamerow and A. MacGregor (eds.), *Image and Power in the Archaeology of Early Medieval Britain*, Oxford, Oxbow.

Hills, C. and Penn, K. (1981). *The Anglo-Saxon Cemetery at Spong Hill, North Elmham. Part II: Catalogue of Cremations*, East Anglian Archaeology 11, Dereham, Norfolk Archaeological Unit.

Hills, C., Penn, K. and Rickett, R. (1987). *The Anglo-Saxon Cemetery at Spong Hill, North Elmham Part IV: Catalogue of Cremations*, East Anglian Archaeology 34, Dereham, Norfolk Archaeological Unit.

Hills, C., Penn, K. and Rickett, R. (1994). *The Anglo-Saxon Cemetery at Spong Hill, North Elmham. Part V: Catalogue of Cremations*, East Anglian Archaeology 67, Dereham, Norfolk Archaeological Unit.

Huntingdon, R. and Metcalf, P. (1991). *Celebrations of Death. The Anthropology of Mortuary Ritual,* 2nd Edition, Cambridge, Cambridge University Press.

Kinsley, A. G. (1989). *The Anglo-Saxon Cemetery at Millgate, Newark-on-Trent, Nottinghamshire,* Nottingham, University of Nottingham.

Kristoffersen, S. (1995). 'Transformation in Migration Period animal art', *Norwegian Archaeological*

Review, 28, 1, 1-18.

Jones A. (1998). 'Where eagles dare. Landscape, animals and the Neolithic of Orkney', *Journal of Material Culture* 3, 3, 301-24.

Jones A. (2003). 'Technologies of remembrance. Memory, materiality and identity in Early Bronze Age Scotland', in H. Williams (ed.), *Archaeologies of Remembrance - Death and Memory in Past Societies,* New York, Kluwer/Plenum.

Leigh, D. (1984). 'Ambiguity in Anglo-Saxon Style I art', *Antiquaries Journal,* 64, 34-42.

Lethbridge, T. C. (1951). *A Cemetery at Lackford, Suffolk,* Cambridge, Cambridge University Press.

Lewis-Williams, J. D. (2001). 'Southern African shamanistic rock art in its social and cognitive contexts', in N. Price (ed.), *The Archaeology of Shamanism,* London, Routledge.

Lindström, T. C. and Kristoffersen, S. (2001). 'Figure it out! Psychological perspectives on perception of Migration Period animal art', *Norwegian Archaeological Review,* 34, 2, 65-84.

MacGregor, A. (1985). *Antler, Ivory and Horn. The Technology of Skeletal Materials since the Roman Period,* London, British Museum.

McKinley, J. (1993). 'Cremated bone', in J. Timby, 'Sancton I Anglo-Saxon cemetery. excavations carried out between 1976 and 1980', *Archaeological Journal,* 150, 243-365.

McKinley, J. (1994). *The Anglo-Saxon Cemetery at Spong Hill, North Elmham. Part VIII: the cremations,* East Anglian Archaeology 69, Dereham, Norfolk Museum Service.

Meaney, A. (1981). *Anglo-Saxon Amulets and Curing stones,* Oxford, British Archaeological Reports British Series 96.

Milner, G. (1853). 'On sepulchral urns found at Newark in 1836', *Journal of the British Archaeological Association,* 8, 192-3.

Myres, J. N. L. (1969). *Anglo-Saxon Pottery and the Settlement of England,* Oxford, Clarendon.

Myres, J. N. L. (1977a). *A Corpus of Anglo-Saxon Pottery of the Pagan Period,* Cambridge, Cambridge University Press.

Myres, J. N. L. (1977b). 'Zoomorphic bosses on Anglo-Saxon pottery', *Studien zur Sachsenforchung,* 1, 281-93.

Myres, J. N. L and Green, B. (1973). *The Anglo-Saxon Cemeteries of Caistor-by-Norwich and Markshall, Norfolk,* London, Society of Antiquaries.

Myres, J. N. L. and Southern, W. H. (1973). *The Anglo-Saxon Cremation Cemetery at Sancton, East Yorkshire,* Hull, Hull Museum Service.

Parker Pearson, M. (1999). *The Archaeology of Death and Burial,* Stroud, Sutton.

Pluskowski, A. (2002) 'Hares with crossbows and rabbit bones: integrating physical and conceptual studies of medieval fauna', *Archaeological Review from Cambridge,* 18, 153-82.

Price, N. (2000). 'Shamanism and the Vikings?', in W. W Fitzhugh and E. I. Ward (eds.), *Vikings. The North Atlantic Saga,* Washington, Smithsonian.

Price, N. (2002). *The Viking Way,* Uppsala, Uppsala University Press.

Ravn, M. (1999). 'Theoretical and methodological approaches to Migration Period burials', in M. Rundkvist (ed) *Grave Matters. Eight Studies of First Millennium AD burials in Crimea, England and southern Scandinavia,* Oxford, BAR International Series 781.

Ravn, M. (2003). *Death Ritual and Germanic Social Structure,* Oxford, BAR International Series 1164.

Richards, J. D. (1987). *The Significance of Form and Decoration of Anglo-Saxon Cremation Urns,* Oxford, BAR British Series 166.

Richards, J. D. (1992). 'Anglo-Saxon symbolism', in M. Carver (ed.), *The Age of Sutton Hoo,* Woodbridge, Boydell.

Salisbury, J. E. (1994). *The Beast Within. Animals in the Middle Ages,* London, Routledge.

Serematakis, N. (1991). *The Last Word. Women, Death, and Divination in Inner Mani,* Chicago, University of Chicago Press.

Speake, G. (1980). *Germanic Animal Art and its Background,* Oxford, Oxford University Press.

Stoodley, N. (1999). *The Spindle and the Spear,* Oxford, BAR British Series 288.

Tilley, C. (1999). *Metaphor and Material Culture,* Oxford, Blackwell.

Timby, J. (1993). 'Sancton I Anglo-Saxon cemetery. Excavations carried out between 1976 and 1980.' *Archaeological Journal,* 150, 243-365.

Vierck, H. (1971). 'Pferdegräber im Angelsächsichen England', in M. Müller-Wille (ed.) Pferdegrab und Pferdeopfer in frühen Mittelalter. *Berichten v.d. Rijksdienst v.h. Oudheidkundig Bodemonderzoek 1971,* 189-99, 218-20.

Vitebsky, P. (1995). *The Shaman,* London, MacMillan.

Wells, C. (1960). 'A study of cremation', *Antiquity,* 34, 29-37.

Wilkinson, L. (1980). 'Problems of analysis and interpretation of skeletal remains', in P.Rahtz, T.Dickinson and L.Watts (eds.), *Anglo-Saxon Cemeteries 1979,* Oxford, BAR British Series 82.

Williams, H. (2001). 'An ideology of transformation: cremation rites and animal sacrifice in early Anglo-Saxon England', in N. Price (ed.), *The Archaeology of Shamanism,* London, Routledge.

Williams, H. (2003). 'Material culture as memory: combs and cremation in early medieval Britain', *Early Medieval Europe,* 12, 2, 89-128.

Williams, H. (2004). 'Death warmed up: the agency of bodies and bones in early Anglo-Saxon cremation rites', *Journal of Material Culture* 9 (3): 263-91.

Williams, P. (1983). *An Anglo-Saxon Cremation Cemetery at Thurmaston, Leicestershire.* Leicester, Leicestershire Museums, Art Galleries and Records Service Archaeological Reports Series No. 8.

Wilson, D. (1992). *Anglo-Saxon Paganism,* London, Routledge.

Zooarchaeology, Artefacts, Trade and Identity: The Analysis of Bone and Antler Combs From Early Medieval England and Scotland

Steven P Ashby

The Role of Zooarchaeology

While the analysis of diet and economy will always be fundamental areas of zooarchaeological research, it is herein argued that faunal analysts may attempt to move into new areas. Zooarchaeology has the potential to contribute to the understanding of social values, culture and ideology, particularly when it is used as part of an integrated approach (*e.g.* Barrett, *et al.* 2000). In this paper, a role for zooarchaeology in the recognition of migration, culture contact and identity is discussed.

There are many means by which valuable contributions to such issues might be made. Biogeographical studies, butchery analysis, morphometric, isotopic and genetic approaches all show great potential (see Ashby 2004). One further area of interest, and one which may perhaps be more seamlessly dovetailed into the 'mainstream' of archaeology, is the analysis of worked bone. To illustrate how such a study may integrate techniques from zooarchaeology, artefact analysis and documentary research, an example is taken from the author's current research.

Bone and Antler Combs in Viking Age England and Scotland

This project aims to elucidate the role of the hair comb in Viking Age England and Scotland (*Figure 4.1*). How were such items produced, and by what means were raw materials acquired? Were combs traded over long distances, or merely produced by local or itinerant craftsmen? Such questions are fundamental to our understanding of these artefacts, but one should also consider the matter of their consumption. Combs probably acted both as visible dress accessories and items of private grooming. As such, they may have played a subtle but important role in the expression of identity. Thus, variations in raw material, style, method and quality of manufacture, and context of deposition are all potentially imbued with meaning, and will be recorded and statistically analysed.

Several in-depth studies of Viking Age combs have been undertaken (see for example Ulbricht 1978; Ambrosiani 1981; Smirnova 2002), and this project builds upon such accomplished work. Indeed, in order to allow backwards

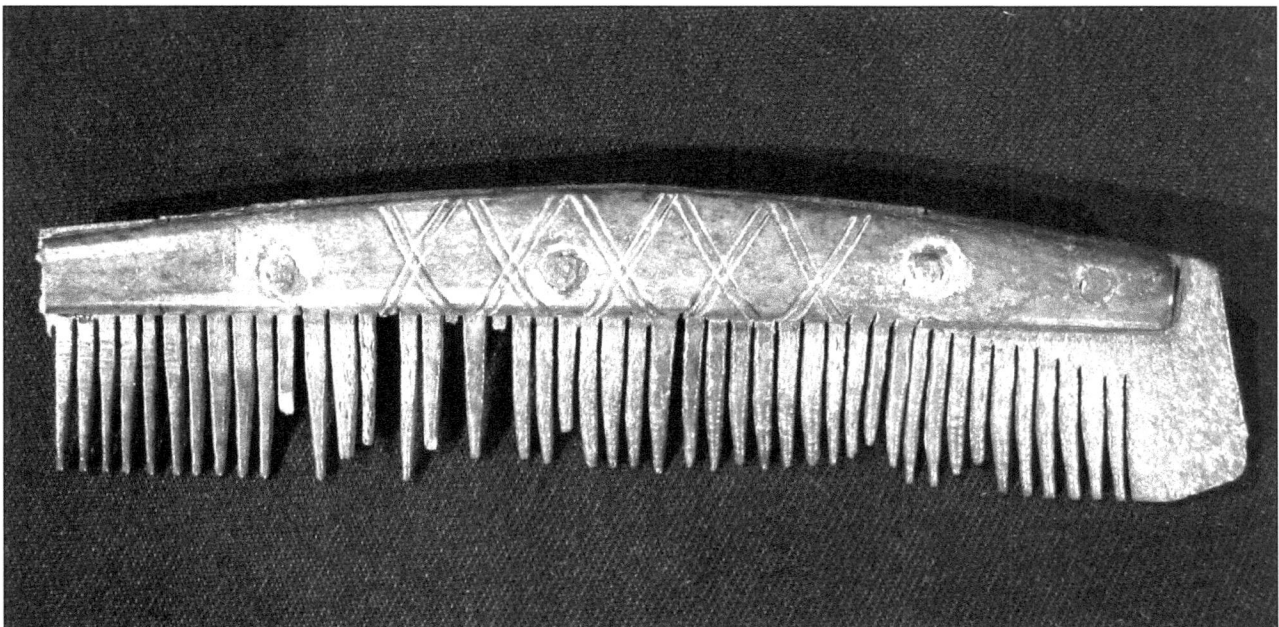

Figure 4.1: Antler Comb from excavations at Lloyd's Bank, York. (Photograph: S. Ashby, courtesy York Museum Trust)

comparability, a number of measures used previously have been applied in this project. However, an explicit focus on combs of skeletal materials, a comparison of corpora from England and Scotland, and the integration of multiple techniques, together make this project unique.

Indeed, a very important component of the project is a survey of documentary sources and ethnohistory. The aim of this facet of the research is to illuminate the role of the comb in early medieval society, most particularly how it was produced, distributed, consumed and disposed of. The aim is not to follow any historical agenda, but to use the documentary record to shed light upon areas of the comb's life that are particularly amenable to literary study. For example, one's understanding of the social contexts in which combs were used, and how they were worn or carried, may benefit from this type of research.

This analysis should inform our knowledge of ethnic relations in the Viking Age, and how the idea of identity was constructed and perpetuated. Such an understanding can only be achieved through the integration of archaeological, zooarchaeological and historical strands of research.

Acknowledgements

Thanks are due to the Arts and Humanities Research Board, funders of this project, and to Terry O'Connor, Julian Richards, James Barrett and Lyuba Smirnova for helpful advice. Particular thanks are due to James Barrett for comments on an earlier draft of the paper presented at Lampeter. Thanks also to York Museums Trust for the use of the photograph in *Figure 4.1*.

References

Ambrosiani, K. (1981). *Viking Age Combs, Comb Making and Comb Makers in the Light of Finds from Birka and Ribe*, Stockholm, Stockholm Studies in Archaeology 2.

Ashby, S.P. 2004. 'Understanding Human Movement and Interaction through the Movement of Animals and Animal Products', in M. Mondini, Muñoz, S. , and Wickler, S. (eds), *Colonisation, Migration, and Marginal Areas: A Zooarchaeological Approach. Proceedings of the 9th ICAZ Conference, Durham 2002*, Oxford: Oxbow, pp 4-9.

Barrett, J. H., Beukens, R. P., Simpson, I., Ashmore, P., Poaps, S. and Huntley, J. (2000). 'What was the Viking Age and when did it happen?', *Norwegian Archaeological Review*, 33, 1-40.

Smirnova, L. (2002). *Comb-making in Medieval Novgorod (950-1450): an Industry in Transition*, unpublished Ph.D. thesis, University of Bournemouth.

Ulbricht, I. (1978). *Die Geweihverarbeitung in Haithabu. Neumunster*, Die Ausgrabungen in Haithabu 7.

The archaeological evidence for equestrianism in early Anglo-Saxon England, c.450-700

By Chris Fern

Studies of the phenomenon of horse burial and of horse equipment, for the early medieval period on the Continent and in Scandinavia, have demonstrated that equestrianism was an important attribute of martial elites in these regions (Müller-Wille, 1970/71; Oexle, 1984; 1992; Rettner, 1997; Sundkvist, 2001). This is evidenced by the widespread practice of sacrificing valuable riding horses to accompany male burials equipped with weaponry, horse harness and prestige goods, and by the related tradition of richly decorating equestrian equipment.   By comparison, the evidence for a parallel custom in early Anglo-Saxon England has been regarded as negligible and peripheral to the main central European distribution, and thus reflective of the relative unimportance of equitation, and by extension the use of horses for warfare, in England in the period (Baldwin-Brown, 1915: 420-423; Härke, 1997). This study seeks to reassess the archaeological data for early Anglo-Saxon England and to demonstrate in opposition to this view that, while small, the archaeological corpus provides definite evidence for an equestrian culture at the top level of society. This is suggested by a tradition of horse harness, which, while related to Continental fashions, also demonstrates distinctly idiosyncratic traits. Furthermore, in line with European trends, on rare occasions such equipment and/or a riding horse was included in the funerary assemblages of Anglo-Saxon elites, in combination with weaponry and luxury goods. The restriction of such rites to this class is interpreted here as a deliberate act intended to signal and at the same time guard equestrian privileges.

Horse and harness burial

Most of our evidence is drawn from the funerary record, and more specifically from the rite of horse inhumation, or the provision of horse equipment as a grave good. In sacrificing horses to accompany the dead the Anglo-Saxon elite were doubtless influenced by Continental burial theatre, where the rite is to be observed at its most explicit. In his study Müller-Wille catalogued over 750 examples of horse inhumation in Europe between the fifth and the eleventh centuries (Müller-Wille, 1970/71). More recently, Oexle's study of Continental horse equipment has catalogued over 600 sets for the Merovingian Period (Oexle, 1992: 17). The earliest horse burials are concentrated east of the Rhine amongst the Saxons, Thuringians and Lombards, though by the seventh century the practice had become popular foremost amongst the Rhineland Franks, Alamanni and Bavarians (Müller-Wille, 1970/71: Abb. 20). It is in these latter regions also that horse harness was most commonly deposited in burials (Oexle, 1984: fig. 1). With a few exceptions, notably the grave of Childeric, the rites of horse burial and bridle burial did not spread

across the Rhine into post-Roman Francia; although a cluster of burials containing spurs west of the Seine is noteworthy (Müller-Wille, 1970/71: Abb. 1; Oexle, 1984: fig. 1; Rettner, 1997: Abb. 4).

In Scandinavia the situation is different. In the Roman Iron Age great sacrificial deposits of horses and horse equipment are evidenced in Denmark and eastern Sweden; yet, these suggest communal ceremonies of a different kind to the individualistic burial of a horse and rider (Müller-Wille, 1970/71: 180-185, Abb. 43). In Sweden the act of cremating horses and putting horse equipment in graves occurs rarely during the Migration Period, but becomes more popular from the mid- to late sixth century, when also the specific act of inhuming horses and their equipment with martial elites begins, a development that is attributed to central European influence (Petré, 1984: 217; Ramquist, 1992: 66-88; Müller-Wille 1999: 10, 18).

In most cases of Continental horse inhumation a single individual was buried, though two, three and occasionally more animals were inhumed, sometimes accompanied by dogs (Müller-Wille, 1970/71: 127-128, 135-138, Abb. 4-5, 8; Prummel, 1992: 137). Usually, the horse was buried whole, though decapitated animals are a particular feature of Thuringian and Alamannic cemeteries, with only the carcass or head buried (Kerth, 2000: 128). In the earliest burials both horse and human could occur in the same large grave with the harness usually on the horse, but from c.600 the rite sees the separation of animal and human into different burials, with the horse equipment typically in the human grave (Oexle, 1984: 123, 139).

In England there are thirty-one[1] instances of inhumed horses (discounting disarticulated remains) and twelve cases of riding equipment[2] deposited as a grave good without associated horse remains (Vierck, 1970/71; English summary see Filmer-Sankey and Pestell, 2001: 256-259; Fern, forthcoming). Most of the horses and

---

[1] Stone I, Bucks.; Little Wilbraham 44, Cambs.; Cornforth, Co. Durham; Great Chesterford I H1, Great Chesterford I 142/H2, Great Chesterford II H1, Great Chesterford II H2, Saffron Walden, Springfield Lyons 8577, Essex; Fairford, Glouc.; Sarre 271, Saltwood 5, Kent; Wanlip, Wigston Magna, Leics.; Caenby, Lincs.; Sporle, Norfolk; Broughton Lodge 15/16/H1, Broughton Lodge 69/H2, Broughton Lodge 88/H3, Broughton Lodge H4, Broughton Lodge 19/20, Notts.; Hardingstone, Marston St. Lawrence, Woodstone, Northants.; Eriswell 0355, Eriswell 4116, Icklingham, Snape 47, Sutton Hoo 17, Warren Hill (Mildenhall), Suffolk; West Heslerton 19/186,Yorks.

[2] Chamberlain's Barn II 45, Beds.; Edix Hill 88, Linton Heath 18, Cambs.; Castledyke 18, Humber.; Bishopsbourne 3, Mill Hill 93, Saltwood 7, Sarre 28, Kent; Kirton-in-Lindsey II, Loveden Hill HB4, Lincs.; Alfriston 91, W. Sussex; Garton II 10, Yorks.

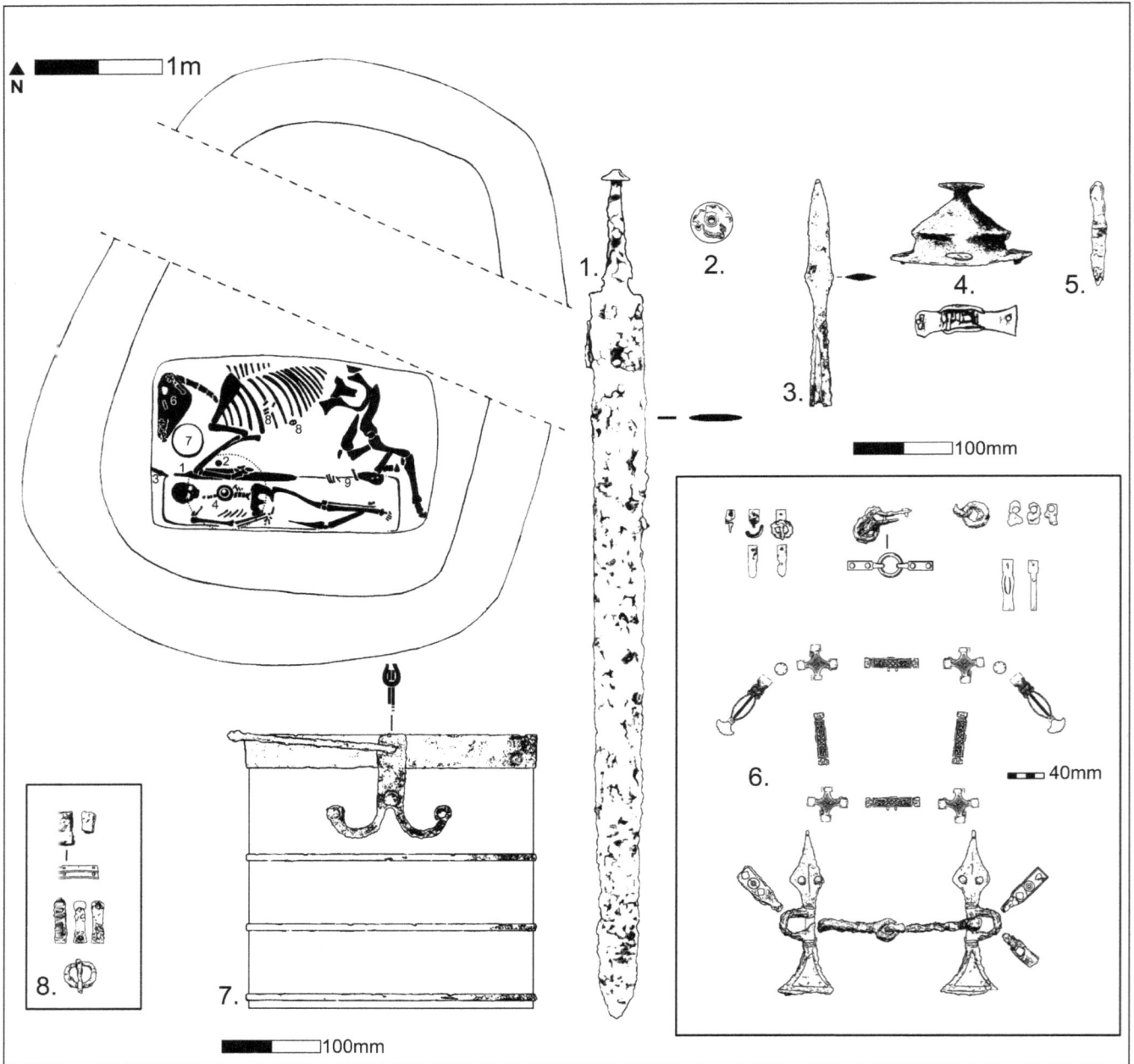

Figure 5.1 The sixth-century horse burial from Eriswell 104 (Lakenheath), grave 4116: 1. Sword 2. Sword-bead 3.
Spearhead 4. Shield 5. Knife 6. Bridle 7.Bucket 8. Saddle fittings 9. Sheep remains

sets of harness have been found buried with, or in association with, adult males with prestige items, such as swords and bronze bowls, and in some cases in graves marked by ring-ditches, posts or mounds (*Figures 5.1-5.3*; Fern, forthcoming).

The Anglo-Saxon rite exhibits notable parallels with the Continental custom. In the sixth century the human and harnessed horse were placed in the same grave, but from the early seventh century the burials are separate. In all cases only a single horse was sacrificed, occasionally by decapitation, with only the head buried (Ibid.). Around half of the horse burials known include bridle

and saddle equipment, and in one third of cases this equipment was found *in situ* on the horse, confirming that these were trained riding animals.[3] After the end of horse burial in England, in the early seventh century, horse harness continued to be buried in human graves, perhaps as a symbol of equestrian status (*Figure 5.3*; Geake, 1997: 101).

---

[3] *On the horse*: Little Wilbraham 44, Great Chesterford I 142/H2, Springfield Lyons 8577, Hardingstone, Marston St. Lawrence, Broughton Lodge 15/16/H1, Eriswell 0355, Eriswell 4116, Snape 47, *In the horse grave*: Broughton Lodge H3, Wanlip, West Heslerton 186, Wigston Magna *In the human grave*: Saltwood 5, Sutton Hoo 17

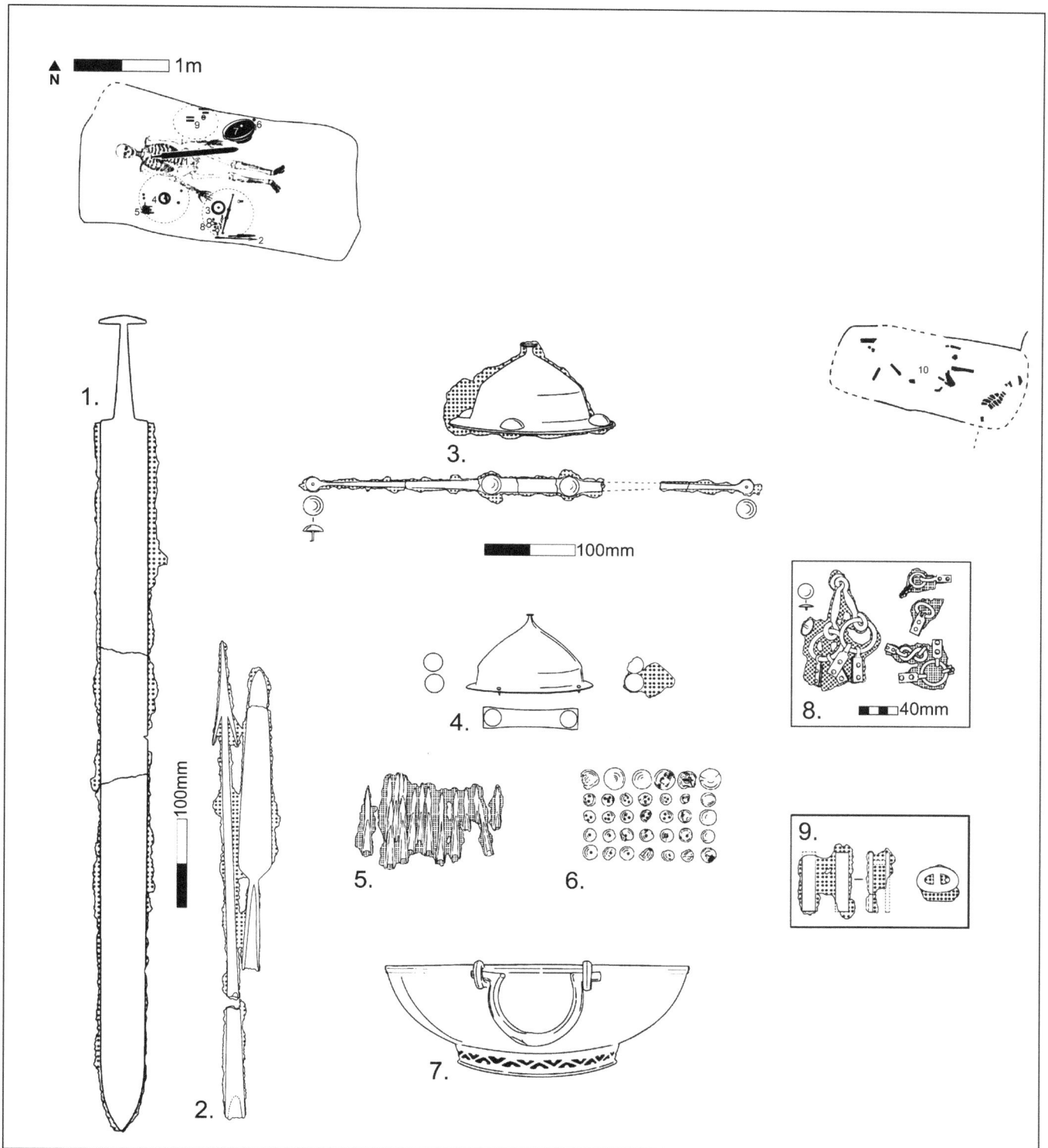

Figure 5.2 The late sixth or early seventh-century horse burial from Saltwood, grave 5 (1-5, 8-9. From x-ray): 1. Sword 2. Spearheads 3. Shield 4. Shield 5. Arrowheads 6. Playing pieces 7. Bronze bowl 8. Bridle 9. Saddle fittings 10. Horse

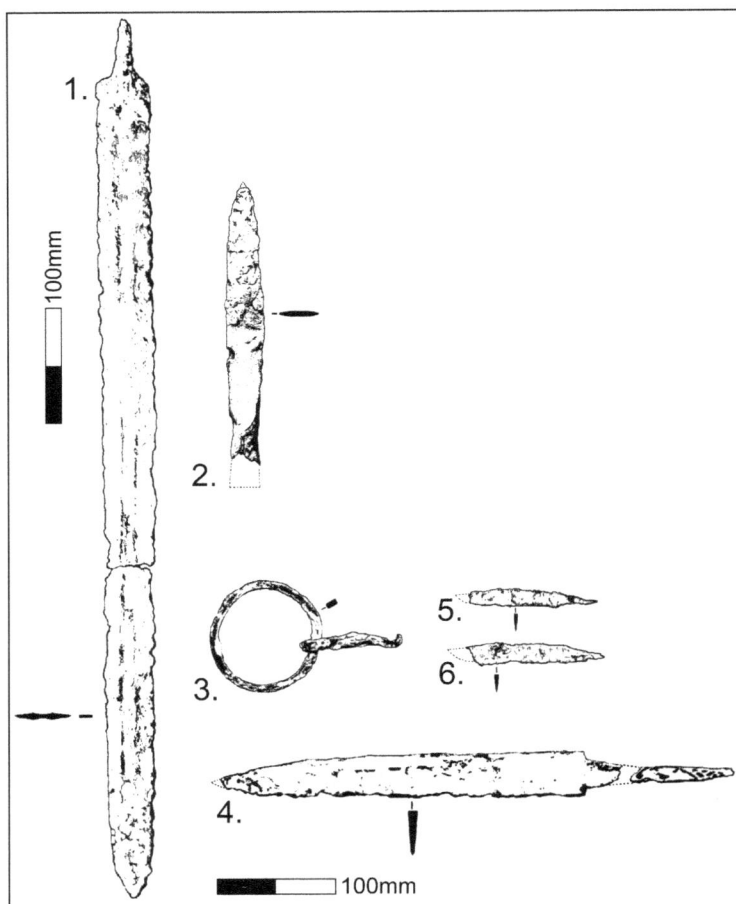

*Figure 5.3 The seventh-century bridle burial from Kirton-in-Lindsey II: 1. Sword 2. Spearhead
3. Snaffle-bit 4. Seax 5. Knife 6. Knife*

In addition, bridle-bits (or parts thereof) and decorated harness suites without a specific context are known from a further nine Anglo-Saxon cemeteries,[4] and from six settlement sites within the British Isles.[5]

A separate class of evidence is the several hundred examples of horse cremation which cluster around the Humber and Wash estuaries, and north Norfolk (Bond, 1996; Fern, forthcoming). In contrast to the inhumation rite, however, in these regions horse sacrifice is not a minority rite, but can occur with around 10 per cent of the buried population, including both males and females, and occasionally children (McKinley, 1994: 66, 99, 123). However, no definite articles of horse equipment have been found with horse remains in a cremation, and the destructive nature of the rite means that the skeletal assemblage can tell us little specifically about the horses themselves. Although some finds of iron rings and bars have been suggested as the remains

of snaffles, all are probably common items from châtelaines (contra Hills, 1999: 153). It is, therefore, difficult to know if these were riding animals or less valuable draft agricultural animals, perhaps sacrificed more for totemic or even cultic reasons (Williams, 2001: 207).

Horse equipment also occurs in burials reused as châtelaine items or brooches. The secondary reuse of horse equipment in this way, particularly in female graves, is a rare phenomenon also evidenced on the Continent (Oexle, 1992: 15-16). In England examples of broken snaffles found employed at the waist as a châtelaine item include East Shefford 9, Berks., and Bishop's Cleeve 7, Glouc.; while Wallingford 12, Oxon., is an example of decorated harness fittings reworked as a pair of brooches (*Figure 5.14*; Peake and Hooton, 1915: 112-113; Leeds, 1938: 97, pl. 5; Dickinson et al, forthcoming). This reuse of decorated horse harness in particular is interesting, since it demonstrates that elaborate harness was more widespread than the few examples in horse and bridle burials attest. In addition, a growing number of decorative mounts have been recovered by metal-detecting, which may represent either casual losses, or destroyed or disturbed burials.

---

[4]   *Snaffles:* Droxford, Hants.; Eastry I (Buttsole), Howletts 36, Kent; Market Overton I, Market Overton II, Rutland; Brixworth II, Duston, Northants., Howick, Yorks. *Harness sets*: Eastry I (Buttsole), Faversham, Kent.

[5]   Lagore, Co. Meath (Ireland); Whithorn, Dumfries.; Wicken Bonhunt, Essex; Thwing, Humber.; Maxey, Northants.; Yeavering, Northum.

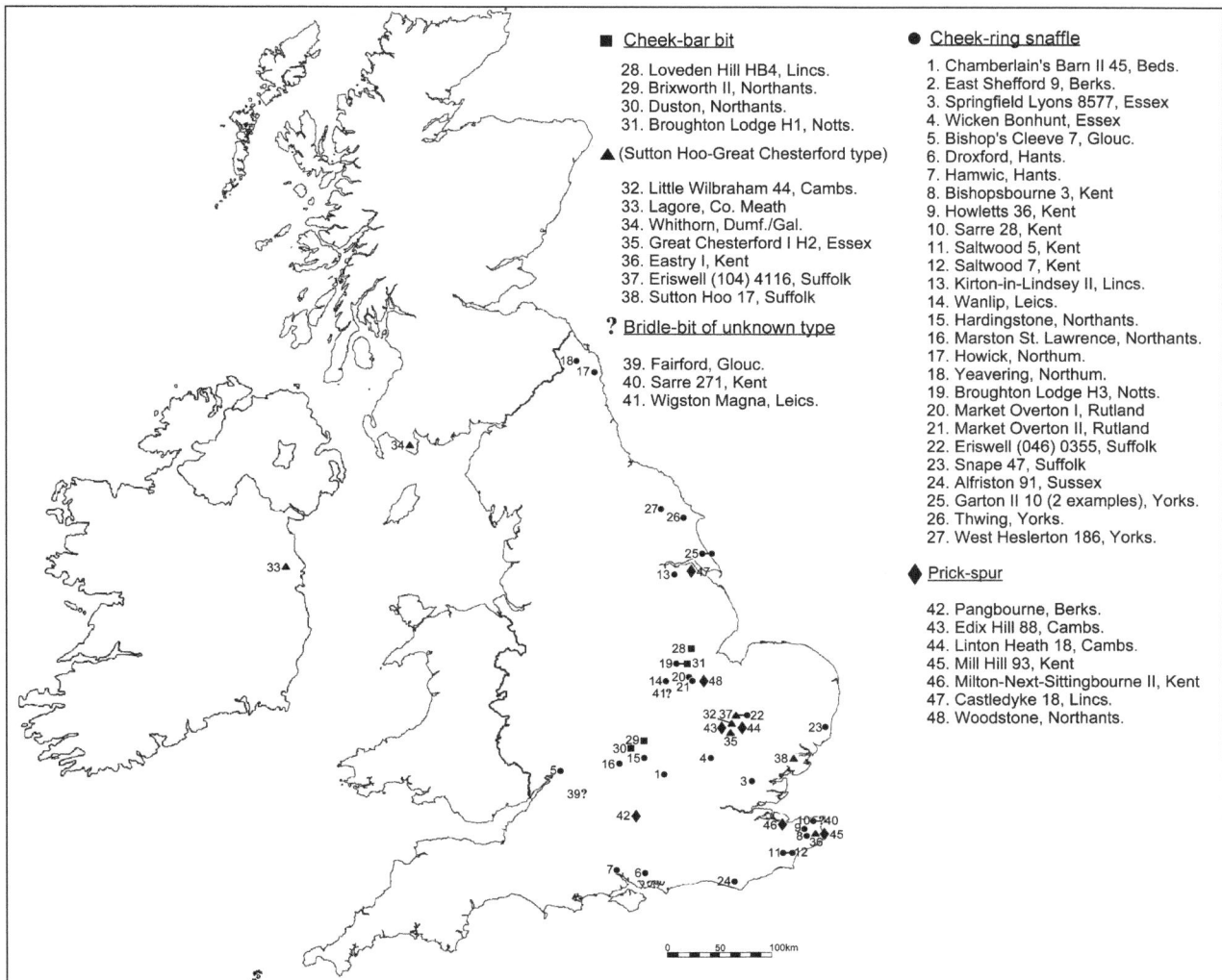

The find locations of horse equipment in England, c.450-700. Map legend:

■ Cheek-bar bit
28. Loveden Hill HB4, Lincs.
29. Brixworth II, Northants.
30. Duston, Northants.
31. Broughton Lodge H1, Notts.

▲ (Sutton Hoo-Great Chesterford type)
32. Little Wilbraham 44, Cambs.
33. Lagore, Co. Meath
34. Whithorn, Dumf./Gal.
35. Great Chesterford I H2, Essex
36. Eastry I, Kent
37. Eriswell (104) 4116, Suffolk
38. Sutton Hoo 17, Suffolk

? Bridle-bit of unknown type
39. Fairford, Glouc.
40. Sarre 271, Kent
41. Wigston Magna, Leics.

● Cheek-ring snaffle
1. Chamberlain's Barn II 45, Beds.
2. East Shefford 9, Berks.
3. Springfield Lyons 8577, Essex
4. Wicken Bonhunt, Essex
5. Bishop's Cleeve 7, Glouc.
6. Droxford, Hants.
7. Hamwic, Hants.
8. Bishopsbourne 3, Kent
9. Howletts 36, Kent
10. Sarre 28, Kent
11. Saltwood 5, Kent
12. Saltwood 7, Kent
13. Kirton-in-Lindsey II, Lincs.
14. Wanlip, Leics.
15. Hardingstone, Northants.
16. Marston St. Lawrence, Northants.
17. Howick, Northum.
18. Yeavering, Northum.
19. Broughton Lodge H3, Notts.
20. Market Overton I, Rutland
21. Market Overton II, Rutland
22. Eriswell (046) 0355, Suffolk
23. Snape 47, Suffolk
24. Alfriston 91, Sussex
25. Garton II 10 (2 examples), Yorks.
26. Thwing, Yorks.
27. West Heslerton 186, Yorks.

◆ Prick-spur
42. Pangbourne, Berks.
43. Edix Hill 88, Cambs.
44. Linton Heath 18, Cambs.
45. Mill Hill 93, Kent
46. Milton-Next-Sittingbourne II, Kent
47. Castledyke 18, Lincs.
48. Woodstone, Northants.

Figure 5.4 The find locations of horse equipment in England, c.450-700

Bridle-bits

Thirty-eight[6] extant bridle-bits (*Figure 5.4*) are known for the early Anglo-Saxon period, as well as three lost examples: 'horse furniture' from Fairford, Glouc.; an 'iron snaffle-bit' from Sarre 271, Kent; and 'something like a snaffle-bit' from Wigston Magna, Leics. (Nichol, 1807: 377; Smith, 1851/52: 79; Brent, 1868: 317). This figure builds significantly on the twenty examples assessed by Vierck in 1970/71; but excludes the erroneous examples from Caenby, Lincs. (a fragment of bucket handle: Webster, pers. comm.), Gilton Ash 83, Kent ('doubtful'), and Linton Heath 47, Cambs. (a châtelaine) (Vierck, 1970/71: 191).

The cheek-ring snaffle (*Figure 5.5*) is the most common bridle-bit, occurring throughout Europe in the period (Oexle, 1992: 17-34; Nawroth, 2001: 77). The form is comprised of paired loose rings linked by a horizontal mouthpiece. It has its origin in the Iron Age, was in use in the Roman period, and is still the basic modern type (Dixon and Southern, 1992: 63). Of the Anglo-Saxon examples all but one has a mouthpiece bar comprising two single jointed elements (*Figures 5.5-5.7*). The exception is that from Chamberlain's Barn II 45, Beds., which has an unbroken bar, a form unknown from Continental contexts (Hyslop, 1963: 184, fig. 15; Nawroth, 2001: 80). Vierck considered this to be possibly a châtelaine, though I would not altogether exclude the possibility that it is a bit (Vierck, 1970/71: 191). In addition, two cheek-ring fittings from the Springfield Lyons 8577 horse-head burial, Essex, were found without evidence for a conjoining mouthpiece bar (Tyler and Major, forthcoming). Possibly in this case the mouthpiece had been made of organic material.

Twenty-two cheek-ring snaffles have been measured to assess their size (*Table 5.1.1*). The results show that most have a mouthpiece measurement of between 110mm and 130mm, with the smallest being the 100mm example

---

[6] This number is based in each case on individual formal examination, with the purpose to exclude examples of châtelaine equipment, which can comprise rings and bars that in appearance are very similar to snaffle-bit components.

from Market Overton II, Rutland, and the largest at 160mm that from Marston St. Lawrence, Northants. (*Table 5.1.1,* dimension C; Dryden, 1885: pl. 25). These measurements accord well with those attained for contemporary Continental and Scandinavian (Vendel and Valsgärde) examples, and are not dissimilar to mouthpiece measurements from Roman snaffles (Hyland, 1990: 139-140; Nawroth, 2001: Abb. 37; Sundqvist, 2001: Tab. 6.1). While the correlation between the withers shoulder height of a horse and its mouth size, and hence fitted snaffle, is not necessarily a direct one, it may serve as a rough guide: by modern standards a 100mm mouthpiece apportions approximately to a 13-13.2 hand (c.1.32-1.37m) horse and one of 110-120mm+ to an animal of 13.2 to 14.2 hands (c.1.37-1.47m) (Hyland, 1990: 140). Although as a cautionary caveat the horse from Marston St. Lawrence, in whose mouth the largest bit was found, was described by its excavator as 'not above 14 hands high' (Dryden, 1885: 330).

Following Vierck's survey, the cheek-rings of the snaffles may be regarded as either small (<79mm) or large (>80mm) in diameter, with the former in the majority (*Table 5.1.1*; Vierck 1970/71: 191). The ring sizes of the English corpus are proportionate with examples of *Ringtrense* (cheek-ring snaffle) from the Continent, where the average diameter was between 40mm and 75mm, with a minimum of 20mm and maximum of 120mm (Oexle, 1992: Abb. 3). The Scandinavian Vendel and Valsgärde cheek-ring snaffles, by comparison, have mainly large rings over 80mm in diameter (Sundqvist, 2001: Tab. 6.1).

The burial contexts of this bridle-bit type demonstrate its use throughout England in the early Anglo-Saxon period: Alfriston 91, E. Sussex, is a fifth-century burial; those from Wanlip, Leics., Broughton Lodge H3, Notts., Eriswell (046) 0355 (Lakenheath), Suffolk, and West Heslerton 186, Yorks., are sixth-century graves; while Bishopsbourne 3, Kent, Saltwood 7, Kent, Kirton-in-Lindsey II, Lincs., Hardingstone, Northants., Snape 47, Suffolk, and Garton II 10, Yorks., are dated to the seventh century (Wright, 1844; Bateman, 1860; Mortimer, 1905: 250, pls. 86-87; Liddle, 1979/80; Welch, 1983: 112, 376, fig. 38; Kinsley, 1993: 48, 53, fig. 90; Haughton and Powesland, 1999: 28-29, 331-333; Filmer-Sankey and Pestell, 2001: 102-111, figs. 75-76 Fern, forthcoming). Others are only datable broadly within the period, such as the uncontexted example from Droxford, Hants., and those from Market Overton I and II (Mearey, 1964: 216-217; Aldsworth, 1979: 141, fig. 46). The examples from settlement sites at Hamwic, Hants., (Six Dials Site: SOU 169.974), Thwing, Yorks., (sf87.194), Wicken Bonhunt, Essex, and Yeavering, Northum., are by comparison all dated between the seventh and ninth centuries (Hope-Taylor, 1977: 189, fig. 89.3; Goodall and Ottoway, forthcoming; Southampton Museum Archaeological Object Database).

The other form of bit employed in the period is the cheek-bar bit, which has two vertical bars instead of, or in addition to, paired rings (*Figure 5.5*; Oexle, 1992: 34-73.). This form is also of probable European Iron Age origin,

but does not appear to have existed in Britain in the Roman period. There are twelve examples of this type, which although related to the equivalent Continental *Knebeltrense* (cheek-bar bit) form, demonstrate distinctly Insular traits in their formal and decorative aspects. The three examples from Loveden Hill HB4, Lincs., Brixworth II, Northants., and Duston, Northants., are non-elaborate in their vertical bars, though the former has slightly flattened 'wing' terminals (*Figure 5.8*; Fennell, 1964: fig. 14). The Brixworth II and Duston bits have 'egg-butt' side joints to their mouthpieces, a development still found in modern forms to prevent pinching to the corners of the horse's mouth (*Figures 5.5, 5.8*). These two bridles also have exceptionally large mouthpieces, which are 180mm and 250mm in length respectively (*Table 5.1.2*). The only explanation for the Duston measurement, which is incongruously large even by modern standards, is that the bit was a symbolic object. In addition, there is the badly corroded example from Broughton Lodge H1, which now exhibits no obvious signs of formal elaboration (Kinsley, 1993; fig. 45).

Seven of the cheek-bar bits belong to a distinctive form defined by a flattened peltaic-shaped lower bar with either a lozenge-shaped upper bar or an off-set disc-head terminal (*Figure 5.5*). Examples with a lozenge-shaped upper bar are those from Little Wilbraham 44, Cambs., Great Chesterford I 142/H2, Essex, and Eriswell (104) 4116 (Lakenheath), Suffolk (*Figures 5.9-5.11*; Neville, 1852: 16, pl. 38; Evison, 1994: 111-112, fig. 54; Caruth and Anderson, 1999; Newman, forthcoming). The two examples with an off-set disc-head to their upper bar are the closely similar bits from Lagore, Co. Meath (Ireland), and Sutton Hoo 17, Suffolk (Hencken, 1950: 101, fig. 36.354; Carver, forthcoming). In addition, a further fragment of cheek-bar, which combines the two features of the lozenge and off-set disc is that from Eastry I (Buttsole), Kent (*Figure 5.12*; Payne, 1894: 179-181, fig. 4).[7] Although this bit type has been found predominantly in the eastern region of Anglian England, a further peltaic cheek-bar fragment from Whithorn, Dumf./Gal., together with the examples from Kent and Ireland, suggest the type is representative of an Insular, rather than a purely Anglo-Saxon tradition; with the Lagore bit a further example of strong Anglo-Saxon influence and contact at this 'royal' site (Whitfield, 2001; Hills, 1997: 421; fig. 49.1).

The cheek-bar bits may be divided further according to whether they are joined to the mouthpiece by an integral ring, as at Great Chesterford I 142/H2 and Sutton Hoo 17, or a D-form loop, as at Brixworth II and Eriswell 4116 (*Figures 5.5, 5.8-5.11*). The D-form loop is well paralleled on the Continent and is a characteristic of the *Knebeltrense Form I* (the earliest of three types), like the example from Newel, Germany (Oexle, 1992: Tafn. 131). However, the Sutton Hoo-Great Chesterford ring form is almost unknown outside Britain, with the only similar example being Orsoy 8, Germany (Oexle, 1992: 44, Tafn. 194).

---

[7]   I am grateful to Dr Tania Dickinson for making this identification.

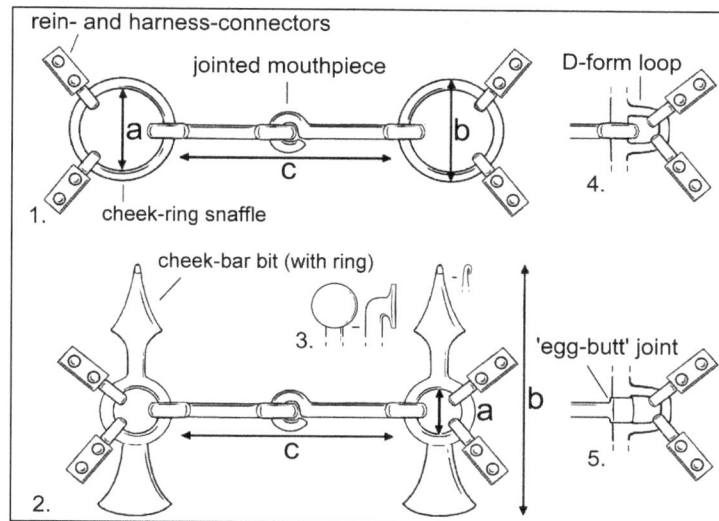

Figure 5.5 Schematic of early Anglo-Saxon bridle-bit forms (scale approx. ¼): 1. Cheek-ring Snaffle 2. Cheek-bar bit 3. Disc-head terminal 4. D-form loop 5. 'Egg-butt' joint

Cheek-ring snaffle	a (*c*.mm)	b (*c*.mm)	c (*c*.mm)
Market Overton II	48	60	100
Bishops Cleeve 7	30	54	100-110
Droxford*	34	45	100-110
Eriswell 0355*	45	55	100-110
Wanlip	40	60	100-110
Chamberlain's Barn II 45	55	70	100-110
Alfriston 91	60	50	110-120
Howletts 36	95	110	110-120
Garton II 10 (ii)	70	90	110-120
Saltwood 5	30	40	110-120
Wicken Bonhunt	-	85	110-120
Broughton Lodge H3	55	70	120-130
Kirton-in-Lindsey II*	80	95	120-130
Snape 47	45	62	120-130
West Heslerton 186	35	50	120-130
Saltwood 7	35	50	120-130
Garton II 10 (i)	85	100	120-140
Hardingstone	45	60	130-140
Market Overton I	40	65	150
Marston St.Lawrence	48	75	160
Springfield Lyons 8577	20	29	-
Yeavering	35	45	-

Table 5.1.1 Dimensions of Anglo-Saxon cheek-ring snaffles in accordance with Figure 5.5.

Cheek-bar bit	a (c.mm)	b (c.mm)	c (c.mm)
Loveden Hill HB4	16	100	100-110
Little Wilbraham 44	15	135	110-120
Great Chesterford I H2	20	131	120
Sutton Hoo 17	25	136	120
Eriswell (104) 4116	18	174	140
Brixworth II	20	110	180
Duston*	30	110	250
Broughton Lodge H1	-	97	-

Table 5.1.2 Dimensions of Anglo-Saxon cheek-bar bits in accordance with Figure 5.5.

Normal = measurement estimated from examination
Italicized = measurement estimated from scaled drawing or photograph
Underlined = measurement estimated from x-ray
* = measurement estimated from incomplete artefact

This suggests that the Sutton Hoo-Great Chesterford type also represents an Insular development, with the possibility that the Orsoy 8 snaffle, with its hint of a peltaic lower bar, is also of Anglo-Saxon manufacture or inspiration. Also of relevance, though probably late Anglian in date, is a cheek-bar fragment from York (3848). Its form is similar to that from Loveden Hill HB4, which argues for the continuity of this local type (Ottoway, 1992: fig. 307).

On the Continent the *Knebeltrense Form I* is dated from the mid-fifth to the end of the sixth century, while the Orsoy 8 bridle is dated to the seventh century (Oexle, 1992: 44-46). These dates agree generally with the Anglo-Saxon examples, with the Great Chesterford I 142/H2, Eriswell 4116 and Little Wilbraham 44 burials all datable to the first half of the sixth century (Evison, 1994: fig. 104; Fern, forthcoming). The Lagore bridle-bit is datable to the seventh century and the Sutton Hoo 17 example to its first quarter (Hencken, 1950: 6-7, 101; Carver, forthcoming).

In addition, three of the cheek-bar bits are decorated: the Eastry I fragment has two applied triangular copper-alloy mounts, each with twin zoomorphic head terminals tipped with gilding; the Eriswell 4116 bit is inlaid with metal strips and ringlets, and is also decorated with silver sheet; and the Sutton Hoo 17 bit has gilded chip-carved Style II animal ornament on its projecting disc and peltaic lower bar (*Figures 5.9, 5.12, 5.18*; Carver, forthcoming; Newman, forthcoming). The fashion for decorated bridle-bits is well-attested on the central Continent and in Scandinavia, with both metal inlay and zoomorphic ornament evidenced, for example, at Niederstotzingen 6, Germany, and Högom 2, Sweden (Ramqvist, 1992: pl. 41; Oexle, 1992: Tafn. 44).

More specifically, the inlaid ringlet ornament on the Eriswell strap-connectors is paralleled on Frankish and Saxon metalwork, such as the brass inlaid bit from

Liebenau, Germany, for which a date around c.500 has been suggested (Hässler, 1981; 77-80).

Decorated harness

The fashion for decorating horse harness in Britain can be traced back to the Iron Age and was prominent in the subsequent Roman period (Bishop, 1988). By comparison, until recently the decorative equestrian traditions of the early Anglo-Saxon period had appeared rather lacklustre (for the last brief survey see Baldwin-Brown, 1915: 423). The two new finds from Eriswell 4116 and Sutton Hoo 17 have in particular served to alter this perception, as well as our understanding of Anglo-Saxon horse harness (Carver, 2005; Newman, forthcoming). Combined with new metal-detector finds and a reappraisal of existing material they demonstrate further the existence of a distinctive equestrian culture.

At Eriswell 4116 the elaborate head harness comprised four cruciform strap-junction mounts, two slightly curved rectilinear mounts set on the brow- and nose-band, two similar rectilinear mounts set on the cheek-straps and two strap-pendants (*Figures 5.9, 5.18*). All were cast in copper-alloy, with chip-carved Style I animal ornament, embellished with gilding and silver sheet in the Bichrome Style. The reverses of these mounts demonstrate rivets and sheet 'washers' for their attachment to, as well as reinforcement of, the leather strap-junctions (*Figure 5.17*). Following this find it has now been possible to identify many similar mounts, from both burials and stray finds, often decorated with chip-carved Style I animal decoration in bichrome fashion, which have previously been misidentified as shield-mounts, belt-fittings and brooches (*Figure 5.13*). Although not an exhaustive list, further examples are: single cruciform mounts from Bishop's Cleeve 13, Glouc., Wakerley 31/32, Northants., and pairs from Easington, Co. Durham, Eastry I, Wallingford 12 and Cheesecake Hill 4, Yorks.; single

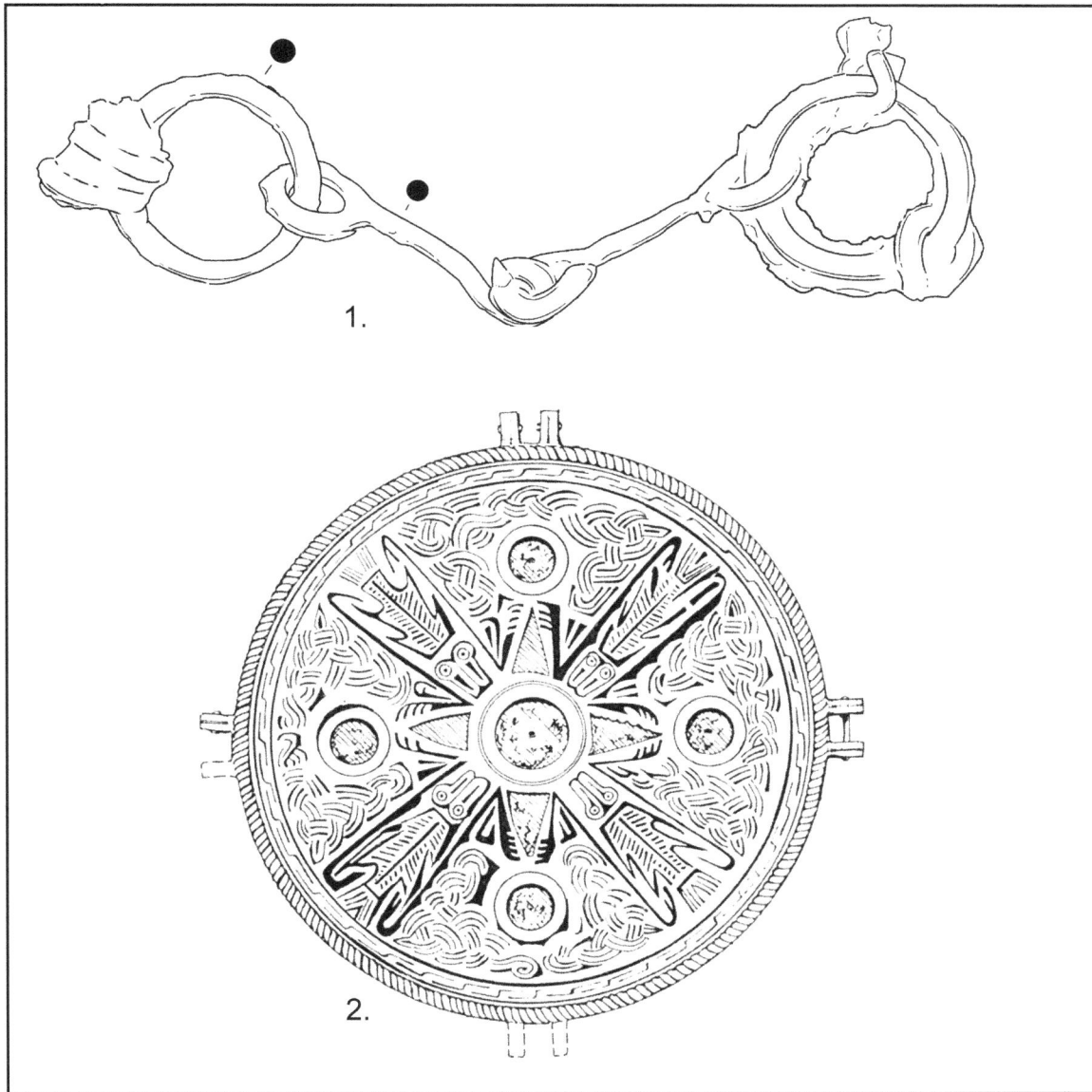

Figure 5.6 Hardingstone: 1. Iron snaffle-bit (scale ½) 2. Gilded copper-alloy disc mount (scale 1/1. After Speake, 1989)

examples of strap-pendant mounts from Beckford B12, Glouc., Lechlade 180, Glouc., Bifrons 92, Kent, Eastry I, and Easington 2; and single finds of rectilinear mounts from Beckford A3, Glouc., Faversham, Kent, Collingham, Notts., Marston St. Lawrence, Loxton,[8] Somerset, and pairs from Eastry I (*Figures 5.12-5.14*; Payne, 1894: 179-181, figs. 1, 3; Mortimer, 1905: 288, fig. 843; Leeds, 1938: 97, pl. 5; Adams and Jackson, 1988/89: 158-159, fig. 31.6; MacGregor and Bolick, 1993: fig 36.6; Hamerow and Pickin, 1995: 45-47, 51-52, figs .5.2, 10.5, 11; Evison and Hill, 1996: 10, fig. 8, 20; Boyle *et al*, 1998: 130-131, fig .5.102; Hawkes, 2000: 61, fig. 36.4; Holbrook, 2000: 71, fig. 6.2; Laing, forthcoming.a). In addition, two circular mounts in Bichrome Style with Style I ornament, possibly originally from horse harness, are those from 'near' Chichester, W. Sussex, and Hadleigh Road 124, Suffolk (Welch, 1983:112-113, fig.127a; West, 1998: 55, fig. 66.1).

---

[8]   I am grateful to Elaine Howard-Jones of the Somerset Portable Antiquities Scheme for bringing this piece to my attention.

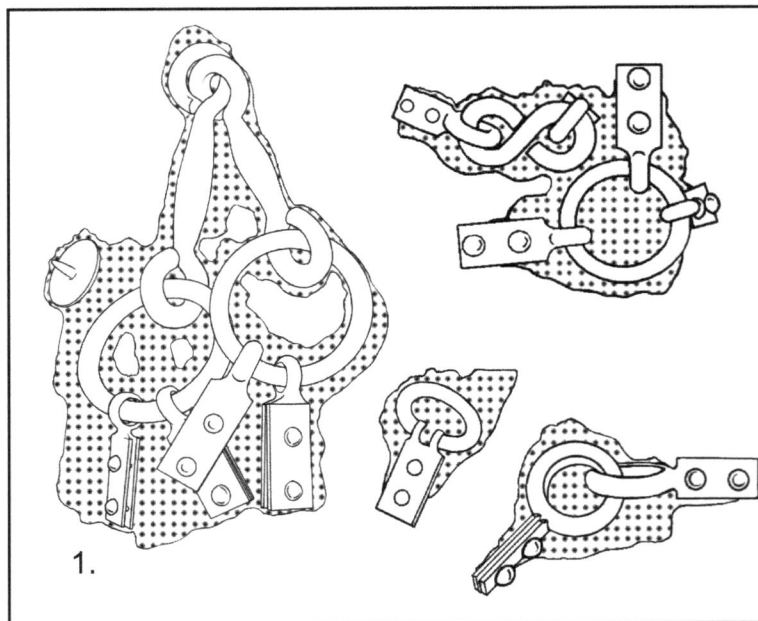

Figure 5.7 Saltwood 5: 1. Iron snaffle-bit, ancillary bridle fittings and copper-alloy rivet (scale ½. From x-ray)

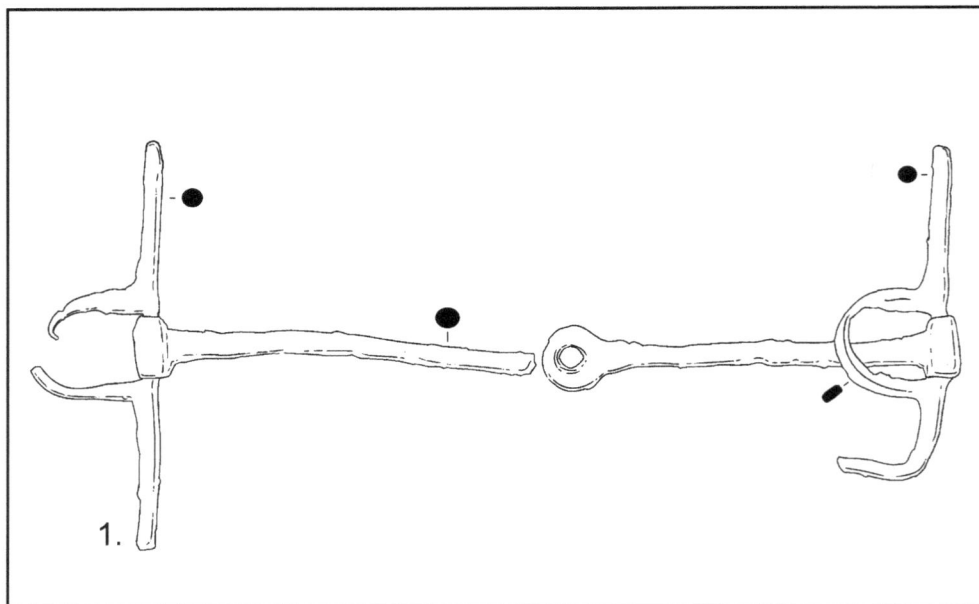

Figure 5.8 Brixworth II: 1. Iron cheek-bar bit (scale ½)

It is possible that the Eastry I mounts and cheek-bar fragment represent a single assemblage from either a bridle or horse burial, though few contextual details survive of this find (*Figure 5.12*; Meaney, 1964: 113). However, many of the other mounts have been found reused as costume accessories in female burials. The original purpose of these mounts and their subsequent adaptation is shown on their reverse by filed-down rivets and evidence for secondary alterations, such as drilled holes and soldering for pin hinges and catches (Dickinson

et al, forthcoming). These modifications can clearly be seen on the illustrated examples from Cheesecake Hill 4 and Wallingford 12, but is also true for the mounts from Beckford A3 and B12, Bishop's Cleeve 13, Hadleigh Road 124, Lechlade 180, and Wakerley 31/32 (Figure 5.14). I would also suggest that the pair of cruciform mounts from the reverse of a shield at Westgarth Gardens 41, Suffolk, may also be an example of the reuse of mounts that initially decorated horse harness (Dickinson and Härke, 1992: 29, fig. 89d).

The bichrome fashioning of many of these mounts and their burial contexts suggest that most were produced and probably buried in Hines' Phase III (c.530-570 AD) (Hines, 1997: 230-234, 240). In support of this date are the Lechlade 180 and Wakerley 31/32 examples, which were buried with herringbone reticella beads. Likewise, the Bifrons 92 mount is from an assemblage with paired keystone disc brooches that date the burial to Brugmann's Kentish Phase III (c.530/40-560/70) (Brugmann, 1999; Hawkes, 2000: n.76). However, in these graves the mounts occur in a context of secondary usage. Only in the Eriswell 4116 burial have such mounts been found unequivocally fulfilling their primary function, as decoration and reinforcement for horse harness. Final dating for this grave is not yet known, though the combination of a low-cone carinated shield-boss, large iron-bound bucket and bichrome metalwork suggest a date for burial in the second quarter of the sixth-century (East, 1983: 587; Dickinson and Härke, 1992; 13-14; Hines, 1997: 230-234, 240).[9] One cruciform mount which is earlier than this date is the recent find from Breamore, Hants., which is a probable Mediterranean import dated to the second half of the fifth or early sixth century, though this mount has little in common with the true Anglo-Saxon harness pieces apart from its cruciform shape (Eagles and Ager, forthcoming).

A less elaborate form of decoration are circular rivets of either iron or copper-alloy, which like those from Great Chesterford I 142/H2 and Little Wilbraham 44 were embellished with tinning and applied silver-sheet (*Figures 5.7, 5.10, 5.11, 5.18*). Like the decorated cruciform mounts they served the functional purpose of reinforcing the orthogonal strap-junctions of the head harness, as the preserved leather with the Little Wilbraham 44 rivet attests. Less certain, but intriguing, is the possibility of the use of Roman coins as decorative mounts. One possible example was found at Gilton Ash 83, Kent, which exhibits three drilled holes positioned to suggest it had been attached to a strap-junction. It is alleged to have been found with other elements of a bridle, although the accompanying illustration of this antiquarian find does not appear to show any other identifiable piece of equestrian equipment (Faussett, 1856: 7, 26-28; Baldwin-Brown, 1915: 422, pl. 100).

A change in decorative harness fashions is evidenced between the late sixth to early seventh century, when the cruciform mount was replaced by the disc mount, or *phalera* (*Figures 5.6, 5.15, 5.16*). This change was accompanied by the transition from Style I to Style II animal art as the decorative aspect. The new style copper-alloy mounts are typified by those from the Sutton Hoo 17 burial, which are heavily gilded, with central Meerschaum settings and associated, but separately cast, peltaic mounts (Carver, 2005). Similar mounts are the well-known examples from the horse burial at Hardingstone and uncontexted examples from Allington Hill, Cambs., and Spelsbury, Oxon. (*Figures 5.6, 5.15*). Like those from Sutton Hoo 17, all demonstrate evidence for attachment rivets arranged at the cardinal points on their reverse, though only the Sutton Hoo examples also preserve the leather strap-arrangement (*Figures 5.15-5.17*; Bateman, 1860; MacGregor, 1993: figs. 47.1, 47.3). Interestingly, like the cruciform mounts, the examples from Allington Hill and Spelsbury both demonstrate evidence for secondary adaptation, in the latter case, probably as a brooch (*Figure 5.15*). Other peltaic mounts are the well-known examples from Barham and Coddenham, Suffolk, as well as more recent metal-detected finds from Dorchester, Dorset, and from an unknown provenance (*Figure 5.15*; West, 1998: figs. 7.70, 21.9; The Searcher, October 2001). These mounts typically demonstrate a triangular arrangement of rivets on their reverse (*Figure 5.17*). Also worthy of note are the Mote of Mark, Dumf./Gal., mould fragments, evidence for the production of disc and peltaic mounts with interlace ornament, that may also be suggested as harness mounts (Speake, 1989: 79, fig. 69; Laing and Longley, forthcoming.b). Furthermore, a stray fragmentary mount from 'near' Ipswich[10] may have been part of a rectilinear-peltaic fitting, of a type attested from eighth-century Irish harness (*Figure 5.15*; Compare with no.113-114 in Youngs 1989: 117, 157). In addition, strap-pendants continued in use, such as the examples from Sutton Hoo 17 and Fincham, Norfolk (Geake, 2001: fig. 1d).

A development from the Sutton Hoo 17 type mounts is represented by the suite of four or five mounts from Faversham and a new metal-detected find from Cowbridge, V. Glam. (*Figures 5.15, 5.16*; Speake, 1989: 77-79, fig. 68; Portable Antiquities Scheme, 2003: 30, fig. 32). On these mounts the peltaic fitting is no longer attached separately, but is cast as one object with the disc mount, together with the addition of three supporting arms. The inspiration for the addition of the three arms can be seen in the development of similar mounts on the Continent (see below). Stylistically the Cowbridge, Faversham and Hardingstone mounts are later than Sutton Hoo 17, probably dating to around the mid-seventh century (Speake, 1980: 64-65).

---

[9] The dating of this burial is based on published chronological schemes. However, new work on the chronology of Anglo-Saxon grave goods, particularly in the area of weaponry forms, is currently being undertaken by Karen Høilund Nielsen and Birte Brugmann. Preliminary results have suggested that the combination of Swanton's Type H spearheads and Dickinson's and Härke's Group 1/2 shield-bosses may be earlier than previously thought, which may lead to an early sixth-century date for the Eriswell 4116 grave and others. Such a conclusion would, therefore, also necessitate a re-evaluation of the dating of the Bichrome Style, based on the finds from this burial. This work has been undertaken in combination with a programme of high-precision radiocarbon dating funded by English Heritage, which will include the Eriswell 4116 horse and rider.

---

[10] This artefact was identified on the internet and its 'find spot' ascertained from the owner.

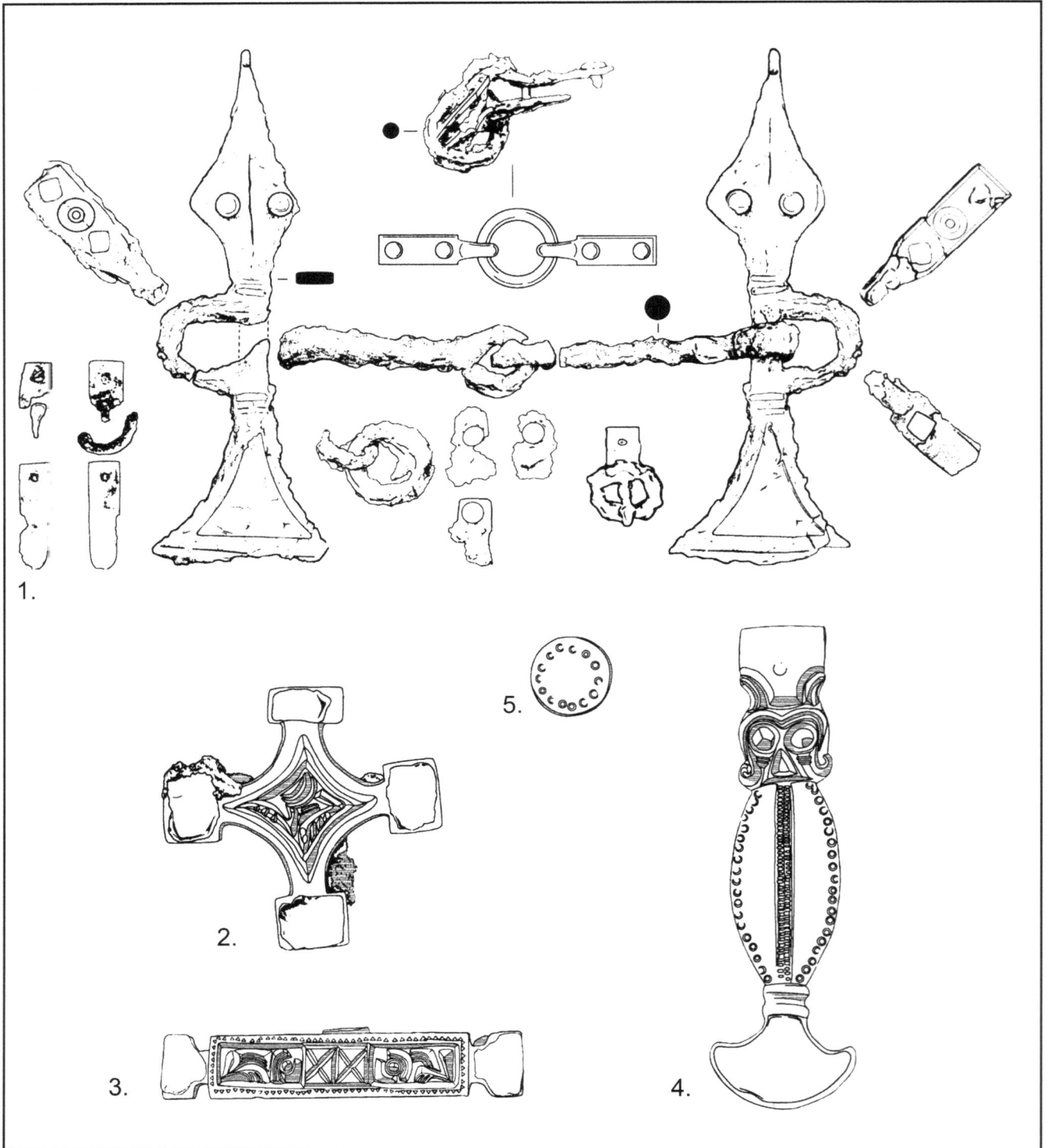

Figure 5.9 Eriswell 4116: 1. Iron cheek-bar bit and ancillary bridle fittings (scale ½)
2. Bichrome copper-alloy cruciform mount (scale 1/1)
3. Bichrome copper-alloy rectilinear mount (scale 1/1)
4. Bichrome copper-alloy pendant mount (scale 1/1) 5. Gilded rivet (scale 1/1)

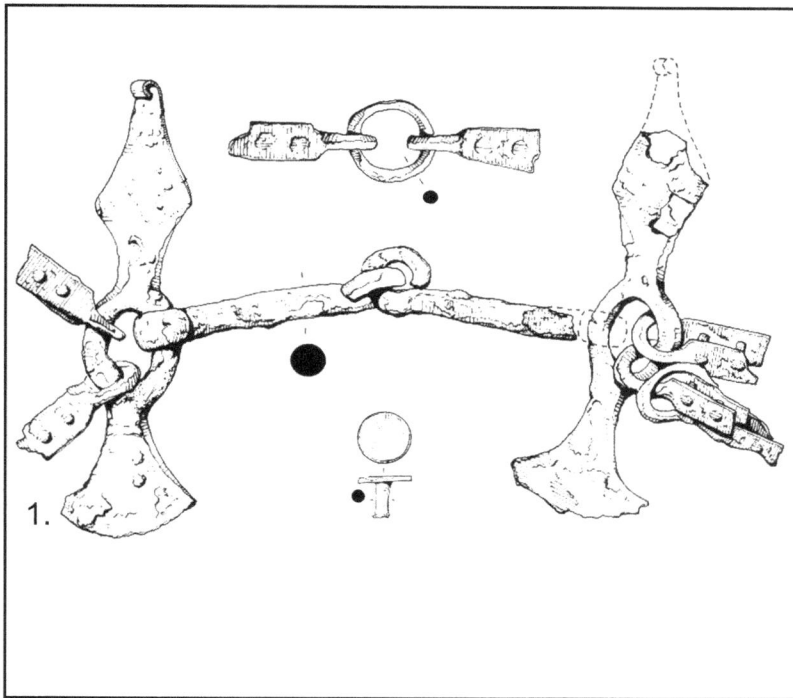

Figure 5.10 Great Chesterford I H2: 1. Iron cheek-bar bit, ancillary bridle fittings and tinned copper-alloy rivet (scale ½. After Evison, 1994)

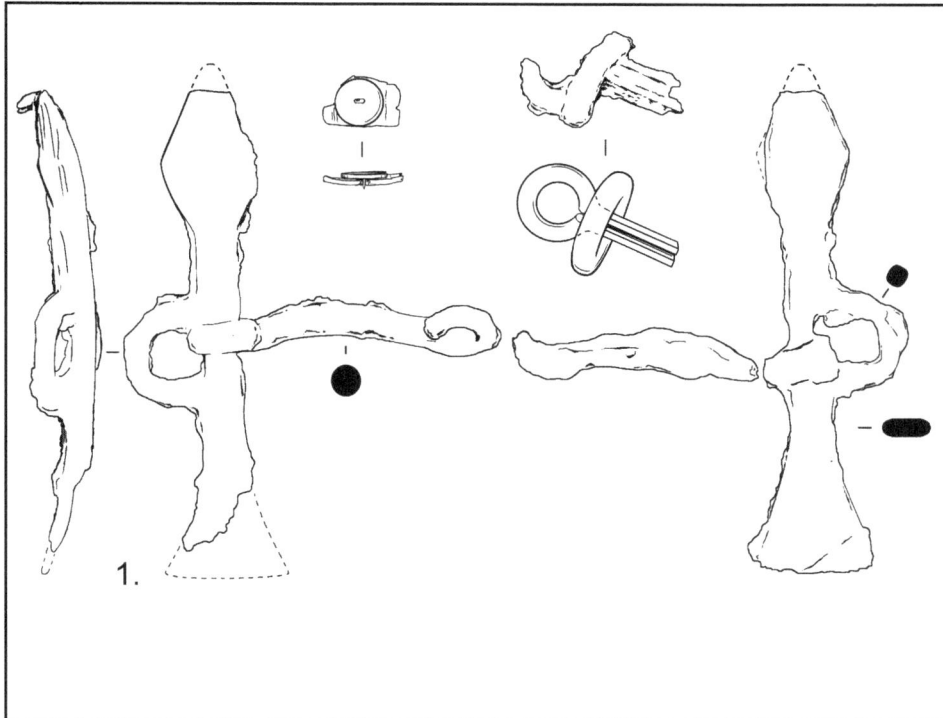

Figure 5.11 Little Wilbraham 44: 1. Iron cheek-bar bit, ancillary bridle fittings and silver-plated copper-alloy stud (scale ½)

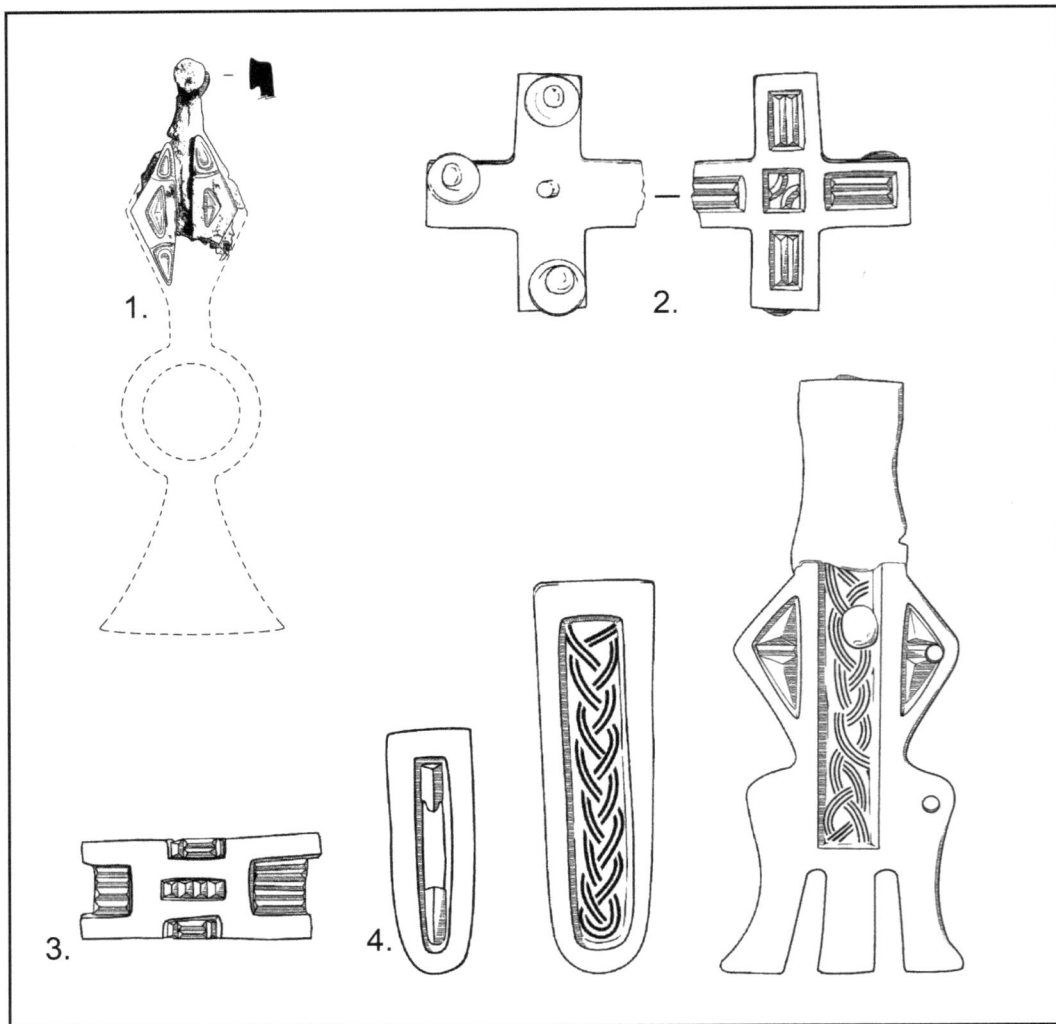

*Figure 5.12 Eastry I (Buttsole): 1. Iron cheek-bar fragment with gilded copper-alloy mounts (scale ½)
2. Gilded copper-alloy cruciform mount (scale 1/1) 3. Gilded copper-alloy rectilinear mount (scale 1/1)
4. Gilded copper-alloy strap-ends and pendant mount (scale 1/1)*

Harness Reconstruction

When addressing the question of harness reconstruction it is important to bear in mind that horse equipment could include both a head bridle and a body harness: the former is concerned principally with preventing the snaffle-bit from falling out of the horse's mouth and with the ability to control the horse; and the latter with keeping the saddle in position on the horse's back, by means of either a breast girth or crupper, or both (*Figure 5.18*). As well as the decorative mounts, dealt with above, there are also a series of iron ancillary fittings that occur with harness assemblages in graves.

No significant problems are presented by the reconstruction of the positions of the decorative mounts on the Eriswell 4116 harness, which was found *in situ* on the horse's head (*Figures 5.1, 5.9, 5.18*; Newman, forthcoming). Suites of cruciform, rectilinear and pendant mounts from head harness are well-attested on the Continent, such as Pfahlheim 20, Germany, though these

mounts have Style II rather than Style I ornament (Oexle, 1992: Tafn. 20).

By comparison, the Sutton Hoo 17 harness was not found on the horse, but in the separate accompanying human grave, a situation which is notable also in the Saltwood 5 burial (*Figures 5.2, 5.7*). It is, therefore, difficult to reconstruct accurately the placing of the decorative mounts on seventh-century harness. Evans' forthcoming reconstruction places all the disc mounts on a head bridle (Carver, 2005). Critically, however, this reconstruction ignores important ancillary body harness fittings also present in the assemblage (see below) and the fact that the peltaic adjuncts to the disc mounts act as strap terminals (*Figure 5.17*). I would instead suggest that these mounts, with the exception of the brow mount, decorated the breast girth and crupper of a body harness (*Figure 5.18*). The large size of the related Faversham and Hardingstone mounts also suggests that these pieces decorated a body harness. This suggested reconstruction also finds support from the Continental evidence, where from the late sixth-century in Frankish-Alamannic regions similarly large disc mounts, which exhibit the same triple arm extensions of the Faversham mounts, appear for the ornamentation of the breast girth, such as those from Olk 18, Germany (Oexle, 1992: Tafn. 21-22, 69, 75, 110, 133-135; Quast, 1993: Abb. 9, Liste 1b; Nawroth, 2001: 100-102).

As well as the decorative mounts the assemblages from horse and bridle burials include an assortment of other purely functional buckles and strap-connectors (Table 5.2). From the position of the buckle in the Eriswell 0355 burial it seems that one buckle fastened the head bridle at the back of the horse's head (Figure 5.18; Newman, forthcoming). Additional buckles, like those on the Sutton Hoo 17 and Eriswell 4116 harnesses presumably functioned to allow for the greater adjustment of the head or body straps, or of the length of the reins (Figure 5.18). Of the other functional fittings six different types are identifiable from twelve assemblages (Table 5.2). The three-way connector from Saltwood 5 and Sutton Hoo 17 may be identified as the central junction fitting for the breast girth (Figures 5.7, 5.18). Although uncommon this fitting is known on the Continent, particularly in Frankish-Alamannic regions (Oexle, 1992: Tafn. 48-50; Quast, 1993: Liste 1c; Nawroth, 2001: fig.45. RV5, RV7). It is possible that the simple metal rings from five of the assemblages fulfilled a similar role, though alternatively they may have functioned as the ring-link, rein-slider, or as strap-junctions.

The Snape 47 horse-head burial provides our best evidence for how many of the other fittings functioned. In this instance the animal's decapitated head, with its harness still in place, was buried in a separate pit immediately adjacent and above the human burial, with the reins found extended and leading down into the grave (Filmer-Sankey and Pestell, 2001: figs. 75-76). In the light of this and illustrative evidence from Insular sculpture, Evans' reconstruction of the Sutton Hoo 17 harness places the remaining, figure-of-eight, double-link, ring-link and rein-slider fittings on the reins (Figure 5.18; Carver, 2005). In particular, the Repton sculpture supports the placing of the ring-link fitting, found with seven harness assemblages, at the mid-reins (Table 5.2; Ibid.). The evidence for the role of the rein-slider comes principally from the surviving Great Chesterford I 142/H2, Little Wilbraham 44, Snape 47 and Sutton Hoo 17 snaffles, where this fitting was found corroded to, or in proximity to, the rein-connectors attached to the snaffle's cheek-rings, indicating that it was intended as a slide adjustment, presumably to facilitate the alteration of the reins' length (Figures 5.10, 5.11, 5.18; Ibid.). The deliberate shortening of the reins may have been appropriate when entering combat, so as to allow the rider's hands to be free for using both weapon and shield, with the ring-link used to anchor the reins to the saddle in some way, a function suggested by some Vendel-period saddles (Arrhenius, 1980: 63-64). The remaining figure-of-eight link and the double-link are again suggested by

their position in the Snape 47 grave as comprising part of the reins (Figures 5.7, 5.18). Their design suggests that they were concerned to prevent the twisting of the reins and to aid their articulation respectively, though admittedly this is not an altogether satisfying explanation.

Parallels for these fittings abroad are difficult to find. The exception are the two bridles from Högom 2, Sweden, both of which include ring-link fittings similar to the English examples, and perhaps also a rein-slider with the cheek-ring snaffle (Ramqvist, 1992: plate 43.26, 44). These Scandinavian parallels in a late fifth-century grave raise the possibility that some of the technical features of Anglo-Saxon harness were not necessarily of Insular invention.

Saddles

On the Continent two types of wooden framed saddle have been identified for the period (Figure 5.18; Nawroth, 2001: 106-113). One is the Prunksättel (parade saddle) type with a high front bow, or board, adorned with decorative metal fittings, typified by that from Wesel-Bislich 446, Germany (Oexle, 1992: Vol. 1, 237-238; Vol. 2, Tafn. 171-173). The other is without metal decorative fittings, such as that from Oberflacht 211, Germany, which had a low front bow (Quast, 1993). Finds of the ornate high bowed variety occur in wealthy burials from the mid- to late fifth century in Ostrogothic Italy, east Francia and east Scandinavia, such as the examples from Krefeld-Gellep 1782, Germany, and Högom 2: it continued to be used throughout the sixth and seventh centuries in all these regions (Arrhenius, 1980: fig. 13; Oexle, 1992: Vol. 1, 247-248; Vol. 2, Tafn. 184-185; Ramqvist, 1992: fig. 48; Quast, 1993: 445-446). The type was probably first introduced to south-east Europe in the late Roman period by steppe nomads, the so-called Huns (László, 1943). By analogy to later medieval war-saddles, its form gave a firm seat to the rider, necessary in the period before the use of stirrups,[11] and served to protect the lower abdomen in combat (László, 1943: 156-157; Hyland 1999: 61-62).

Examples of Oberflacht type saddles are less well known, since the lack of decorative fittings means that generally little evidence of them survives. However, though the organic remains of the frame have usually disintegrated, Quast has demonstrated for the Continental corpus that the original presence of wooden framed saddles can be inferred from remaining iron girth buckles and other body harness fittings; but in such circumstances it is impossible to know if originally the saddle had a low or high front bow (Quast, 1993: Abb.1, 3 and 6; Listen 4, 5).

---

[11] There is no evidence for the widespread use of the iron stirrup in England before the eleventh century, excepting two possible Scandinavian imports of the ninth century. While leather stirrups remain a possibility they are not demonstrable in the material or literary record (Seaby and Woodfield 1980). Similarly, the use of the horseshoe cannot be unequivocally demonstrated before the late Anglo-Saxon period (Clark, 1995).

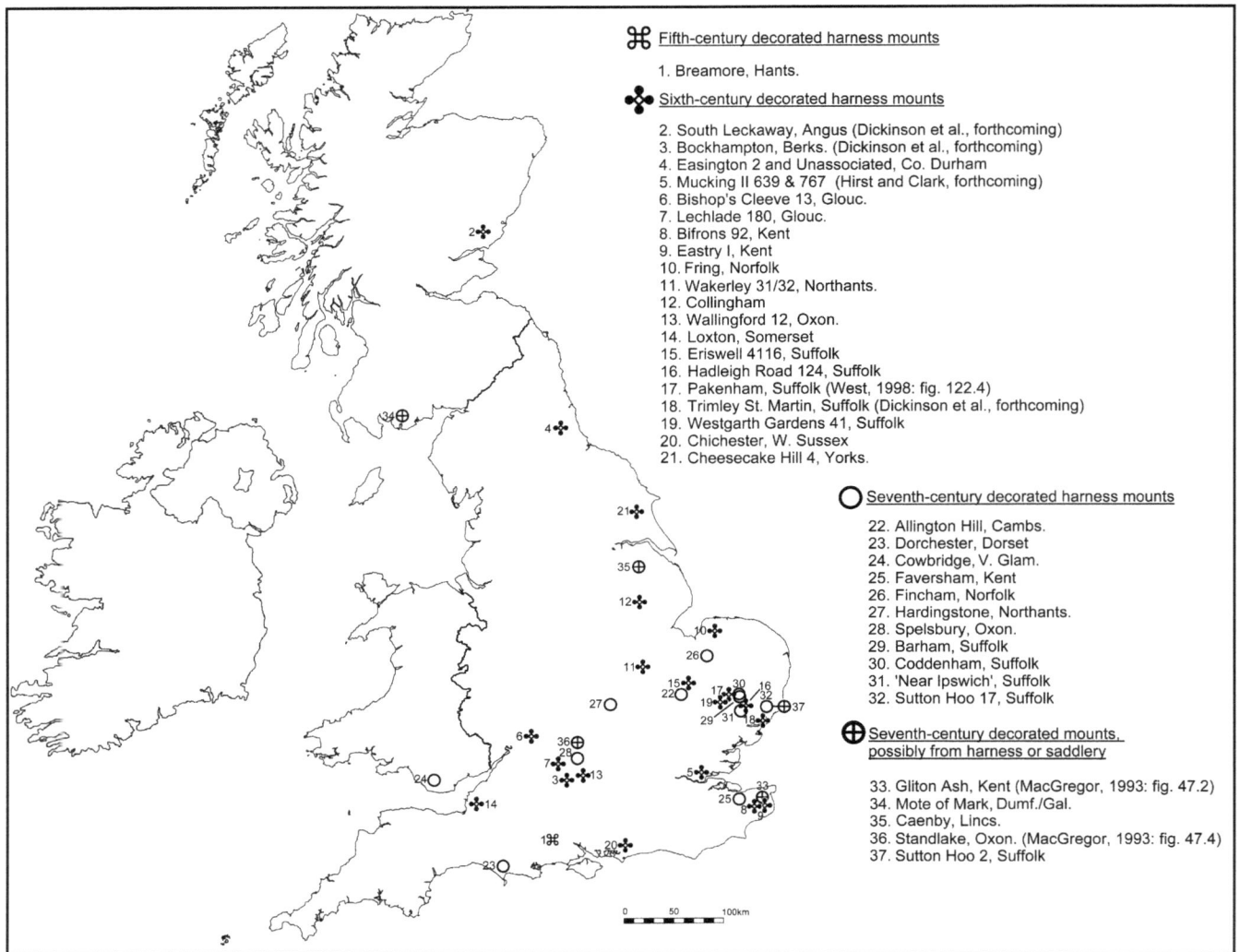

Figure 5.13 The find locations of decorated harness fittings in England, c.450-700

By applying Quast's method to the smaller Anglo-Saxon corpus a saddle can be identified as part of the original horse equipment in six burials. In the two horse graves from Eriswell a girth buckle was found on the horse's ribs and at Marston St. Lawrence 'on the rump' of the animal, indicating that saddles had been placed on the horses before burial (Dryden, 1885: 332). The excavator of the horse burial at Warren Hill also remarked on the presence of 'a small buckle' found with the horse, but mentioned no other bridle equipment, suggesting a possible girth buckle (Prigg and Fenton, 1888: 57). With the Eriswell 4116 burial was found also on the ribs three or four iron clamp-brackets with preserved wood between them (*Figures 5.1, 5.19*). A very similar fitting, identified as from a saddle, was found on a horse's back together with a girth buckle in the ship-burial at Valsgärde 8, Sweden, a grave datable to the late sixth century (Arwidsson, 1954: 75-76; Abb. 51). It seems probable that such

brackets secured the girth strap to the seat of the saddle (*Figure 5.18*). A comparable pair of fittings was found close to a large oval buckle, to the left of the deceased, in the Saltwood 5 burial, which may be all that survives of a wooden saddle (*Figures 5.2, 5.19*). This rich weapon grave also contained a horse's harness and is to be associated with an unbridled horse buried in a separate aligned pit five metres to the east. A similar situation existed in the case of the separate burials of a human and horse, under a single mound, at Sutton Hoo 17, with the saddle placed in the north-west corner of the human grave (Carver, 1993: fig. 3). Here too an iron clamp-bracket and a large iron oval girth buckle were found. In addition, the excavator of the Great Chesterford I cemetery suggested a saddle in the burial of Horse 1, from the evidence of copper-alloy edge strips and a buckle that had been burnt *in situ* at the horse's hindquarters (Evison, 1994: 29).

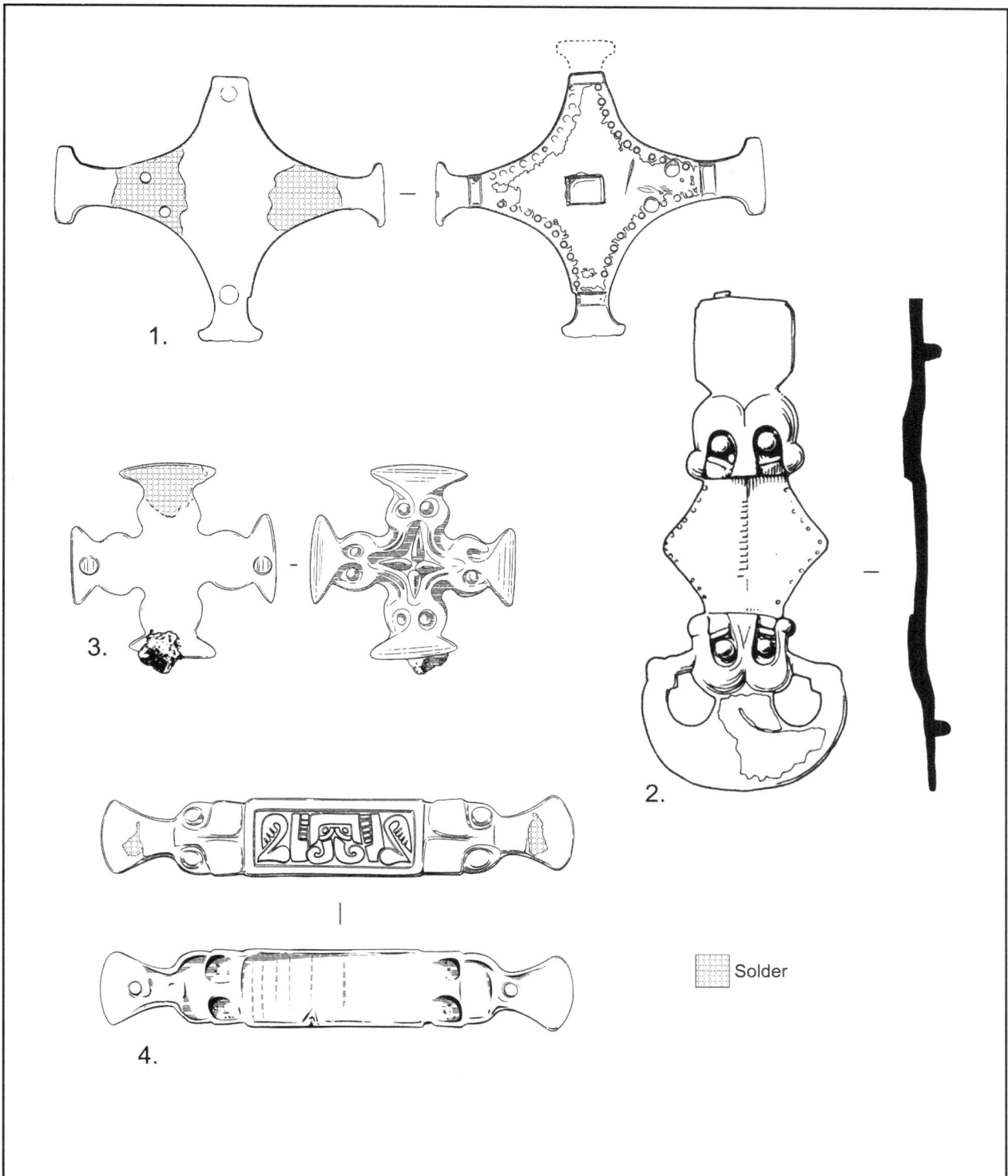

Figure 5.14 Sixth-century gilded copper-alloy harness mounts (scale 1/1):
1. Cheesecake Hill 4 2. Lechlade 180 (After Boyle et al, 1998) 3. Wallingford 12 4. Loxton

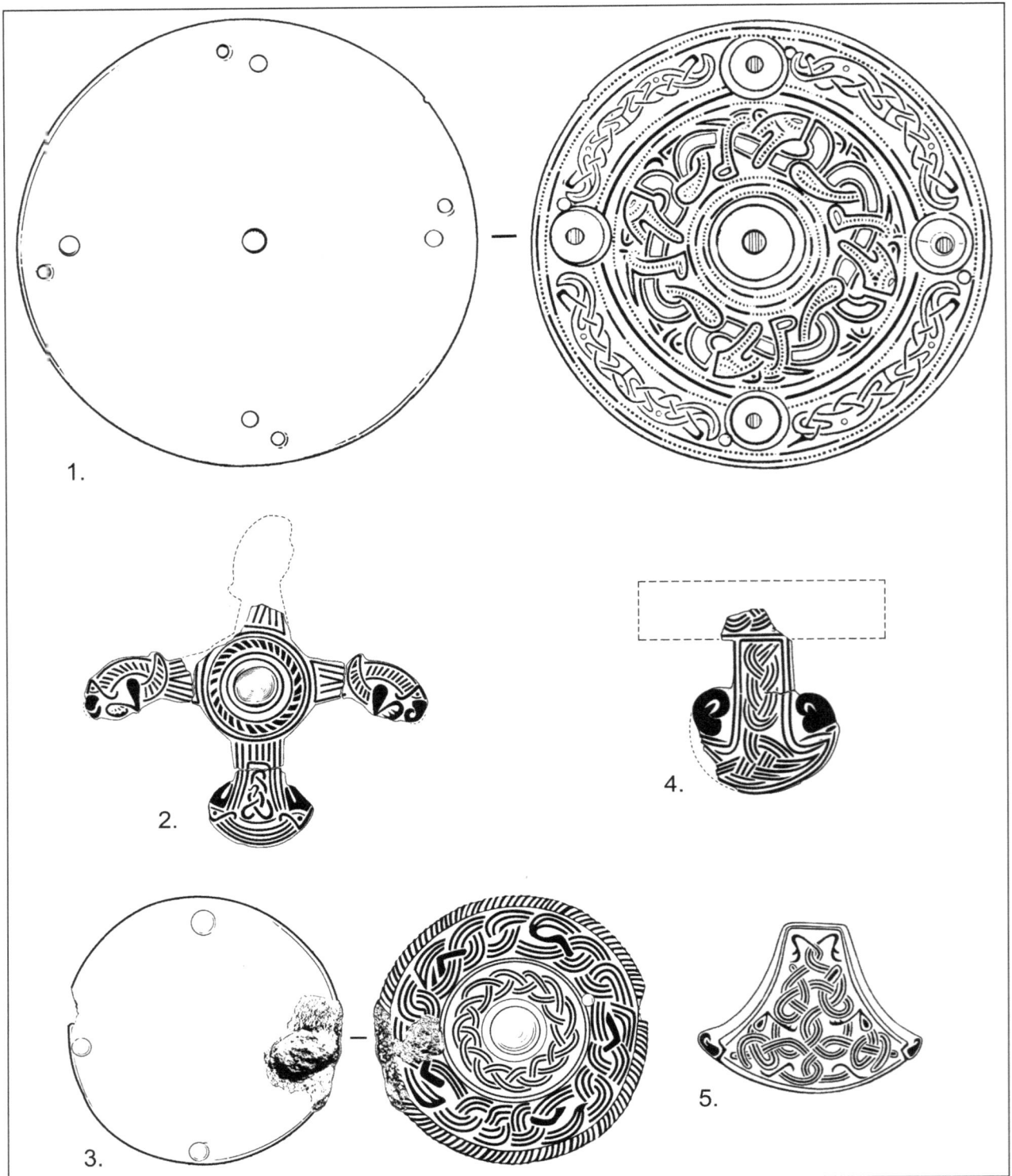

Figure 5.15 Seventh-century decorative gilded copper-alloy harness fittings (scale 1/1, except 5 for which the scale is unknown): 1. Allington 2. Cowbridge 3. Spelsbury 4. 'Near Ipswich' 5. Unprovenanced

Figure 5.16 Faversham (scale 2/3. After Speake, 1989):
1. Gilded copper-alloy disc mount with integrated peltaic and arm appendages

Regarding the form of these Anglo-Saxon saddles, the example from Hillquarter, Ireland, is apposite; as is the elaborately carved wooden saddle bow fragment with silver studs from York (Tweddle et al, 1999: 258-259; fig. 81; Kelly, 2001). The latter is of ninth-century date, but is significant as it demonstrates the use of the high bowed saddle in England in the subsequent period. The early seventh-century Hillquarter saddle has been reconstructed with the high front bow of *Prunksättel* type from its surviving decorative metal fittings. A possible example of this type of saddle in a seventh-century Anglo-Saxon context may be represented by the gilded copper-alloy and silver mounts attached to a degraded wooden object, found collapsed over the body in the burial at Caenby, a 'princely' weapon grave, which also contained horse remains (Jarvis, 1850: 37-38). Another may be suggested from the gilded disc mounts, found riveted to wood, together with lengths of pinned and swaged silver strip, from the Sutton Hoo Mound 2 burial (Bruce-Mitford, 1975: figs.115-117; Carver 2005). Ultimately, there are no conclusive statements that can be made about the form of the Anglo-Saxon saddle in this period, though it would seem unlikely that

Insular wooden saddle traditions could have existed independently of the forms prevalent in the rest of Europe, which appear to have reached as far as Ireland by the seventh century (*Figure 5.18*).

No examples of saddle blankets, a necessary accessory to prevent injury to a horse's back, have survived from Anglo-Saxon England, though the remnants of one was found on the back of a horse at Ammerbuch-Entringen, Germany, demonstrating their use in the period (Hald and Laux, 1999: 148).

Prick-spurs

In Europe the prick-spur is of Iron Age origin, though in Britain they are first attested from the Roman period, such as the late fourth or early fifth-century examples from Bitterne, Southampton (Shortt, 1959). On the Continent and in Scandinavia their continued use in the post-Roman period is attested by finds in burials and cremations, though they do not occur in fifth-century Anglo-Saxon contexts (Saggau, 1986: 61-62; Ramqvist, 1992: 86-87; Hässler, 1994: 48, Abb. 22; Rettner, 1997).

Fitting Type/Burial	Triple-link	Figure-eight	Double-link	Ring-link	Rein-slider	Ring	Buckle
Broughton Lodge H3				?		?	x
Bishopsbourne 3				x			x
Eriswell 4116				x	?		x
Eriswell 0355						x	x
Garton II 10						x	x
Great Chesterford I H2				x	x		
Howletts 36						x	
Little Wilbraham 44					x		
Marston St. Lawrence		x		x		x	x
Saltwood 5	x	x	x				x
Saltwood 7		x	x	x			x
Snape 47		x	x	x	x		
Sutton Hoo 17	x	x	x	x	x		x

Table 5.2 Ancillary harness fittings

Horse Burial	Sex	Age (years)	Withers (cm)	Trauma	Reference
Broughton Lodge H1	♂	3.5	135-139*	-	Harman, 1993
Broughton Lodge H3	♂	6	130-134*	-	Harman, 1993
Broughton Lodge H4	-	>3.5	-	-	Harman, 1993
Eriswell (046) 0355	-	9	130-135	-	O'Connor, Unpublished
Eriswell (104) 4116	♂	5	140-145	x	O'Connor, Unpublished
Great Chesterford I H1	♂	<2.5	126	-	Serjeantson, 1994
Great Chesterford I H2	♂	4-7	140-144	-	Serjeantson, 1994
Marston St.Lawrence	-	-	c.140	-	Dryden, 1885
Saltwood 5	♀	4-6	-	-	Bendrey, 2002
Snape 47	♂	20-30	-	-	Davis, 2001
Sutton Hoo 17	♂	5-6	140-144	-	O'Connor, 1994
West Heslerton 186	♀	3	-	-	Haughton and Powesland, 1999

* Estimates calculated using Kieswalter and Boesneck (Müller 1955). All others are reproduced as given in the relevant literature.

Table 5.3 Physical characteristics of horses from Anglo-Saxon burials

Two forms of spur were employed between the fifth and seventh centuries in Europe: the *Bügelsporen* (bow-spur), a derivative of late Roman forms, characterized by a shallow heel form and integral goad; and the simple *Plattensporen* (disc-spur), which comprises a simple rivet pushed through the reverse of a boot or strap to form a goad (Rettner, 1997). Manufactured in both copper-alloy and iron, they normally occur singularly in male weapon graves (though pairs are known), although with no apparent preference for the right or left foot (Ibid.; Tab. 1). In this period, the spur was probably employed to quickly turn the horse, allowing the rider to attack with his weapons or missiles, and then to retreat from danger (Baldwin-Brown, 1915: 421).

Compared to the seventy central European spur examples for the period up to c.600 AD, only seven possible spurs are recorded from early medieval burials in England, of which three survive only as cursory notes for the cemeteries of Pangbourne, Berks., Milton-Next-Sittingbourne, Kent, and Woodstone, Northants.(Urban, 1838: 650; Walker, 1899: 345; Smith, 1908: 374; Rettner, 1997: 134).[12] The best known surviving example of purported early Anglo-Saxon date is the iron spur from Linton Heath 18, Cambs., said to have been found in a female burial with a cruciform brooch of late fifth or sixth-century date (*Figure 5.20*; Neville, 1854: 99-100). This spur has long ankle stems and an integral prick goad, a form known in the Roman period in Britain, but which

---

[12] The examples identified by Baldwin-Brown from Pakenham, Suffolk, and Richborough, Kent, are of late Anglo-Saxon date (Baldwin-Brown, 1915: 422).

did not re-emerge in central Europe in the form of *Schlaufensporen* (loop-spur) until the seventh century (Shortt, 1959; Koch, 1982: 65). Furthermore, the buckle-loop terminals of the Linton Heath spur are a characteristic best paralleled by examples from late Anglo-Saxon settlement contexts and Carolingian Europe, particularly the uncontexted example from Kingston-upon-Thames (Boon 1959: 95. Koch, 1982: 68. Ellis, 1984. Ottoway, 1992: Fig. 304). Hence, it would appear that the Linton Heath spur is an intrusive find within its early Anglo-Saxon cemetery context, since it is typologically considerably later than the grave in which it is alleged to have been found.

Another, recent spur find, is that from Castledyke 18, Lincs., which occurred with an unremarkable double burial of two adolescents (Drinkall and Foreman, 1998: 251, figs. 14, 59). While it bears comparison with seventh-century Continental types, alone it is sparse evidence for the use of *Schlaufensporen* in early Anglo-Saxon England, and it could be a Roman object, or intrusive. More convincing are two recently identified *Plattensporen* from male weapon burials at Edix Hill 88, Cambs., and Mill Hill 93, Kent (Parfitt and Brugmann, 1997: 153-154, fig. 50, 73; Malim and Hines, 1998: 79-80, figs. 3.59-3.60, 3.81; Parfitt et al, 2000). The former is a sixth-century grave and the latter dates to the end of the same century. Ultimately, however, the fact of the rarity of this item of equestrian equipment and, moreover, its absence from the English corpus of bridle and horse burials, suggests that it was not commonly used in England before at least the eighth century, the date of two prick-spurs from Hamwic (Andrews, 1997: 226; Southampton Museum Archaeological Object Database: SOU 32.20, SOU 169.2184).

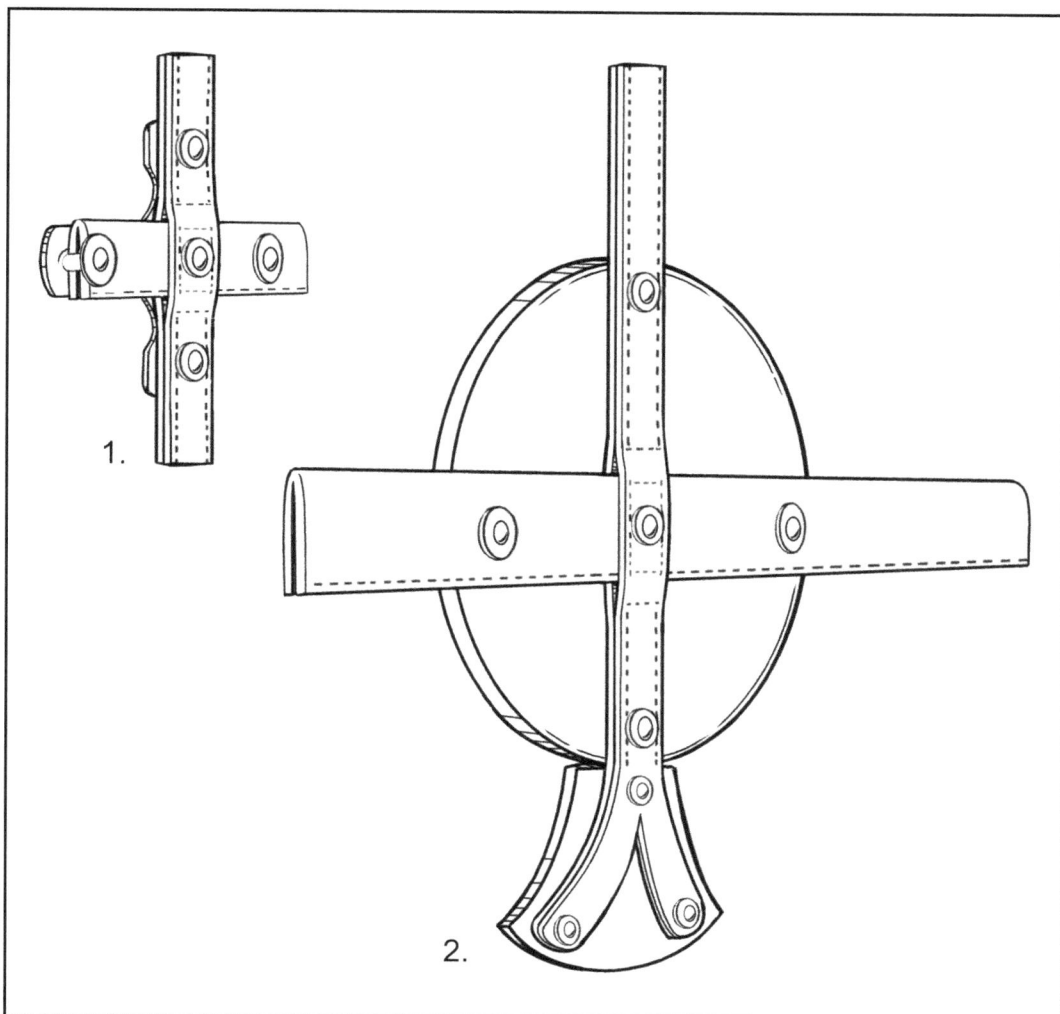

Figure 5.17 Schematic demonstrating the method of attachment for harness mounts (scale approx. 1/1): 1. Sixth-century cruciform mount 2. Seventh-century disc and peltaic mounts

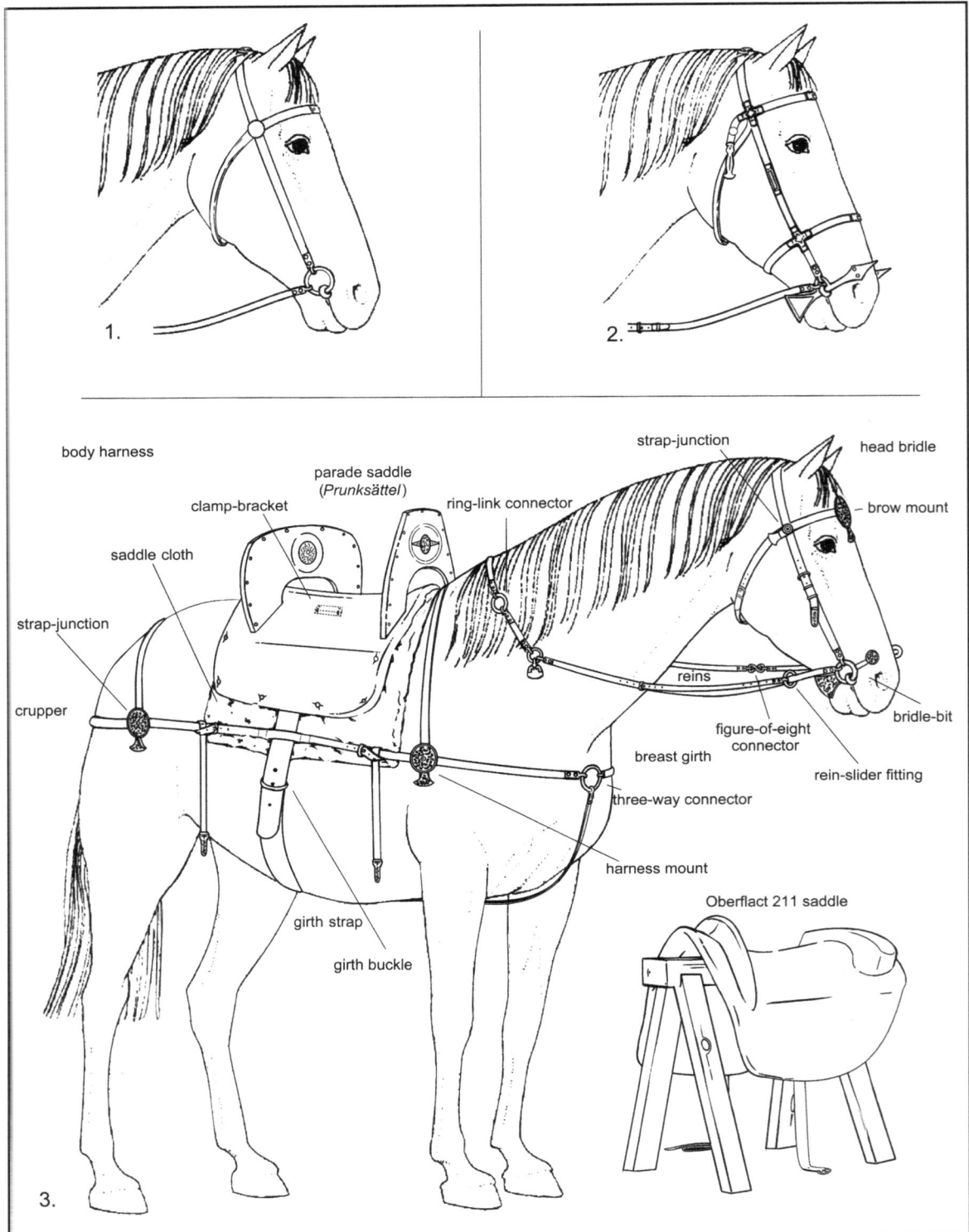

Figure 5.18 Reconstruction of horse harness (adapted from Bishop, 1988):
1. Head harness with rivet fittings, cf. Saltwood 5 2. Sixth-century head harness with decorative mounts,
cf. Eriswell 4116 3. Seventh-century harness with decorative mounts, cf. Sutton Hoo 17.

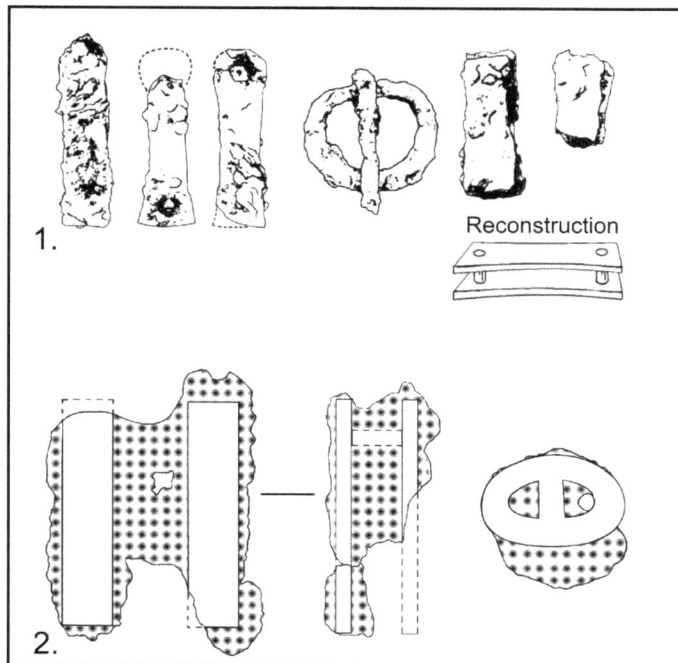

Figure 5.19 Iron saddle brackets and girth buckles (scale ½): 1. Eriswell 4116 2. Saltwood 5 (from x-ray)

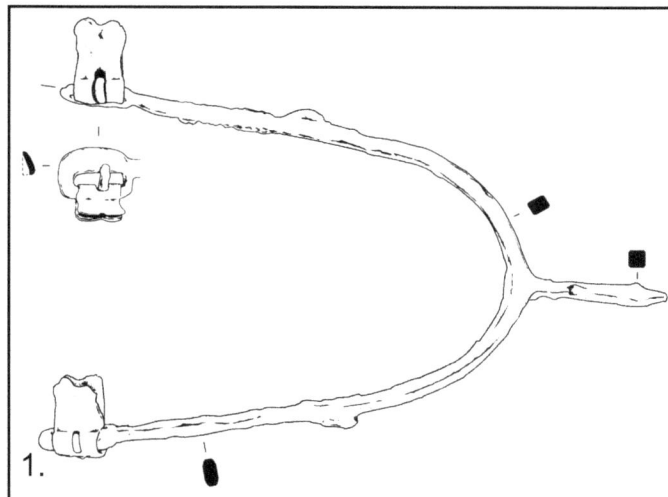

Figure 5.20 Iron prick-spur (scale ½): 1. Linton Heath 18

The Horse[13]

Remains of horses from contemporary settlements have demonstrated a normal withers height in this period for mature animals of around 13 hands, with a minority of individuals as small as 11.2 hands (1.18m), and some just under 14 hands (Crabtree, 1989: table 37). The records for twelve horses from burials provide details of the types of animals that were chosen for sacrifice (*Table 5.3*; Dryden, 1885: 330; Harman, 1993; O'Connor, 1994; Serjeantson, 1994; Haughton and Powesland, 1999: 331; Davis, 2001; Bendrey, 2001; O'Connor, unpublished). The size of eight individuals shows that over half were between 13.2 and 14 hands (c.1.37-1.44m) at the withers and of a robust build. They are the horses from Broughton Lodge H1, Eriswell 4116, Great Chesterford I H2, Marston St. Lawrence and Sutton Hoo 17. Smaller animals of between 12.2 and 13 hands (1.26-1.32m) are Broughton Lodge H3, Eriswell 0355 and the immature

---

[13] By modern standards anything below 15 hands is a pony. The term 'pony' is not used here, however, since the Anglo-Saxon vocabulary has no equivalent word, that first came into use in the eighteenth century and comes from the French *poulenet*, a derivative of the word for a foal which probably came into use to denote a horse of small stature.

individual from Great Chesterford I H1. It may be concluded from this evidence, therefore, that the horses selected for burial were often the largest available in society, though it has been suggested that the animal from Eriswell 4116 might have had a partially limp, and so was perhaps a preferable sacrifice (O'Connor, unpublished). Furthermore, of nine individuals for which sex has been determined, seven were males and two females (based on the absence of canine teeth), although it has not been possible to differentiate stallions from geldings. This preference may be due to the generally larger stature of male horses, though a symbolic dimension may also be possible. In terms of age, most were between 3½ and 7 years at death, indicating that they were killed in their prime. The exception is Snape 47, where the animal was between 20 and 30 years.

These findings from the admittedly small corpus of Anglo-Saxon horse burials compare favourably with horses from burials elsewhere in Europe (*Figure 5.21*). The surviving horse remains from the great ship-burials at Vendel and Valsgärde, Sweden, also suggest animals

of between 13 and 14 hands (Lundholm, 1949: Tabn. 7-8). Similarly, the study of over fifty central European horses from cemeteries has also shown that most were of this size, with a few larger individuals of between 14 to 15 hands, and occasional evidence of lameness (Müller, 1980: 150, Tab. 1). Stallions and geldings were also favoured for burial in Europe (a preference for males is also apparent for dog burial), though mares are known, and indeed make up a significant proportion of the horses from funerary contexts in Vendel-period Sweden (Ibid.; Oexle, 1984: fig. 11; Prummel, 1992: 143; Kerth, 2000; Götherström 2002).

Empirical observation of the animals from cemetery contexts thus creates the impression that the horse burial rite in Europe in this period was very concerned with the visual quality of the animal, with its size, sex and perhaps pedigree, all important aspects, though it was not necessarily the best riding animal available, and probably not the personal steed of the deceased. Obviously, the more impressive was the animal, however, the greater the statement of status.

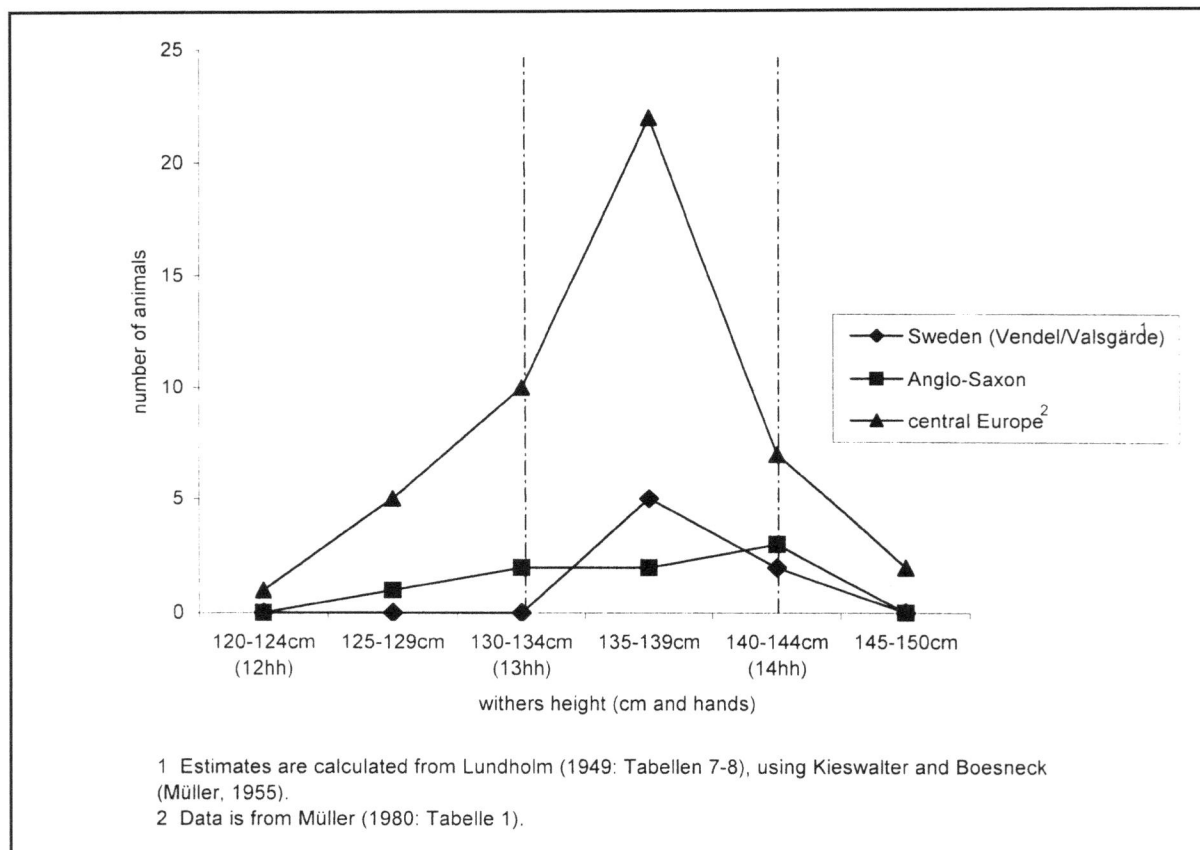

1 Estimates are calculated from Lundholm (1949: Tabellen 7-8), using Kieswalter and Boesneck (Müller, 1955).
2 Data is from Müller (1980: Tabelle 1).

Figure 5.21 Withers estimates for central and north European horses from funerary contexts in the early medieval period.

Conclusion

The very fact of the rarity of the sacrifice of a riding horse and of horse equipment in the inhumation rite in early Anglo-Saxon England may be interpreted as a statement on the value of equestrianism in contemporary society. Indeed the riding horse is much rarer than the prized sword as a grave good. This may ultimately be a reflection of the fact that in the period after Roman rule in Britain, the diminished institutions of land, labour and agriculture, provided only an elite minority with the considerable economic resources necessary to breed, train and feed quality riding animals. In addition, the value of an equestrian status is suggested by the tendency for such groups to decorate their horses' harness with rich materials and in the elite animal styles of the period (Hedeager, 2000: 45, 50-51).

Finally, the association of horse inhumation with the rite of weapon burial raises inevitably the question of whether or not horses were employed in warfare in this period in England. This is difficult to conclude from the archaeological record alone, though Continental, and to a lesser extent Anglo-Saxon and British, historical sources detail the limited use of horses in battle, even if the concept of cavalry warfare is premature before the late Anglo-Saxon period (Bacharach, 1985; Hooper, 1993; Halsall, 2003: 180-188). Concerning the method of fighting from horseback in the period, both the historical and pictorial evidence, such as the famous Sutton Hoo helmet rider-motif, depict the use of the spear in an over-arm fashion, as a thrusting or throwing weapon, a technique that was also employed by Roman cavalry (Cessford, 1993; Hyland, 1993: 142-143; Gaimster, 1998: fig. 47). The option of fighting from horseback, in a period when most combatants fought on foot, would have provided elite warleaders with obvious advantages in battle, a prerogative which archaeologically, it may be argued, we find expressed in the burial record.

Acknowledgements

The author would like to thank those individuals who provided unpublished material to the benefit of this study, together with staff at museums and other institutions that allowed me to examine and draw artefacts in their collection. They are Sue Anderson, Robin Bendrey, Chris Chippendale, Angela Evans, Elizabeth Hartley, Kevin Leahy, John Newman, Arthur MacGregor, Jacqueline Minchinton, Terry O'Connor, Phil Rainer, Ian Riddler, Susanne Ryder, Fleur Shearman, Sue Tyler and Leslie Webster. Particular thanks are due to Martin Carver, Annette Roe, Suffolk County Council Archaeological Service and Union Railways South, for allowing examination of records, reports and artefacts relating to the Sutton Hoo, Eriswell (046 and 104) and Saltwood cemeteries respectively. Also, special gratitude is extended to Malin Holst for her invaluable assistance with German translations, to Dieter Quast for his assistance with the Continental corpus and particularly to Tania Dickinson for her advice and incisive observation of the pre-published manuscript. Illustrations are by the author except where stated.

References

Adams, B. and Jackson, D. (1988/89). 'The Anglo-Saxon cemetery at Wakerley, Northamptonshire. Excavations by Mr D Jackson, 1968-9', *Northamptonshire Archaeological Journal*, 22, 69-178.

Aldsworth, F. (1979). 'Droxford Anglo-Saxon cemetery, Soberton, Hampshire', *Proceedings of the Hampshire Field Club and Archaeological Society*, 35, 93-182.

Andrews, P. (1997). *Excavations at Hamwic Volume 2: excavations at Six Dials* (Council for British Archaeology Research Report, 109, York.

Arrhenius, B. (1980). 'The chronology of the Vendel graves', in P. Lamm, and H. Å. Nordström, (eds) *Vendel Period Studies*, Stockholm, Statens Historika Museum Studies, 2, 39-70.

Arwidsson, G. (1954). *Die Gräbfunde von Valsgärde, 3: Valsgärde 8*, Uppsala.

Arwidsson, G. (1977). *Die Gräbfunde von Valsgärde, 1: Valsgärde 7*, Uppsala.

Bachrach, B. S. (1985). 'Animals and warfare in early Medieval Europe', *Settimane di Studio*, 31, 1: 707-751.

Baldwin-Brown, G. (1915). *The Arts in Early England – Saxon Art and Industry in the Pagan Period*, Vol. 3, London, John Murray.

Bateman, T. (1860). 'Anglo-Saxon antiquities in the possession of T. Bateman, Esq.', *Reliquary*, 1, 189-190.

Bendrey, R. (2002). 'Assessment of the animal bone', in *Archaeological Investigations at Saltwood Tunnel, Near Folkstone, Kent. Detailed Archaeological Works Assessment Report*, Vol. 3, Unpublished Report.

Bishop, M. C. (1988). 'Cavalry equipment of the Roman army in the first century AD', in J. C. Coulston (ed.) *Military Equipment and the Identity of Roman Soldiers*, Oxford, British Archaeological Reports International Series 394, 67-196.

Bond, J. (1996). 'Burnt offerings: animal bone in Anglo-Saxon cremations', *World Archaeology*, 28,1, 76-88.

Boon, G. C. (1959). 'A bronze spur from the Thames at Kingston', *The Antiquaries Journal*, 39, 95.

Boyle, A., Jennings, D., Miles, D. and Palmer, S. (1998). *The Anglo-Saxon Cemetery at Butler's Field, Lechlade, Gloucestershire*, Vol. 1, Thames Valley Landscapes 10, Oxford, Oxbow books.

Brent, J. (1868). 'Account of the Society's researches in the Anglo-Saxon cemetery at Sarr', *Archaeologia Cantiana*, 7, 307-321.

Bruce-Mitford, R. (1975). *The Sutton Hoo Ship-burial*, Vol. 1, London, British Museum Publications.

Brugmann, B. (1999). 'The role of Continental artefact-types in sixth-century Kentish chronology', in J. Hines, K. Høilund Nielsen and F. Siegmund (eds), *The Pace of Change: Studies in Early-Medieval Chronology*, Oxford, Oxbow Books, 37-64.

Caruth, J. and Anderson, S. (1999). 'RAF Lakenheath Saxon Cemetery', *Current Archaeology*, 163, 244-250.

Carver, M. O. H. (1993). 'The Anglo-Saxon cemetery: an interim report', *Bulletin of the Sutton Hoo Research Committee*, 8, 11-19.

Carver, M. O. H. (2005). *Sutton Hoo: A Seventh-century princely burial ground and its context*, London, British Museum Publications.

Cessford, C. (1993). 'Cavalry in early Bernicia: a reply', *Northern History*, 29, 185-187.

Clark, J. (1995). 'Horsehoes', in J. Clark (ed.) *The Medieval Horse and its Equipment c.1150-c.1450: Medieval finds from excavations in London*, 5, London, Museum of London, 75-123.

Crabtree, P. J. (1989). *West Stow, Suffolk: Early Anglo-Saxon Animal Husbandry*, Gressenhall, East Anglian Archaeology Report, 47.

Davis, S. (2001). 'The horse head from grave 47', in W. Filmer-Sankey and T. Pestell, *Snape Anglo-Saxon Cemetery: Excavations and Surveys 1824-1992*, Gressenhall, East Anglian Archaeology Report, 95, 231-232.

Dickinson, T. M. and Härke, H. (1992). *Early Anglo-Saxon Shields*, London, The Society of Antiquaries of London, *Archaeologia*, 110.

Dickinson, T. M., Fern, C. and Hall, M. A. (forthcoming). 'An early Anglo-Saxon bridle fitting from South Leckaway, Forfar, Angus, Scotland', *Medieval Archaeology*.

Dixon, K. R. and Southern, P. (1992). *The Roman Cavalry. From the First to the Third Century AD*, London, Routledge.

Drinkall, G. and Foreman, M. (1998). *The Anglo-Saxon Cemetery at Castledyke South, Barton-on-Humber*, Sheffield, Sheffield Excavation Reports, 6.

Dryden, H. (1885). 'Excavation of an ancient burial ground at Marston St. Lawrence, co. Northamptonshire', *Archaeologia*, 48, 327-339.

Eagles, B. and Ager, B. (forthcoming). 'A mid-5th to mid-6th century bridle-fitting of Mediterranean origin from Breamore, Hampshire, England, with a discussion of its local context', in M. Lodewijckx (ed.), *Bruc ealles Well: Archaeological Essays concerning the Peoples of North-west Europe in the First Millennium AD*, Leuven.

East, K. (1983). 'The tubs and buckets', in R. Bruce-Mitford *The Sutton Hoo Ship-burial Vol. III Part II*, London, British Museum Publications, 554-594.

Ellis, B. (1984). 'Spurs', in A. Rogerson and C. Dallas, *Excavations in Thetford 1948-59 and 1973-80*, Gressenhall, East Anglian Archaeology Report, 22, 101-104.

Evison, V. I. (1994). *An Anglo-Saxon Cemetery at Great Chesterford, Essex*, York, Council for British Archaeology Research Report, 91.

Evison, V. I. and Hill, P. (1996). *Two Anglo-Saxon Cemeteries at Beckford, Hereford and Worcester*, York, Council for British Archaeology Research Report, 103.

Fennell, K. R. (unpublished). *The Anglo-Saxon Cemetery at Loveden Hill (Hough-on-the-Hill) Lincolnshire and its significance in relation to the Dark Age settlement of the East Midlands*, Nottingham, University of Nottingham Ph.D. Thesis.

Fern, C. (forthcoming). 'Early Anglo-Saxon horse burials of the fifth to seventh centuries AD ', in S. Semple and H. Williams (eds) *Anglo-Saxon Studies in Archaeology & History*, 14.

Filmer-Sankey, W. and Pestell, T. (2001). *Snape Anglo-Saxon Cemetery: Excavations and Surveys 1824-1992*, Gressenhall, East Anglian Archaeology Report, 95.

Gaimster, M. (1998). *Vendel Period Bracteates on Gotland: on the Significance of Germanic Art*, Lund, Acta Archaeologica Lundensia, 8, 27.

Geake, H. (1997). *The Use of Grave-Goods in Conversion-Period England c.600-850*, Oxford, British Archaeological Reports British Series, 261.

Geake, H. (2001). 'Portable Antiquities Scheme', *Medieval Archaeology*, 45, 236-251.

Goodall, I. H. and Ottoway, P. (forthcoming). *Excavations at Wicken Bonhunt*, Gressenhall, East Anglian Archaeology Report.

Götherström, A. (2002). 'The value of stallions and mares during the Early Medieval time in upper-class Svealand', *Journal of Nordic Archaeological Science*, 13, 75-78.

Hald, J. and Laux, U. (1999). 'Zwei Pferdebestattungen im alamannischen Gräberfeld von Ammerbuch-Entringen, Kreis Tübingen', *Archäologische Ausgrabungen in Baden-Württemberg*, 147-149.

Halsall, G. (2003). *Warfare and Society in the Barbarian West, 450-900*, London, Routledge.

Hamerow, H. and Pickin, J. (1995). 'An early Anglo-Saxon cemetery at Andrew's Hill, Easington, Co.Durham', *Durham Archaeological Journal*, 11, 35-66.

Harman, M. (1993). 'The animal burials: discussion', in A. G. Kinsley, *Excavations on the Romano-British Settlement and Anglo-Saxon Cemetery at Broughton Lodge, Willoughby-on-the-Wolds, Nottinghamshire 1964-8*, Long Eaton, Nottingham Archaeological Monographs, 4, 58-61.

Härke, H. (1997). 'Early Anglo-Saxon military organisation: an archaeological perspective', in A. Nørgård Jørgensen and B. L. Clausen (eds), *Military Aspects of Scandinavian Society in a European Perspective, AD 1-1300*, Copenhagen, The National Museum Studies in Archaeology and History, 2, 93-101.

Hässler, H-J. (1981). 'Inlaid metalwork of the late Migration period and the Merovingian period from Lower Saxony', in V. I. Evison (ed.) *Angles, Saxons and Jutes. Essays presented to J. N. L. Myres*, Oxford, Clarendon Press: 72-95.

Hässler, H-J. (1994). *Neue Ausgrabungen in Issendorf, Ldkr.Stade Niedersachsen*, Hannover, Studien zur Sachsenforschung, 9.

Haughton, C. and Powesland, D. (1999). *West Heslerton. The Anglian Cemetery*, Nottingham, Landscape Research Centre Archaeological Monograph Series, No. 1, Vol. 1.

Hawkes, S. C. (2000). 'The Anglo-Saxon cemetery of Bifrons, in the parish of Patrixbourne, East Kent', *Anglo-Saxon Studies in Archaeology and History*, 11, 1-94.

Headeger, L. (2000). 'Migration Period Europe: the formation of a political mentality', in F. Theuws and J. L. Nelson (eds), *Rituals of Power: From Late Antiquity to the Early Middle Ages*, Leiden, Brill: 15-57.

Hencken, H. (1950). 'Lagore crannog: an Irish royal residence of the 7th to 10th centuries AD', *Proceedings of the Royal Irish Academy*, 53, 1-247.

Hines, J. (1997). *A New Corpus of Anglo-Saxon Great Square-Headed Brooches*, Woodbridge, Reports of the Research Committee of the Society of Antiquaries, 51, Boydell Press.

Hills, C. (1999). 'Did the people of Spong Hill come from Schleswig-Holstein?', *Studien zur Sachsenforchung*, 11, 145-154.

Hills, P. (1997). *Whithorn and St. Ninians: The Excavation of a Monastic Town, 1984-91*, Stroud, Sutton Publishing.

Hirst, S. M. and Clark, D. (forthcoming). *Excavations at Mucking, Vol. 3: The Anglo-Saxon Cemeteries*, London.

Hope-Taylor, B. (1977). *Yeavering: an Anglo-British Centre of Early Northumbria*, London, Department of the Environment Archaeological Report, 7.

H olbrook, N. (2000). 'The Anglo-Saxon cemetery at Lower Farm, Bishop's Cleeve: excavations directed by Kenneth Brown, 1969', *Transactions of the Bristol and Gloucestershire Archaeological Society*, 118, 61-92.

Hooper, N. (1993). 'The Aberlemno Stone and cavalry in Anglo-Saxon England', *Northern History*, 29, 188-196.

Hyland, A. (1990). *Equus: The Horse in the Roman world*, London, Batsford.

Hyland, A. (1993). *Training the Roman Army: from Arrian's Ars Tactica*, London, Sutton.

Hyland, A. (1999). *The Horse in the Middle Ages*, Trowbridge, Sutton.

Hyslop, M. (1963). 'Two Anglo-Saxon cemeteries at Chamberlain's Barn, Leighton Buzzard, Bedfordshire', *Archaeological Journal*, 120, 161-200.

Jarvis, E. Rev. (1850). 'Account of the discovery of ornaments and remains, supposed to be of Danish Origin, in the Parish of Caenby, Lincolnshire', *Archaeological Journal*, 7, 36-44.

Kelly, E. P. (2001). 'The Hillquarter, Co. Westmeath mounts: an early medieval saddle from Ireland', in M. Redknap, N. Edwards, S. Youngs, A. Lane and J.

Knight (eds) *Pattern and Purpose in Insular Art*, Oxford, Oxbow Books, 261-274.

Kerth, Von K. (2000). 'Die Tierbeigaben aus vier frühmittelalterlichen Gräberfeldern in Unterfranken', *Germania*, 78, 1, 125-138.

Kinsley, A. G. (1993). *Excavations on the Romano-British Settlement and Anglo-Saxon Cemetery at Broughton Lodge, Willoughby-on-the-Wolds, Nottinghamshire 1964-8*, Long Eaton, Nottingham Archaeological Monographs, 4.

Koch, R. (1982). 'Stachelsporen des frühen und hohen mittelalters', *Zeitschrift für Archäeologie des Mittelalters*, 10, 63-83.

Laing, L. (forthcoming.a). 'Some Anglo-Saxon artefacts from Nottinghamshire', in S. Semple and H. Williams (eds) *Anglo-Saxon Studies in Archaeology & History*, 14.

Laing, L. and Longley, D. (forthcoming.b). *The Mote of Mark. A Dark Age Hillfort in South-West Scotland*, Society of Antiquaries of Scotland Monograph.

László, G. (1943). 'Der Grabfund von Koroncó und der altungarische Sattel', *Archaeologica Hungarica*, 27, 107-191.

Leeds, E. T. (1938). 'An Anglo-Saxon cemetery at Wallingford, Berkshire', *Berkshire Archaeological Journal*, 42, 93-101.

Liddle, P. (1979/80). 'An Anglo-Saxon cemetery at Wanlip, Leicestershire', *Trans. of the Leicestershire Archaeol. and Hist. Soc.*, 55, 11-21.

Lundholm, B. (1949). 'Abstammung und Domestikation des Hauspferdes', *Zoologiska Bidrag Från Uppsala*, 27, 1-287.

MacGregor, A. and Bolick, E. (1993). *Ashmolean Museum, Oxford: A Summary Catalogue of the Anglo-Saxon Collections (Non-ferrous metals)*, Oxford, British Archaeological Reports British Series, 230.

Malim, T. and Hines, J. (1998). *The Anglo-Saxon cemetery at Edix Hill (Barrington A), Cambridgeshire*, York, Council for British Archaeology Research Report, 112.

McKinley, J. (1994). *Spong Hill Part VII: The Cremations*, Gressenhall, East Anglian Archaeology Report, 69.

Meaney, A. (1964). *A Gazetteer of Early Anglo-Saxon Burial Sites*, London, Unwin.

Mortimer, J. R. (1905). *Forty Years' Researches in British and Saxon Burial Mounds of East Yorkshire*, London.

Müller, H-H. (1955). 'Bestimmung der Höhe im Widerist bei Pferden', *Jahresschrift fürMitteldeutsche Vorgeschichte*, 39, 240-244.

Müller, H-H. (1980). 'Zur Kenntnis der Haustiere aus Völkerwanderungszeit im Mittelelbe – Saale-Gebiet', *Zeitschrift für Archäologie*, 14, 145-172.

Müller-Wille, M. (1970/71). *Pferdegrab und Pferdeopfer im frühen Mittelalter*, Berichten van de Rijksdienst voor het Oudheidkundig Bodemonderzoek Jaargang, 20-21.

Müller-Wille, M. (1999). 'Das Frankenreich und der

Norden. Zur Archäologie wechselseitiger Beziehungen während der Merwinger- und frühen Karolingerzeit' in U. von Freeden, U. Koch and A. Wieczovek (eds), *Völker au Nord- und Ostee und die Franken*, Bonn, 1-18.

Nawroth, M. (2001). *Das Gräberfeld von Pfahlheim und das Reitzhubehör der Merowingerzeit*, Nürnberg, Germanisches Nationalmuseum.

Newman, J. (forthcoming). *Anglo-Saxon Cemeteries at PAF Lakenheath, Suffolk*, Gressenhall, East Anglian Archaeology Report.

Neville, R. C. (1852). *Saxon Obsequies*, London.

Neville, R. C. (1854). 'Anglo-Saxon Cemetery on Linton Heath, Cambridgeshire', *Archaeological Journal*, 11, 95-115.

Nichols, J. (1807). *The History and Antiquities of the County of Leicester*, Vol. 4, 1, London.

O'Connor, T. (1994). 'A horse skeleton from Sutton Hoo, Suffolk, U.K.', *Archaeolzoologia*, 7, 1, 29-37.

O'Connor, T. (unpublished). 'Animal bones from Lakenheath, Suffolk (ERL046, 104, 114)', Archive report to Suffolk CC Archaeology Unit.

Oexle, J. (1984). 'Merowingerzeitliche Pferdebestattungen – Opfer oder Beigaben?', *Frühmittelalterliche Studien*, 18, 122-172.

Oexle, J. (1992). *Studien zu merowingerzeitlichem Pferdegeschirr am Beispiel der Trensen*, Mainz, Germanische Denkmäler der Völkerwanderungszeit, Serie A, 16.

Ottoway, P. (1992). *Anglo-Scandinavian Ironwork from 16-22 Coppergate*, York, The Archaeology of York, 17: The Small Finds, Fascicule 6, Council for British Archaeology.

Parfitt, K and Brugmann, B. (1997). *The Anglo-Saxon Cemetery on Mill Hill, Deal, Kent*, Leeds, Society for Medieval Archaeology Monograph, 14.

Parfitt, K, Brugmann, B. and Rettner, A. (2000). 'Anglo-Saxon spur from the Mill Hill, Deal, Cemetery', *Kent Archaeological Review*, 140, 229-230.

Payne, G. (1894). 'Note', *Proceedings of the Society of Antiquaries of London*, 15, 178-183.

Peake, H. and Hooton, E. A. (1915). 'Saxon graveyard at East Shefford, Berks.', *Journal of the Royal Anthropological Institute*, 45, 92-130.

Petré, B. (1984). *Arkeologiska undersökningar på Lovö Del 4*, Studies in North-European Archaeology 10, Stockholm, Acta Universitatis Stockholmiensis.

Prigg, H. and Fenton, S. (1888). 'The Anglo-Saxon graves, Warren Hill, Mildenhall', *Proceedings of the Suffolk Institute of Archaeology*, 6, 57-72.

Prummel, W. (1992). 'Early medieval dog burials among the Germanic tribes', *Helinium*, 32, 132-194. *Portable Antiquities Scheme Annual Report 2001/02-2002/03* (2003), Re:source: The Council for Museums, Archives and Libraries.

Ramqvist, P. H. (1992). *Högom. The Excavations 1949-1984.* Neumünster, Högom, 1, University of Umeå.

Rettner, A. (1997). 'Sporen der Ältern Merowingerzeit', *Germania*, 75, 1, 133-157.

Faussett, B. (1856). *Inventorium Sepulchrale: an Account of some Antiquities dug up at Gilton, Kingston, Sibertswold, Barfriston, Beakesbourne, Chartham, and Crundale, in the County of Kent, from AD 1757 to AD 1773*, ed. by C. Roach-Smith, London.

Saggau, H. E. (1986). *Bordesholm. Der Urnenfriedhof am Brautberg bei Bordesholm in Holstein*, Neumünster, Offa-Bücher, 60.

Seaby, W. A. and Woodfield, P. (1980). 'Viking Stirrups from England and their Background', *Medieval Archaeology*, 24, 87-122.

Serjeantson, D. (1994). 'The animal bones', in V. I. Evison, *An Anglo-Saxon Cemetery at Great Chesterford, Essex*, York, Council for British Archaeology Research Report, 91, 66-70.

Shortt, H. de. S. (1959). 'A provincial Roman spur from Longstock, Hants., and other spurs from Roman Britain', *The Antiquaries Journal*, 39, 61-76.

Smith, C. R. (1851/52). 'Notes on Saxon sepulchral remains found at Fairford, Gloucestershire', *Archaeologia*, 34, 77-82.

Smith, R. A. (1908). 'Anglo-Saxon Remains', in W. Page (ed.), *The Victoria History of the County of Kent*, Vol. 1, London, 339-387.

Southampton Museum Archaeological Object Database: http://sccwww1.southampton.gov.uk/archaeology/search.asp

Speake, G. (1980). *Anglo-Saxon Animal Art and its Germanic Background*, Oxford, Clarendon Press.

Speake, G. (1989). *A Saxon Bed Burial on Swallowcliffe Down*, London, Historic Buildings and Monuments Commission for England Archaeological Report, 10.

Sundkvist, A. (2001). *Hästarnas Land: Aristokratisk hästhållning och ridkonst I Svealands yngre järnålder*, Uppsala, Uppsala universitet.

Quast, D. (1993). 'Das hölzerne Sattelgestell aus Oberflacht Grab 211: Bemerkungen zu merowingerzeitlichen Sätteln', *Funderberichte aus Baden-Württemberg*, 18, 437-464.

Tweddle, D., Moulden, J. and Logan, E. (1999). *Anglian York: A Survey of the Evidence*, York, The Archaeology of York, 7 Fascicule 2, Council for British Archaeology.

Tyler, S. and Major, H. (forthcoming). *The Early Anglo-Saxon Cemetery and Late Saxon Settlement at Springfield Lyons, Essex*, Gressenhall, East Anglian Archaeology Report.

Urban, S. (1838). 'Discovery of Roman skeletons', *The Gentleman's Magazine*, 10, New Series, 650. Vierck, H. (1970/71). 'Pferdegräber im angelsächsischen England', in M. Müller-Wille, *Pferdegrab und Pferdeopfer im frühen Mittelalter*, Berichten van de Rijksdienst voor het Oudheidkundig Bodemonderzoek Jaargang, 20-21, 189-199.

Welch, M. (1983). *Early Anglo-Saxon Sussex*, Oxford, British Archaeological Reports British Series 112.

West, S. (1998). *A Corpus of Anglo-Saxon Material from Suffolk*, Gressenhall, East Anglian Archaeology Report, 84.

Williams, H. (2001). 'An ideology of transformation: Cremation rites and animal sacrifice in early Anglo-

Saxon England', in N. Price, *The Archaeology of Shamanism*, London, Routledge, 193-212.

Whitfield, N. (2001). 'The earliest filigree from Ireland', in Redknap, N. Edwards, S. Youngs, A. Lane and J. Knight (eds), *Pattern and Purpose in Insular Art*, Oxford, Oxbow Books, 141-154.

Wright, T. (1844). 'An account of the opening of barrows in Bourne Park, near Canterbury', *Archaeological Journal*, 1, 253-256.

Youngs, S. (1989). '*The Work of Angels*': *Masterpieces of Celtic Metalwork, 6th-9th Centuries AD*', London, British Museum Publications.

Hunting for the Anglo-Normans:
Zooarchaeological Evidence for Medieval Identity

Naomi Sykes

Introduction

Eleventh- and twelfth-century documents suggest that the Normans perceived themselves as a people, or 'Gens', regardless of their geographical location (Loud, 1982; Bliese, 1991; Potts, 1995; Shopkow, 1997) but archaeological absence of a distinct material culture led some scholars to question whether the Normans did indeed possess a common identity (Davis, 1976; Rowley, 1999: 13). It is now widely recognised that, although material culture is frequently invoked in expressions of ethnicity, there is not a fixed one-to-one relationship between ethnic groups and artefact typology (Jones, 1997). Instead symbolic assertions of ethnicity are fluid, situational and generally enmeshed with a group's existing cultural practices and social, economic and political structure. Archaeological identification of ethnicity requires, therefore, the adoption of a contextual and historical approach that considers changing patterns in the production, distribution and consumption of material culture. Such approaches have been applied to the study of the Roman Conquest (Jones, 1997) and the Migration Period (Hines, 1993) but similar investigation of Norman England has been neglected, perpetuating the belief that the Conquest of 1066 is archaeologically invisible (Rowley, 1997).

Recent examination of animal-bone data, synthesised from almost 300 assemblages from fifth- to fourteenth-century sites in England and France, demonstrated the archaeological record to be a better medium for the detection of Norman influence than has previously been accepted (Sykes, 2001), and it seems likely that animal bone studies may be equally profitable for the detection of Anglo-Norman identity. To date, zooarchaeological investigations of ethnicity have lagged behind other specialist fields of archaeology. Up to now they have generally been founded in period- or site-specific studies of diet, notably the analysis of species presence/absence or butchery patterns (for instance Langenwalter, 1980; Ijzereef, 1989; Scott, 1996). It is perhaps for this reason in particular that attention has focused on just one aspect of the production-distribution-consumption process, that studies of ethnicity which are based on zooarchaeology have been largely unsuccessful (for examples see Crabtree, 1991). By drawing on work that has followed the 'social life' of different animals and their products (Sykes, 2001), I hope in this paper to highlight the potential of zooarchaeological analysis for the detection of ethnic identity.

Norman England is an ideal case-study for the examination of ethnicity for several reasons. The events of 1066, which saw the Norman aristocracy appropriate positions of social, economic, religious and political power, produced precisely the kind of climate that can lead to heightened ethnic consciousness (Hodder, 1979; Kimes et al., 1982). As a result, there is every possibility that expressions of identity were particularly overt in Norman England and thus potentially archaeologically detectable. Guidance to the spheres in which the expressions may have been objectified is provided by the large number of eleventh- and twelfth-century histories written or commissioned by the Normans. The self-image projected by these texts is one of ethnic and moral superiority founded, above all, on the Normans' perceived 'God-given' military virtues (Bliese, 1991). Whilst at face value ethnic identity based on martial supremacy would appear to be inaccessible to zooarchaeological research, there is a well-documented association between warfare and hunting (Kent, 1989), an activity for which the Anglo-Normans are also traditionally famed. Beyond the connection with warfare, hunting, as a social action, is an activity worthy of study in its own right. Indeed, as a mechanism for generating identity, hunting is receiving increasing attention (Kent, 1989; Cartmill, 1993; Marvin, 2001; Hamilakis, 2003) and it is now acknowledged that patterns of wild-animal exploitation mirror social and political change (Wickham, 1994: 161). For this reason, the Normans's use of hunting to negotiate power and authority forms the focus of this paper. Initially I shall present the zooarchaeological evidence that confirms the Normans 'love of hunting' before considering the meaning and symbolism behind this apparent passion.

Love of the chase

The Norman Conquest of 1066 has come to be viewed as a significant watershed in the history of English hunting, with William I applying Forest Law to vast areas of common and privately owned land, restricting use of the wild animals that inhabited them. Despite this, few modern books on the subject actually examine the Norman contribution to the development of British hunting. Instead, most authors concentrate on the peculiarities of later medieval English hunting practices — in particular their preoccupation with ritual, terminology and etiquette — without considering why they should differ so much from continental traditions

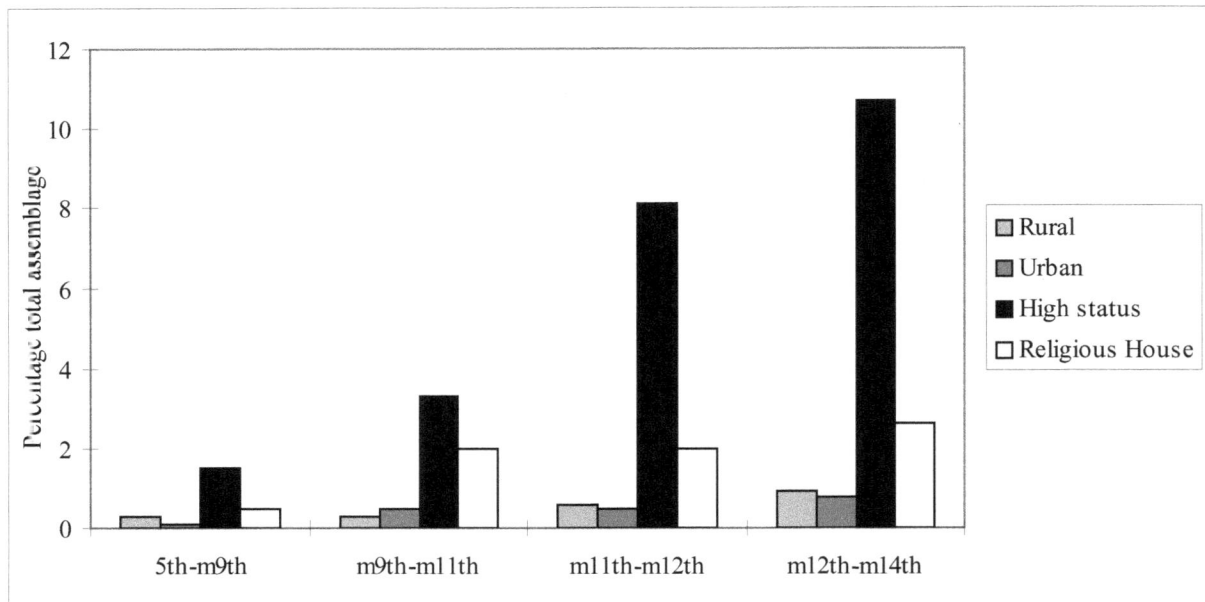

Figure 6.1: Inter-period variation in wild mammal representation on sites of different type. Frequencies are expressed as a percentage of the total fragment count (excluding fish)

(Cummins, 1988; Rooney, 1993 and Almond, 2003). To ignore the evolution of medieval hunting is a significant oversight if we are to understand the changing social and symbolic meaning of this form of wild-animal exploitation. Lack of early medieval texts concerning hunting may put these questions beyond the scope of historical investigation but they can be answered through zooarchaeological analysis. Animal-bone studies have, for instance, demonstrated that the origins of many later medieval hunting traditions can be traced directly to the decades after 1066 (Sykes, 2001; in press). At the most basic level this is reflected by changing frequencies in game representation, with high-status sites showing a post-Conquest increase in the abundance of wild mammals disproportionate to that seen for other settlement types (*Figure 6.1*).

Unprecedented shifts in species representation are also apparent for eleventh- and twelfth-century assemblages. Not only do fallow deer appear for the first time but long-standing ratios of roe deer to red deer also change on many site-types: assemblages from castles and manor-houses demonstrate a pre- to post-Conquest move away from roe deer towards red deer whilst those from urban settlements show an equally dramatic shift in the opposite direction (*Figure 6.2*).

Perhaps most significantly, studies of medieval deer assemblages have highlighted clear changes in anatomical representation that occur shortly after 1066: deer from pre-Conquest assemblages, regardless of site-type are represented by all parts of the body whereas those from post-Conquest high-status sites show a dearth of the pelvis and elements of the upper forelimb but an over-representation of foot bones, particularly from the hindquarters (*Figure 6.3*).

These shifts in skeletal patterning have been linked to the introduction of new hunting rituals, in particular the 'unmaking', in which the deer was skinned, disembowelled and butchered in a highly formulaic manner (Sykes, 2001; in press). As part of this ceremony, certain portions of the carcass were given to particular individuals. For instance, the 'corbyn bone' (the pelvis) was cast away at the kill-site as an offering to the 'corbyn' (raven); the left shoulder was presented to the forester or parker as his fee and the right shoulder was often given to the best hunter, hence the under-representation of these elements in assemblages from high-status sites. By the end of the twelfth century, knowledge of the unmaking rituals and, in particular, the French terminology surrounding them was deemed to be a mark of nobility. This is made clear by John of Salisbury who wrote that 'the scholarship of the aristocracy consists in hunting jargon' (Policraticus 1.4 (I,.23)).

All of these pre- to post-Conquest changes could be interpreted as evidence for the importation of a 'Norman Package'; that the new foreign elite brought their own hunting traditions and preferences from pre-Conquest Normandy. Certainly there is evidence that Normandy possessed a forest system by the early eleventh century (Gilbert, 1979; Debord, 1990) and that red, as opposed to roe, deer were the favoured quarry of the aristocratic deer hunt (Sykes, n.d; Yvinec, 1993). Such an interpretation is, however, too simplistic, being little advanced from the culture-historical approach adopted by the archaeologists

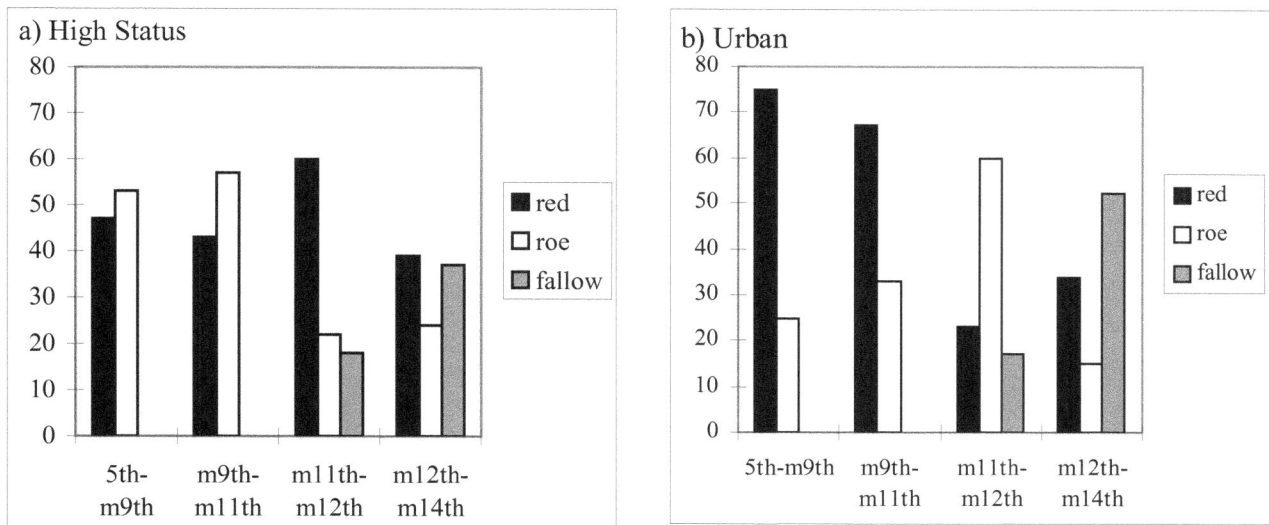

Figure 6.2: Inter-period variation in red, roe and fallow deer representation for a) high-status and b) urban sites

of the twentieth century, which assumed that cultural similarity equates to ethnic identity. Though there were affinities between the hunting practices of pre-Conquest Normandy and post-Conquest England, they reveal nothing of the activity's symbolism within these two milieu; there is every possibility that the apparently similar traditions conveyed very different meanings in these separate contexts. Below I consider the social and cultural significance of the pre- to post-Conquest changes in English hunting.

Symbolism and meaning

In many respects the pre-to post-Conquest changes in hunting are symptomatic of the time, being linked to widespread changes in social structure. The significant rise in aristocratic hunting can, for instance, be seen as reflecting the increasing social division that typified the eleventh and twelfth centuries. This was also a period of growing gender definition, with emphasis being placed increasingly on masculinity and military activity (Coss, 1999), and hunting, with its references to warfare and male identity, must be symbolic of this. In England the origins of these social trends pre-date 1066 but the extent to which they were accelerated by the Conquest, is important. Differences in the social and cultural structures of inter-dependent groups are frequently the foundation for feelings and expressions of ethnicity (Jones, 1997), thus any slight variation between Saxon and Norman social structure could have been magnified by the Conquest and employed as a signifier of Norman identity. There is some evidence to suggest that society in pre-Conquest Norman was more patriarchal, at least in terms of inheritance, than was the case in Saxon England (Bates, 1982; Coss, 1999: 21). Combine this with the fact

that the Conquest saw a male-dominated Norman elite dispossess a Saxon aristocracy that, as a result of the battle-depleted male line, was female-dominant, and it seems likely that masculine identity amongst the Normans of post-Conquest England would have been strong, being enmeshed with warfare, social status and authority. Anthropological studies have shown repeatedly that hunting is a mechanism for asserting precisely these traits (Kent, 1989), and historical evidence demonstrates that this was certainly true in medieval England (Rooney, 1993; Almond, 2003). I suggest that the sudden and dramatic post-Conquest increase in high-status wild resource exploitation (*Figure 6.1*) reflects Anglo-Norman deployment of hunting as a device for demonstrating power over the subjugated population. This theory is born out by the imposition of Forest Law, which fundamentally altered perceptions of hunting space but also challenged ideology concerning the 'chain of being'; the relative position of animals to humans.

In pre-Conquest England most aristocratic hunting was centred on enclosed wooded parks (see for instance Liddiard, 2003), 'wild' spaces that were deemed distinctly separate from the domestic landscape. It was only within these reserves that restrictions were placed on hunting, elsewhere people were largely free to exploit wild resources. This fact is clear from article number 80 of Canute's law (issued between 1020 and 1030) which states that 'It is my will that every man shall be entitled to hunt in the woods and fields of his own property' but that ' everyone, under pain of incurring the full penalty, shall avoid hunting in my preserves' (Attenborough, 1922). Under this system all humans, regardless of social status, were classified as higher beings than animals (*Figure 6.4*).

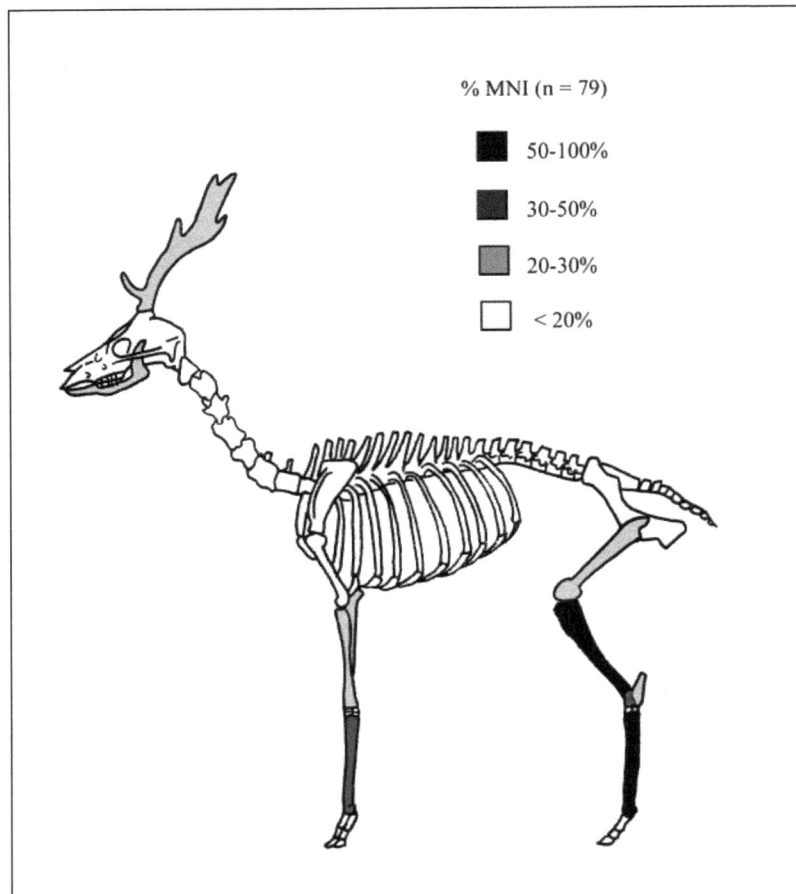

Figure 6.3: Inter-site variation in the representation of deer remains, shown as a percentage of the total count of mammal bone fragments.

	Landscape Model			Chain of Being	
Key	Perceived Wild Perceived Domestic			**Category 1**	**Category 2**
Pre-Conquest	Low-status High-status Acess Permitted Restricted			Human	Animal
Post-Conquest	All Restricted	High-status Low-status		High-status human (Anglo-Norman) Game animals	Low-status human (Saxon) Domestic animals

Figure 6.4: Pre- to post-Conquest changes in perceptions of landscape and human-animal relationships.

76

With the introduction of Forest Law, geographic definition of wild and domestic space became blurred as the Anglo-Normans superimposed their own hunting landscape over the existing domestic one. By restricting hunting rights to the elite, the 'wild' became associated with high social status whereas 'domestic' equated to the lower classes. Rather than all humans having domination over nature, Forest Law placed game animals in the same macro-category as the aristocracy, a category above the peasantry who were now essentially classified together with domestic animals (*Figure 6.4*)

It has been suggested elsewhere (Sykes, 2001; in press) that these shifts in hunting landscape – with emphasis moving from enclosed woodland parks to unbounded forests – were the impetus for the observed decline in roe deer, and the uptake of the red deer, as the premier beast of the aristocratic chase (*Figure 6.2*). This argument was based on the behavioural ecology of the two species, roe deer being adapted for woodland living whilst the red deer is better suited to open landscapes (Legge and Rowley-Conwy, 1988:13-16). On its own, this interpretation is flawed by its environmentally deterministic approach. Hunting is not passive in its selection of quarry but, as Cartmill (1993: 29) has argued, it involves special sorts of animals, killed in specific ways for particular reasons. The pre- to post-Conquest shift from roe deer to the hunting of red deer reflects, therefore, a deliberate decision on the part of the hunters and can be understood only as symbolic behaviour. Altered perceptions of hunting landscapes, together with the fact that red deer were the preferred deer of the French Norman aristocracy, could be part of the explanation but it may also be significant that in medieval iconography and literature there is an association between the stag and Christ (Cummins 1988: 68-74; Payne, 1990: 38). Piety was a character trait that the Normans actively sought to project – as is evidenced by their histories (Shopkow, 1997) and their dynamic foundation of religious houses (Taylor, 1996; Bull, 1988) – and it seems fitting that they chose to hunt species that were imbued with religious symbolism.

The late eleventh-century introduction of fallow deer added a further dimension to post-Conquest hunting – one of trade and 'luxury' (see van der Veen, 2003). Recent research (Sykes, 2004) confirms that the Anglo-Normans conveyed this species to England but suggests that, rather than being brought from Normandy, fallow deer were actually amongst a suite of elements imported from Sicily (for other imports see Moffett, 1989; Sykes, 2001; Hieatt, 2002: 28). The Normans of Sicily were held in great esteem by the Anglo-Normans who used the achievements of their Mediterranean kinsmen to bolster their own identity (Jameson, 1938; Hermans, 1979: 80). Members of the Anglo-Norman aristocracy travelled regularly to Sicily and, in England, the adoption of elements of the Sicilian lifestyle, such as the maintenance of fallow deer in pleasure parks, would have been an additional feature which enhanced social standing.

Anthropological studies (for instance Goody, 1982) have shown that goods and ideas from 'outside' are often incorporated into assertions of social power and in the medieval World, the ownership of exotic animals frequently formed part of this display. Henry I, for example, maintained a variety of foreign beasts in his menagerie at Woodstock, a collection that served as a statement of his international status (Bartlett, 2000: 670).

It has recently been pointed out that status derived from hunting skill is, likewise, frequently associated with long-distance travel (Helms, 1993; Hamilakis, 2003). For the medieval period, this association appears to find literary expression in Gottfried von Strassburg's story of Tristan (written c. AD 1210). In the hunting scene, which is set in Cornwall, the King's party had caught a red deer and was beginning to dress the carcass according to the traditions of the country when Tristan, a well-travelled Frenchman, arrives. Tristan is horrified by the huntsmen's uncouth butchery techniques and proceeds to instruct them in the 'correct' manner of 'excoriating' the deer, as well as introducing them to the terminology of the procedure (von Strassburg, 1967: 78-82). So impressed are the hunters that they praise Tristan's breeding, nobility and courtliness and take him to meet the King. The excoriation outlined in the story is the earliest known description of the 'unmaking', the techniques that, according to skeletal representation studies, appear in England shortly after 1066. As has been noted above, their coincidence with the timing of the Conquest strongly promotes the Anglo-Normans as the importers of these rituals. Absence of zooarchaeological evidence for their presence in pre-Conquest Normandy, however, undermines the assumption that they formed part of a pre-existing Norman package (Sykes, 2001). In France it is not until at least the thirteenth century that the unmaking rituals become apparent in the zooarchaeological record and, interestingly, their appearance there is synchronous with the arrival of fallow deer. There appears to be a link between fallow deer and the unmaking rituals and it may be no coincidence that, to date, the only place in which skeletal representation patterns akin to those of deer from post-Conquest England (Figure 3) have been idemtified is in Sicily, notably at site of Brucato (Bossard-Beck, 1984; Sykes, 2001). Further investigation is required but the probability is that the unmaking rituals were Sicilian traditions brought to England, along with fallow deer, by members of the Anglo-Norman elite.

It seems improbable that the Sicilian meaning behind the unmaking traditions was retained after their uptake in England. This is supported by the fact that none of the Middle English hunting texts clarify the symbolism of, or reason for, the rituals; even Gottfried's Tristan does not explain why his excoriation techniques are superior to those of the Cornish huntsmen (Rooney, 1993: 88). Traditions are dynamic, frequently being invented or manipulated in order to legitimise change (Eisenstadt, 1969). I would argue that the Sicilian unmaking rituals were adopted and modified by the Anglo-Normans as a device to reinforce their social and political authority. As such, the original significance of the unmaking ceremony became irrelevant, with the rituals being given new meaning. In post-Conquest England emphasis was placed on the etiquette and terminology of the hunt, and it was the ability to participate in the rituals, rather than an understanding of their original symbolism, that marked a person as noble. This was reinforced by the fact the language of the hunt was French, something that was clearly socially and ethnically divisive. It is here where we begin to see that hunting, high social rank and Norman identity were enmeshed in post-Conquest England, a subject to which I now turn.

Hunting and ethnicity

Within most farming societies the significance of hunting extends beyond the desire to obtain meat; instead it is a symbolic action, a social and political 'performance' (Marvin, 2001; Hamilakis, 2003). Whilst different groups may employ hunting for similar reasons, the purpose and meaning of hunting is not cross-culturally uniform: for instance Hamilakis (2003) in his study of Neolithic and Bronze Age Greece has proposed that hunting was linked to perceptions of time and space and employed as a strategy for negotiating gender and social power; Kensinger (1993) has interpreted hunting in Cashinahua society as embodying masculinity; and Marvin (2000) has explained modern English fox hunting in terms of the social and cultural identity of rural communities. In the case of the post-Conquest England I suggest that hunting was used as a mechanism for the generation of power and authority but that this was also tied to expressions of Anglo-Norman ethnicity.

After 1066, when the Normans took the positions of power, ethnicity and social class essentially became enmeshed, with Norman identity being associated with the social elite whereas the term 'English' was used to denote people of lesser rank (Williams, 1997: 5; Gillingham, 1995: 78). Pre- to post-Conquest changes in hunting laws, landscape and rituals served to reinforce this divide operating as they did on a basis of social exclusion. Imposition of Forest Law both restricted legitimate wild resource exploitation to the elite, in other words the Norman elite, but it also stamped Norman authority on the landscape. This is of particular significance as it is increasingly being recognised that landscape is a platform upon which group identity is inscribed and through which it is expressed (see for example Knapp and Ashmore, 2000). As a reference point for the assertion of identity, the introduction of fallow deer was also significant in landscape terms. The parks which had been built to retain them placed not only legal but also physical barriers on the hunting landscape, and the creation of fallow deer parks would have combined allusions to travel and the exotic with a strong statement of authority, rank and social exclusion (Herring, 2003).

Although largely the preserve of the Anglo-Norman aristocracy, these post-Conquest hunting restrictions did not totally exclude the wealthy Saxon lords who retained their lands and position after 1066 – they were presumably still entitled to hunt. How the Normans set out to differentiate their hunting from that of the native aristocracy was to introduce new and complex rituals that were steeped in French terminology, thus imposing a linguistic hurdle to outside involvement. It must be assumed that, in much the same way as is depicted by Gottfried's story of Tristan, these 'French' rituals were suggested to be more 'correct' than, even morally superior to, the Saxon techniques. This situation may explain the apparent peculiarity of Middle English hunting literature compared with its continental equivalents; the English texts' concern with hunting language and etiquette being a fossilization of Anglo-Norman traditions.

Hunting, and in particular the introduction of the unmaking rituals, provided the Anglo-Normans with outlet through which they could project everything they wished to emphasise about themselves, their 'Frenchness' and social superiority being just two of many traits. Male status and the Normans' belief in their martial supremacy went hand in hand with hunting ability, thus it is no wonder that the zooarchaeological record suggests a phenomenal post-Conquest increase in wild animal exploitation. The Normans also prided themselves on their piety and it may be for this reason that their favoured quarry was the red deer, a species deemed to symbolise many aspects of the Christian faith. Pride in the Norman Empire is reflected by the introduction of fallow deer and the associated arrival of the unmaking techniques, both of which appear to have been of Sicilian origin.

Hunting just one of many mechanisms through which the Anglo-Normans could have marked their identity but by embedding social status and ethnicity in law, landscape and language it would have been one of considerable power. These statements of identity would have been reproduced through the consumption of venison, an act that was also highly ritualised (Sykes in press). It is therefore, little wonder that hunting has come to be a character trait that is so frequently attributed to them.

References

Almond, R. (2003). Medieval Hunting, Stroud, Sutton.

Attenborough, F. L. (1922). Laws of the Earliest English Kings, London, Cambridge University Press.

Bartlett, R. (2000). England Under the Norman and Angevin Kings 1075-1225, Oxford, Clarendon Press.

Bates, D. (1982). Normandy Before 1066, London, Longman.

Bliese, J. R. E. (1991). 'The courage of the Normans. A comparative study of battle rhetoric', Nottingham Medieval Studies, 35, 1-27.

Bossard-Beck, C. (1984). 'Le mobilier ostéologique et botanique', in J-M. Pesez (ed.), Brucato: Histoire et Archéologie d'un Habitat Médiéval en Sicile, Rome, Collection de l'Ecole Française de Rome.

Bull, M. (1998). Knightly Piety and the Lay Response to the First Crusades: The Limousin and Gascony, c.970-c.1130, Oxford, Clarendon Press.

Cartmill, M. (1993). A View to a Death in the Morning: Hunting and Nature Through History, Cambridge, Harvard University Press.

Coss, P. (1999). The Lady in Medieval England 1000-1500, Stroud, Sutton.

Crabtree, P. (1991). 'Zooarchaeology and complex societies: some uses of faunal remains for the study of trade, social status and ethnicity', in M. Schiffer (ed.), Archaeological Method and Theory 2, Tucson, University of Arizona Press.

Cummins, J. (1988). The Hound and the Hawk: the Art of Medieval Hunting, London, Weidenfield and Nicholson.

Davis, R. H. C. (1976). The Normans and their Myth, London, Thames and Hudson.

Debord, A. (1990). 'Châteaux et forêts en France aux XIe and XIIe siècle', in A. Chastel (ed.), Le Chateau, La Chasse et la Foret, Luçon, Sud Ouest.

Eisenstadt, S. N. (1969). 'Some observation on the dynamics of traditions', Comparative Studies in Society and History, 11, 451-475.

Gilbert, J. (1979). Hunting and Hunting Reserves in Medieval Scotland, Edinburgh, John Donald.

Gillingham, J. (1995). 'Henry of Huntingdon and the twelfth-century revival of the English nation', in S. Forde, L. Johnson and A. Murray (eds.), Concepts of National Identity in the Middle Ages, Leeds, School of English, University of Leeds.

Goody, J. (1982). Cooking, Cuisine and Class: A Study in Comparative Sociology, Cambridge, Cambridge University Press.

Hamilakis, Y. (2003). 'The sacred geography of hunting: wild animals, social power and gender in early farming societies', in E. Kotjabopoulou, Y. Hamilakis, P. Halstead, C. Gamble and V. Elafanti (eds.), Zooarchaeology in Greece: Recent Advances, London, British School at Athens.

Helms, M. (1993). Craft and the Kingley Ideal: Art, Trade and Power, Austin, Texas University Press.

Hermans, J. (1979). 'The Byzantine view of the Normans - another Norman myth?', Anglo-Norman Studies, 2, 78-92.

Herring, P. (2003). 'Cornish medieval deer parks', in R. Wilson-North (ed.), The Lie of the Land: Aspects of the Archaeology and History of the Designed Landscape in the South West of England, Exeter, The Mint Press.

Hieatt, C. B. (2002). 'Medieval Britain', in M. Weiss Adamson (ed.), Regional Cuisines of Medieval Europe: A Book of Essays, London, Routledge.

Hines, J. (1996). 'Britain after Rome: between multiculturalism and monoculturalism', in P. Graves-Brown, S. Jones and C. Gamble (eds.), Cultural Identity and Archaeology: The Construction of European Communities, London, Routledge.

Hodder, I. (1979). 'Economic and social stress and material culture patterning', American Antiquity, 44, 3, 446-54.

Ijzereef, G. F. (1989). 'Social differentiation from animal bone studies', in D. Serjeantson and T. Waldron (eds.), Diet and Crafts in Towns: The Evidence of Animal Remains from the Roman to the Post-Medieval Periods, Oxford, BAR British Series 199.

Jameson, E. (1938). 'The Sicilian Norman kingdom in the mind of Anglo-Norman contemporaries', Proceedings of the British Academy, 24, 237-85.

John of Salisbury (1909). Policraticus (ed. C. C. J. Webb) Oxford.

Jones, S. (1997). The Archaeology of Ethnicity: Constructing Social Identities in the Past and Present, London, Routledge.

Kent, S. (ed.) (1989). Farmers as Hunters: The Implications of Sedentism, Cambridge, Cambridge University Press.

Kessinger, K. M. (1989). 'Hunting and male domination in Cashinahua society' in Kent, S. (ed.), Farmers as Hunters: The Implications of Sedentism, Cambridge, Cambridge University Press.

Kimes, T., Haselgrove, C. and Hodder, I. (1982). 'A method for the identification of the location of regional cultural boundaries', Journal of Anthropological Archaeology, 1, 113-31.

Knapp, A. B. and Ashmore, W. (2000). 'Archaeological landscapes: constructed, conceptualized, ideational', in W. Ashmore and A. B. Knapp (eds.), Archaeologies of Landscape: Contemporary Perspectives, Oxford, Blackwell.

Langenwalter, P. E. II (1980). 'The archaeology of 19th century Chinese subsistence at the lower China store, Madera County, California', in R. L. Schuyler (ed.), Archaeological Perspectives of Ethnicity in America, New York, Baywood.

Legge, A. J. and Rowley-Conwy, P. A. (1988). Star Carr Revisited, London, The Archaeological Laboratory Centre for Extra-Mural Studies, Birkbeck College.

Liddiard, R. (2003). 'The deer parks of Domesday Book', Landscapes, 4, 1, 4-23.

Loud, G.A. (1981). 'The 'Gens Normannorum': myth or reality?', Anglo-Norman Studies 4, 104-16.

Marvin, G. (2001). 'The problem of foxes: legitimate and illegitimate killing in the English countryside', in J. Knight (ed.), Natural Enemies: People-Wildlife Conflict in Anthropological Perspective, London, Routledge.

Moffett, L. (1989). 'The archeobotanical evidence for free-threshing tetraploid wheat in Britain', in S. Vytlacock (ed.), Palaeoethnobotany and Archaeology: International Work-Group for Palaeoethnobotany 8th Symposium Nitra-Nové Vozokany 1989, Nitra, Archaeological Institute of the Slovak Academy of Sciences.

Payne, A. (1990). Medieval Beasts, London, British

Library.

Potts, C. (1995). 'Atque unum ex diversis gentibus populum effecit: historical tradition and the Norman identity', Anglo-Norman Studies, 17, 139-175.

Rooney, A. (1993). Hunting in Middle English Literature, Woodbridge, Boydell Press.

Rowley, T. (1997). Norman England. An Archaeological Perspective on the Norman Conquest, London, Batsford.

Rowley, T. (1999). The Normans, Stroud, Tempus.

Scott, E. M. (1996). 'Who ate what? Archaeological food remains and cultural diversity', in E. J. Reitz, L.A. Newsom and S. J. Scudder (eds.), Case Studies in Environmental Archaeology, London, Plenum Press.

Shopkow, L. (1997). History and Community: Norman Historical Writing in the 11th and 12th centuries, Washington D.C, Catholic University of America Press.

Sykes, N. J. (2001). The Norman Conquest: A Zooarchaeological Perspective, unpublished Ph.D. thesis, University of Southampton.

Sykes, N. J. 2004. 'The Introduction of fallow deer (Dama dama): a zooarchaeological perspective', Environmental Archaeology: The Journal of Human Palaeoecology, 9 pp.75-83.

Sykes, N. J. in press. 'The impact of the Normans on hunting practices in England', in C. Woolgar, D. Serjeantson and T. Waldron (eds.), Food in Medieval England: History and Archaeology, Oxford, Oxford University Press.

Sykes, N. J. (nd). The Animal Remains from Vatteville Castle, Normandy.

Taylor, M. (1996). 'The impact of the Norman ecclesiastical revival in Britain after 1066 - a summary', in X. Delestre and A. Woodcock (eds.), Proximus, Dieppe, Archaeological Round Table.

Veen, M. van der (2003). 'When is food a luxury?', World Archaeology, 34, 3), 405-427.

Von Strassburg, G. (1960). Tristan, London, Penguin (Hatto, A. T. trans.).

Wickham, C. (1994). Land and Power; Studies in Italian and European Social History, 400-1200, London, British School at Rome.

Williams, A. (1997). The English and the Norman Conquest, Woodbridge, Boydell and Brewer.

Yvinec, J.-H. (1993). 'La part du gibier dans l'alimentation du haut Moyen Âge', in J. Desse and F. Audoin-Rouzeau (eds.), Rencontres Internationales d'Archéologie et d'Histoire d'Antibes (13e: 1992: Ville d'Antibes): Exploitation des animaux sauvages a travers le temps, Juan-les-Pins, Éditions APDCA.

Prowlers in Wild and Dark Places?
Mapping Wolves in Medieval Britain and Southern Scandinavia

Aleksander Pluskowski

Introduction

The wolf is often invoked in the popular media as one of the most potent symbols of fear in the minds of medieval Europeans, a nightmare haunting the darkest woods in a world 'lit only by fire' (Manchester 1993). The wolf's association with woodland in the historical past is sometimes taken for granted in both the public and academic sphere, perhaps unsurprisingly given that in popular fairy tales, wolves typically inhabit this type of environment and that stories such as *Little Red Riding Hood*, always set in the woods, are thought by some to derive from the experiences of medieval Europeans (Pluskowski 2005; forthcoming a). Ecologists on the other hand are actively promoting a new understanding of wolf biogeography:

> 'Wolves appear to cope well with extreme wilderness, but they also inhabit crowded agricultural lands at the outskirts of towns and villages' (Mech and Boitani, 2003: 343)

Yet the link between wolves and woodland cited in general works on medieval society (e.g. Le Goff, 1990: 133), is found as a recurring *topos* in north European medieval literature. For example, a line from the late-thirteenth century *Norwegian Runic Poem* states that: 'føðesk ulfr í skóge' – 'the wolf lives in the woods' (Dickins, 1915: 25), whilst in the fable of 'The wolf and the dog' composed by Marie de France in the latter half of the twelfth century, the wolf concludes his conversation with the dog by saying 'Va a la vile, jeo vois al bois!' – 'You fare to town; to woods I'll go' (Spiegel, 1994:96-7). From a modern ecological perspective 'vegetation type makes little difference to wolves as long as populations of hoofed prey are available' (Fuller *et al*, 2003: 163), and both of these literary examples can be 'read' on a number of levels, which taken together appear to represent the interaction between physical experience and conceptual thought. This relationship has rarely been explored in studies of medieval landscapes and species biogeography. Scholars have tended to separate into two camps – those studying the physical landscape through pollen analysis, cartography and land charters, and those studying the landscape in literature, art and attempting to access the medieval imagination. Moreover, both groups rarely consider the presence and movement of fauna in any detail.

Focusing on the biogeography of wolves in Britain and southern Scandinavia during the eighth to fourteenth centuries AD, this paper offers a synthesis of 'physical' and 'conceptual' perspectives to demonstrate how the real and perceived distribution of animals is of cultural, as well as ecological significance in furthering our understanding of medieval societies. There is not enough space to touch on all the aspects of this relationship, but the resulting synthesis aims to provoke further discussion from a range of disciplines. Primary sources for wolf biogeography in medieval Britain and Scandinavia are subdivided into place names, skeletal remains recovered from archaeological contexts and written sources, including both observed and perceived wolf presence. These fragmentary primary sources will be complemented by modern ecological studies, with the aim of presenting a holistic model of wolf biogeography in medieval northern Europe.

The name of the wolf in the landscape

There are many place names incorporating the term 'wolf' in Britain and Scandinavia, associated with a variety of topographical features: in England derived from Old English *wulf* or Old Norse *ulfr*, with a handful of examples of Cornish *bleit*, in Wales derived from Old Welsh *bleidd* as well as the Old English term, and in Scotland derived from Gaelic *maddie* and the Old Norse term. In southern Scandinavia, elements include *ulfr* and *vargr*, for example in Sweden, Vargarn, Vargberget, in Norway Ulvdal and in Denmark, Ulvehøj and Ulvemose. These names are sometimes cited as evidence for the ubiquity of wolves in a particular region (Finberg, 1967: 40) as well as regional patterns of extinction (Dent, 1974: 99-134), however, their interpretation can be problematic and they are not straightforward snapshots of historical wolf biogeography. Firstly, they may refer to an individual named 'wolf' (Wulf, Úlfr etc.) rather than the animal, although it is possible to differentiate between the two (Aybes and Yalden, 1995). Secondly, it may be difficult to specify a particular use of 'wolf' for any given place name, even where examples are explicitly associated with topographical features such as valleys or hills. Thirdly, if they do refer to the animal, there is no indication of how long this name functioned for, or the purpose of its application to a particular point in the landscape. In addition, the naming may be related to a metaphorical rather than a physical use of the animal; for example, Rackham (1997: 34) provides a modern analogue: a 'wolf tree' is what modern foresters call a tree that grows inordinately fast to the detriment of its neighbours, rather than a landscape feature associated with wolves. This type of usage should not be excluded from the range of interpretations for place names. Fourthly, the distribution of place names cannot refer to the abundance or lack of wolves in any given area; there is no evidence for any preference in choosing rare or common species.

Bearing all of this in mind, a comprehensive list of lupine place names in the British Isles has been compiled by Aybes and Yalden (1995) (*Figure 7.1*). The highest numbers are found in the northern counties of Cumberland, Westmoreland and West Yorkshire. The elements associated with these names include hills, clearings, valleys, woods and enclosures, but the largest single category is of 'wolf pits', the majority of which are field names interpreted as the sites of pit traps (*ibid*: 205). The place-name evidence suggests that 'wolf pit' names occur at varying proximity to settlements, and this corresponds with both the intermittent placement of traps by communities in response to the local presence of wolves, and with the sustained trapping campaigns of professional wolf hunters in, for example, royal forests (see below). Since these traps represented a hazard to both human and animal health, it was useful to know their whereabouts in the landscape. Sometimes this was a legal obligation; the mid-fourteenth century Swedish King Magnus Eriksson's Law of Homicide (2, 6) required those who set traps in the woods to announce their location at the local parish church, both before and after their construction (Donner, 2000: 117).

Added to this list are names interpreted as referring to wolf cubs (e.g. Whelpstone Crag, West Yorkshire), all in mountainous areas and at higher altitudes in close proximity to other place-name records of wolves. Wolf place-names are frequently compounded with wood and hill elements and Aybes and Yalden (1995: 221) found a strong positive correlation between wolf place-names and high ground but no comparable pattern with woodland. They interpreted this pattern as signifying that wolves had been largely exterminated from most of lowland England by the Norman Conquest, whilst settlement in the northern counties rarely penetrated the uplands enabling wolves to find shelter and breed, with encounters between humans and wolves frequent enough for landscape features to be named accordingly (*ibid*: 222) As a point of comparison, the distribution of wolf place-names in medieval Scandinavia is being currently mapped by the author and will be published in due course (Pluskowski, forthcoming a).

Wolf remains in medieval archaeological contexts

Wolf remains in Britain and Scandinavia are extremely limited in both number and contextual information (*Figure 7.2*). This is partly due to the problems in distinguishing between wolves and dogs, and it is difficult to suggest how many misidentified canid remains have been documented, and how many have been ignored on grounds of poor or fragmentary preservation (Pluskowski, forthcoming b). Although relatively more wolves have been found in Continental medieval contexts, for example in north Germany, Poland and Hungary (Pluskowski, 2003: figs. 18 and 19; Wolsan,

Bienieck and Buchalczyck, 1992: 376; Bökönyi, 1974: appendix), the overall numbers are too small for any quantitative analysis or detailed study of wolf populations. Nonetheless the limited evidence represents an essential element in this synthesis.

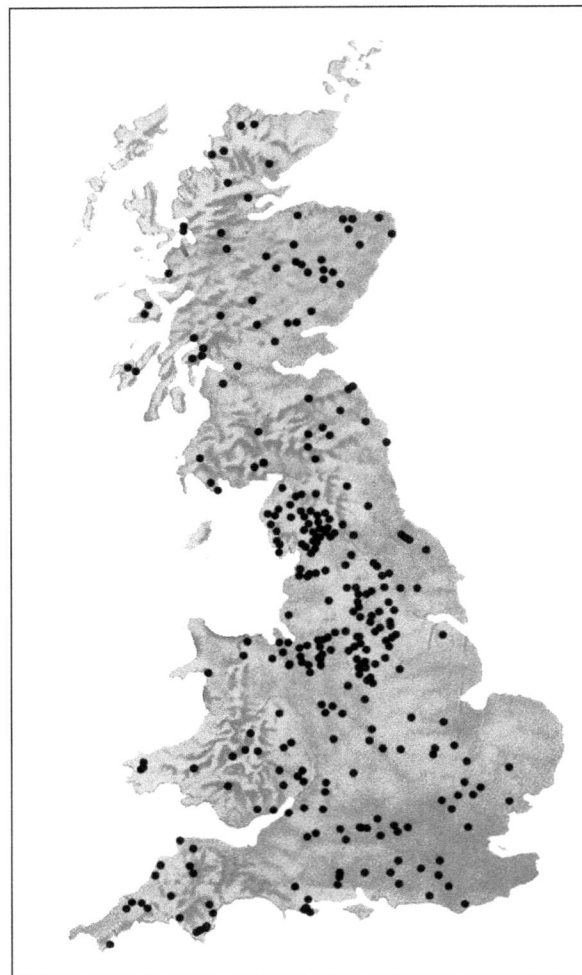

Figure 7.1: Major, minor and Celtic place names in Britain relating to wolves (aft. Aybes and Yalden 1995)

In the British Isles, early medieval faunal assemblages rarely contain wolf remains; examples of *Canis lupus* have been documented from Middle Anglo-Saxon contexts at Ramsbury (Wiltshire) (Coy, 1980). In high medieval contexts, reports of wolf remains are frequently anecdotal in nature and unfortunately not wholly reliable. Early scholarship contains occasional references to wolf bones recovered from hasty excavations of medieval sites, for example, claims of remains discovered during the construction of the reservoirs at Walthamstow cannot be verified, but if accurate, implies that the species was found (but not necessarily in abundance as suggested) in the Forest of Essex – a vast area in itself (Fisher, 1880: 189). A single bone has been identified at Lyveden as evidence of a rare wolf present in the Forest of Rockingham (Northamptonshire) in the thirteenth century (Steane, 1985: 167). Likewise, the cited presence of wolf

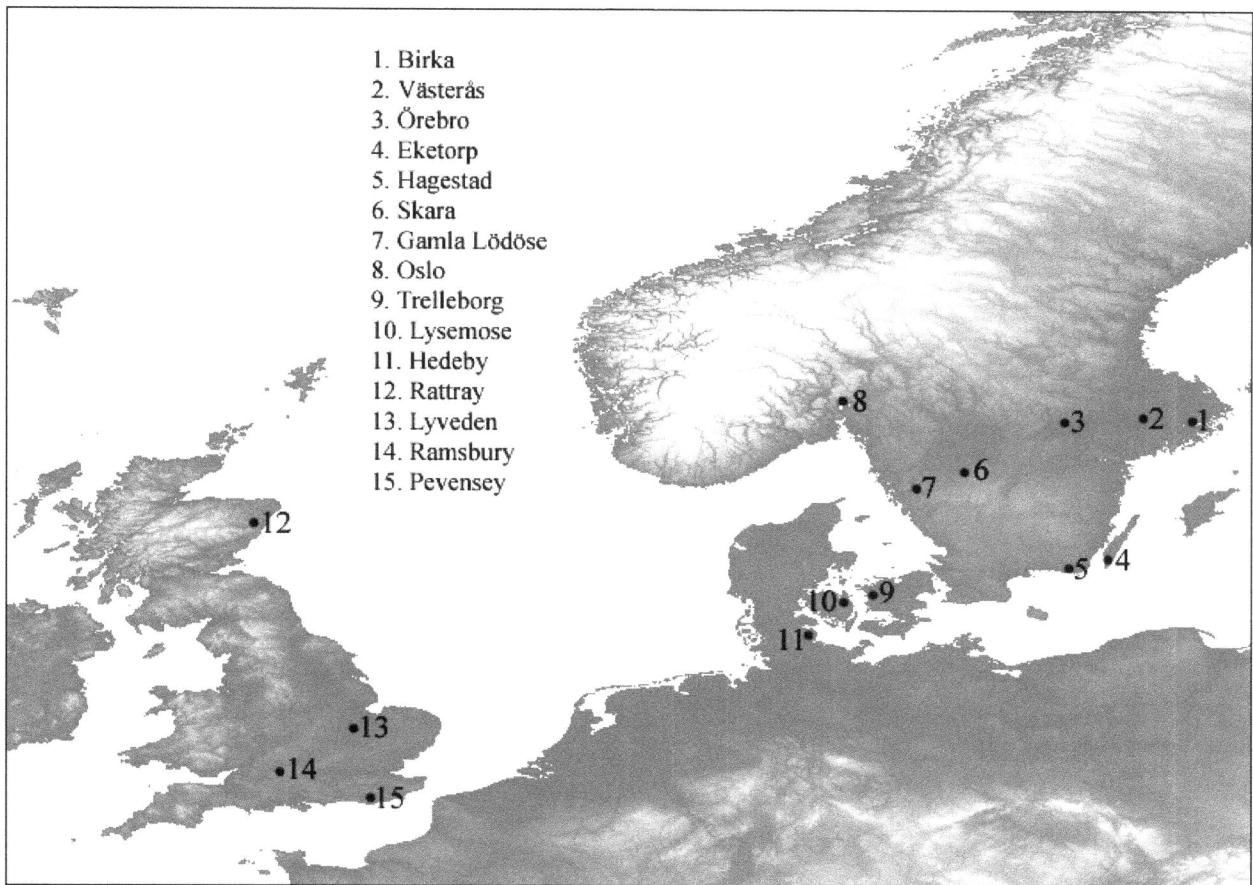

1. Birka
2. Västerås
3. Örebro
4. Eketorp
5. Hagestad
6. Skara
7. Gamla Lödöse
8. Oslo
9. Trelleborg
10. Lysemose
11. Hedeby
12. Rattray
13. Lyveden
14. Ramsbury
15. Pevensey

Figure 7.2: Wolf remains recovered from medieval contexts in Britain (excluding Ireland) and southern Scandinavia

remains at Pevensey (Sussex), as well at Rattray (Aberdeen) offer very little additional information, even if accurate (Yalden, 1999: 147). This limited body of data can be used to indicate the possible presence of wolves in the locality of their recovered remains, but in relation to the representation of other species in faunal assemblages it also hints at their value.

In southern Scandinavia, remains of *Canis lupus* appear in early, high and later medieval contexts, however these are generally fragmentary, and in some cases individual elements cannot be verified as those of a wolf or large dog. Traces of wolf have been found at Birka (Sweden), a trading settlement on an island in Lake Mälaren occupied in the ninth and tenth centuries, amongst the largest collection of fur-bearing animal bones in Scandinavia. They are only represented by three third phalanges (claws, dated c. 840-60) and it is likely the rest of the bones were left where the animal was skinned – at the site of the kill (Wigh, 1998: 86-88; 2001: 127). These remains suggest the preparation and use of wolf pelts by local households, and do not necessarily indicate the presence of wolves in the immediate *environs* of Birka. In a comparable likely trading association, a range of wolf bones (mandibles, scapula, limbs) have also been identified in the harbour of Hedeby, a settlement on the southern Baltic coast of the Jutland Peninsula occupied

from the eighth to the eleventh century (Reichstein, 1991: 37-39). Wolf remains (cranial elements and limbs) tentatively identified at the fortifications of Trelleborg (Denmark) and Eketorp (Sweden), and dated to the late Viking era (Norlund, 1948: 262; Boessneck, 1979: 189), may reflect any number of activities associated with wolves in the nearby or distant landscape. In high medieval contexts, wolf remains recovered from urban centres have been interpreted in relation to their hinterland; the presence of wolf (six individuals dated to the period 1025-1225), bear, lynx and deer bones in eleventh and twelfth century layers in Oslo have been related to deforestation in the town's hinterland (Schia, 1991: 186; 1994: 7). In Sweden, one wolf bone has been recovered from Skara, dated to the fourteenth century (Lepiksaar, 1976), four bones from Örebro dated to the period 1250-1350 (Johansson 1990), three bones from Västerås dated to the period 1350-1420 (Vretemark and Sten, 1995), and wolf remains have also been reported in Hagestad and Gamla Lödöse within the territory of medieval Denmark (Lepiksaar, 1975: 231-232). Whilst acknowledging the limitations of such a data set, it may be initially suggested that the relatively limited distribution of wolf remains compared to other wild carnivores reflects infrequent hunting, an idea that becomes increasingly plausible when integrated with other forms of evidence.

Written sources I: the wolf and wilderness

It has been argued that understandings of animal behaviour in the Middle Ages were limited by the poor acquisition of accurate reports and the widespread belief that animals had no intelligence (Sobol, 1993). However many, if not all, written accounts of animal behaviour can be attributed to those individuals who were likely to have relatively limited contact with the natural world. People who did have regular contact with animals – notably shepherds, farmers and hunters – rarely recorded their experiences, but the few that have survived indicate a more informed understanding of animal behaviour based on working relationships with both wild and domestic fauna. Moreover, perceptions of animal behaviour were likely to be more accurate in the case of those species present in nearby landscapes – as they would be based to some extent on direct or indirect experience – in contrast to perceptions of animals found only in distant lands. In this light it is unsurprising to find consistent relationships between wolves and their environment recorded in medieval north European written sources. Modern observations of wolves indicate their adaptive success in being able to survive in virtually any environment, but only certain habitats are referred to in both early and high medieval written sources – the most recurring being woodland. Many examples, such as the two quoted in the introduction, are likely to contain multiple meanings, and however formulaic and removed from a specific experience, they are informative by associating wolves with particular spaces. Literary references tend to be brief (surveyed in detail in Pluskowski, 2003 and forthcoming a), and contain little in the way of ecological descriptions; for example in the Old English poem *Maximus II* 'the wolf belongs in the woods' (Bradley, 1995: 513). Descriptions of wolf hunting, which may otherwise have provided an environmental context, are rarely encountered in Middle English literature, whilst *The Vision of Piers Plowman* and *Gawain and the Green Knight* refer to wolves, woodland and waste without much elaboration. Further survivals of this association crop up in a number of contexts, for example, in proverbs (Wilson, 1977: 205), although the woods of romance literature have limited lupine denizens – with the exception of the occasional werewolf.

Unsurprisingly, wolves feature relatively frequently in Old Norse literature and their relationship with woodland is found in a number of contexts: mythology, romance and epithet. The sagas, a literary genre encompassing a number of variants, were predominantly written down in the twelfth and thirteenth centuries, however they contain borrowings from earlier oral literature which, depending on the content, may be dated to the late Viking Age, whilst also serving high medieval audiences (Pulsiano, 1993: 592-594). In this respect the relationship between wolves and woods represents a persisting literary motif comparable to the association between wolves and

battlefields. Most references to the association between wolves and woodland are brief, such as in the two Eddic poems of *Helgi Hundingsbani*:

:

'You lay under the home hay stacks, used to wolves' howling, out in the woods'
(*First Poem of Helgi Hundingsbani*, verse 41, Larrington, 1996: 119)

More evocative descriptions of this relationship, incorporating many layers of meaning can also be found, as in *Volsunga Saga* written down between 1200-1270 (Byock, 1993: 41). Turning to a retrospective view of pagan Scandinavian cosmology, Snorri Sturluson's *Edda*, referring directly to the Eddic poem *Voluspa*, outlines the sinister origins of the wolves Skoll and Hati:

'A certain giantess lives east of Midgard in a wood called Iarnvid (Ironwood). In that wood live trollwives called Iarnvidiner. The ancient giantess breeds as sons many giants and all in wolf shapes, and it is from them that these wolves are descended.' (*Gylfaginning*, Faulkes, 1987: 15)

Snorri continues in *Skaldskaparmal* – Geri, a wolf with a series of associations, is enticed 'from the north out of the wood' (*ibid*: 135), whilst in his list of names for wolves, Snorri refers to 'Hroduifnir and heath-dweller' and 'Freki and wood-dweller' (*ibid*: 164). In both Old English and Old Norse literature, the wolf, particularly in the context of woodland is used as a metaphor for outlaw – but here the environment plays a more explicit role in designating marginal status than the animalisation of the individual. What is relatively clear is that medieval English and Scandinavian literature is not explicitly recording the distribution of wolves in the landscape, but preserving a recurring conceptual link between the wolf and the woods that is ultimately ousted by a romance forest typically free of wolves. Wolf associations with other types of wilderness are recorded, but not to the same extent. In *King Harald's Saga* in *Heimskringla*, Snorri inserted a verse by the eleventh century poet Bolverk Arnorsson which includes the line 'whilst wolves howled in the mountains' (Magnusson and Pálsson, 1970: 47), whilst a verse copied down in the thirteenth century refers to enemies fleeing the hero Helgi 'just as panicking goats run before the wolf down from the mountain filled with fear' (*The Second Poem of Helgi Hundingsbani*, Larrington, 1996: 138). An alternative epithet for the wolf is associated with fens, heaths and marshes; in the early Eddic poem *Atlakvida*, the wolf is referred to as 'heath-wanderer' (Larrington, 1996: 211), whilst the monstrous wolf's name Fenrir can be translated as 'fen-dweller' (Orchard, 1998: 42). These conceptualised links can be set alongside relationships between wolves and landscapes recorded in documentary sources.

Written sources II: wolves and royal forests

Although wolves are noted in a string of early medieval documentary sources (Pluskowski, forthcoming a), they are most frequently recorded within the bounds of royal English forests (*foresta*) in the twelfth and thirteenth centuries (*Figure 7.3*). These represented perhaps the most sophisticated form of controlled hunting space in medieval Europe, and given their focus on preserving deer habitat, included woodland as an important (but not exclusive) topographic feature (Young, 1979: 3). From at least the late eleventh century in England, it was common royal practise to grant land in exchange for, amongst other things, obligations to keep it free of 'wolves'; for example Robert de Umfraville was granted lordship of Riddesdale in Northumberland by William I, on condition of defending the region from 'enemies and wolves' (Harting, 1994: 20), whilst Robert Ferrers the Earl of Derby was granted lands at Heage by the crown in the early twelfth century in return for driving wolves out of Belper, within Duffield Chase (Derbyshire), which afterwards became a royal forest (VCH Derby 1: 405). Although lands continued to be held by serjeanty of killing wolves into the reign of Henry VI, this information cannot be used to map the distribution of wolves in the late medieval period; the overwhelming evidence points to a significant depletion of wolf populations in England by the late fourteenth century and the obligation to hunt wolves was probably preserved as a sinecure. Nonetheless, when coupled with examples of occasional hunting grants which include wolves (e.g. from King John to William de Briwere across the whole of Devonshire), they indicate consistent royal interest in the persecution of wolves from the time when Anglo-Norman seigneurial hunting culture, and its obsession with the wolf's natural prey, was developing alongside the institutionalisation of controlled hunting space.

This pattern is emphasised by evidence of direct action taken against wolves within royal forests, which helpfully contribute to our understanding of wolf biogeography in medieval England. Although established in the late eleventh century, the institution only appears to have become fully operational on a national level by the mid-twelfth century and reached its height in the thirteenth century. In 1156, the Sheriff of Hampshire arranged for an allowance from the Exchequer to pay for the livery of the royal wolf hunters operating in the New Forest and the Forest of Bere (Madox, 1969: 204). Their efforts to reduce wolf numbers in the county were limited – a roll from 1212-1213 refers to a payment of 5s in May 1212 for a wolf caught within the bounds of the Forest of Freemantle, also in Hampshire, and in the same year two wolves were captured in the Forest of Irwell in Lancashire (Harting, 1994: 25).

Further north, payments to wolf hunters from the Peak Forest (Derbyshire) are listed in 1160-1, 1167-8 and in the latter half of the thirteenth century (VCH Derby 1:398, 403, note 1), whilst wolf depredations are

described in the accounts of Gervase de Bernake, bailiff of the Peak Forest, in 1255-6 and in the earliest extant Gloucestershire Forest Eyre of 1258 for the Forest of Dean (VCH Gloucester 2:268, note 8). Patent rolls for 1280 indicate that John Gifford was empowered to destroy all wolves within royal forests (Harting, 1994: 28). In 1281, wolf depredations on deer are recorded at Cannock Chase (Staffordshire) (VCH Shropshire 1:490, note 51), and in the same year, Richard Talbot was given license to hunt wolves with nets in the Forest of Dean, so long as no deer were taken and no warrens were coursed (Hart 1971: 37), and lastly – and perhaps most famously – a writ of aid was issued for Peter Corbet to take and destroy all wolves in the forests, parks and 'other places' in Gloucestershire, Herefordshire, Worcestershire, Shropshire and Staffordshire (Calendar Patent Rolls, May 14, 1281). Wolves remained in Dean; a year later, the Forest Eyre fined two men for taking venison mauled by wolves, whilst the most detailed account of wolf hunting is dated to 1285 (*ibid*). Lands continued to be held by serjeantry of hunting wolves into the 1290s (Harting 1994: 30).

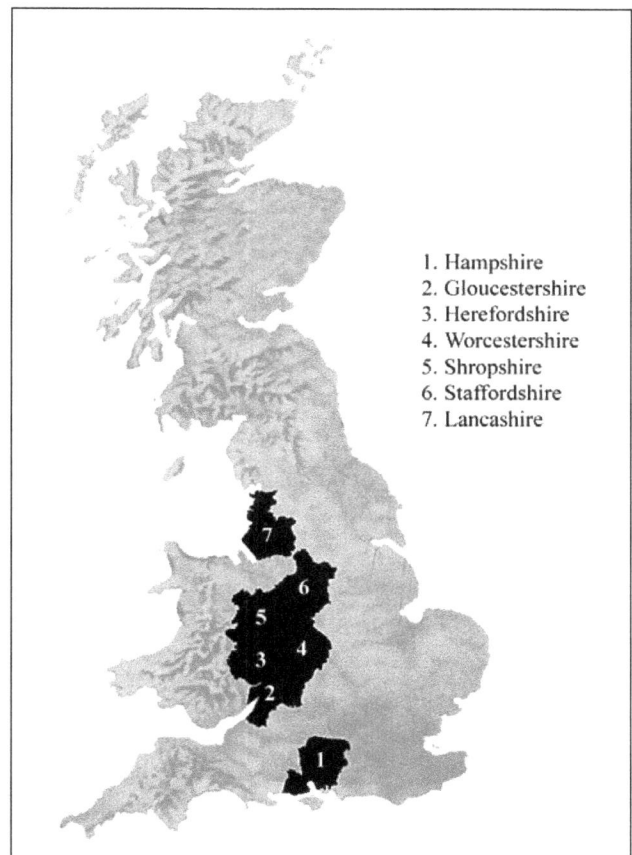

1. Hampshire
2. Gloucestershire
3. Herefordshire
4. Worcestershire
5. Shropshire
6. Staffordshire
7. Lancashire

Figure 7.3: English counties where wolf presence documented in royal forests is referred to in the text

In 1281, Edward I had ordered the underwood in the wood of Hope Mansel to be cut down, as it was unfit to support deer and provided shelter for 'wolves and other malefactors...by reason of its density', after which it was to be enclosed with a hedge (Calendar Patent Rolls, May 23, 1281; VCH Gloucseter Vol 2:270, note 1). This encouragement of coppicing in the Forest of Dean indicates a more aggressive approach to wildlife management which may have partially motivated woodland clearance elsewhere. Coppicing has a clear physical and visual impact on woodland with variable foliage density determined by harvesting cycles (fig. 4). There is further evidence that the effective use of dense vegetation by both animal and human predators was recognised; earlier, Edward I had ordered highways between towns to be cleared of woodland and hedges to reduce shelter for thieves and protect travellers (Calendar Patent Rolls, June 18, 1278). This tactic was also used during the English conquest of Wales where strategic woodland clearance was carried out to reduce the possibility of ambushes (Linnard, 1982: 21-29). That wolves were still active in northern England by the late thirteenth century is suggested by an assemblage of roe deer bones in Rawthey cave, Cumbria, interpreted as being accumulated by wolves and dated no later than c. 1300 (Hedges *et al*, 1998: 440-1). The reign of Edward I marked the most aggressive period of wolf persecution in England and subsequent references to both wolves and royal attempts to control them are sparse.

The forest documentation is interesting, not least because it provides some details on wolf hunting and depredations, but also because it offers an insight into medieval wolf biogeography. Although they were contested and occupied spaces, royal forests included actively maintained habitats for deer, and in doing so restricted settlement, woodland clearance and permanent human activity – particularly in the Peak Forest and Dean. The presence of significant herds of deer in these areas undoubtedly attracted wolves – indeed both animals would have affected each other's distribution and behaviour to a certain extent – with the result of providing alternative and undoubtedly irritating competition to the royal chase. In Scotland, comparable persecution of wolves by the royalty is only evident in the high medieval period from a reference to a wolf hunter in Stirling in 1283 – in close proximity to a number of royal parks – whilst more extensive laws for the destruction of wolves were passed in the fifteenth century (Gilbert 1979). In medieval Scandinavia, there is some evidence of royal control of game particularly on the Danish islands, but also in Swedish laws from the fourteenth century, which mention roe deer as 'the king's animals' (Andrén, 1997: 472) and forbid the catching of deer in wolf nets (Donner, 2000: 55). But in comparison to England, references to royal promotion of wolf hunting are sparse and comparatively late (Pluskowski, 2003: 192-193).

Away from the wilderness: wolves in and around human settlements

Whilst wolves moved through landscapes of hamlets and villages, there is also evidence that they approached major urban centres, which were immediately accessible to the countryside, even with developing suburbs. For example, Matthew Paris refers to a grant of church lands by Abbot Leofstan to Thurnoth and others on the condition of keeping the woods between the Chiltern Hundreds and London free from wolves (Riley, 1867: 39-40). From the north to the south of the Continent, wolves are occasionally recorded near or sometimes within towns; in Bremen in 1072, wolves howling in packs in the suburbs vied 'with horned owls in horrific contest' (Adam of Bremen, *Gesta Hammaburgensis ecclesiae pontificum*, 3, 63, Tschan, 1959: 171), whilst Slimbene of Parma's chronicle records how during the winter of 1247-8, ravenous wolves howled for hours outside the city walls at night and even occasionally entered the town (Fumagalli, 1995: 107). Although rabies was not a significant problem in north European urban areas until the seventeenth century, a few examples are documented in medieval towns. In 1166, the *Annales Cambriæ* record that a rabid wolf in the town of Carmathen (Wales) had bitten twenty-two people (Ithel, 1860: 51-52), whilst rabid wolves are recorded invading towns and villages in 1271 in Franconia (Steele and Fernandez, 1991: 4). These are amongst a number of examples cited in Continental written sources, and if they are to be taken as documentary, rather than literary conceptualised juxtapositions between the embodiments of human achievement – urbanism and wilderness – they suggest that wolves could and did approach urban centres. In the light of recent observations from across Europe of wolves penetrating significantly built-up areas, it is not unreasonable to suggest a comparable situation for certain medieval towns. In southern Scandinavia, archaeological evidence points to potentially similar proximities. A number of bricks excavated from medieval contexts in Stockholm, tentatively dated to the fourteenth century, contain a range of wild and domestic animal prints created when the bricks were still soft and had been set out to dry (unpublished, but housed in the Stockholms Medeltidsmuseum). Wolf prints have been identified on some of these, and whilst they may also be the prints of large dogs (although there are typically diagnostic differences between the two), the possibility of wolves approaching the town should not be dismissed (Benneth pers. comm.). These events reinforce the close relationships between urban and rural areas across medieval Europe outlined by detailed studies of medieval urban hinterlands, contrasting with conceptualisations of urban centres as ideals of civilisation, particularly when juxtaposed with, and seemingly separate to, the 'primitive' and 'barbaric' countryside.

So far the evidence considered has been relatively anthropocentric, presenting wolves as components of human systems of spatial organisation – whether perceived and recorded by contemporaries, or recovered and reinterpreted as the end product of human activity such as hunting. In order to 'consider wild animals seeking to stay wild in wild places' (Philo and Wilbert,

2000: 20), it is important to complement this with an ecological understanding of wolf biogeography, focusing on wolves as primary agents within a broader community of organisms that includes humans as well as other animals and plants.

Incorporating modern ecological analogues into medieval wolf biogeography

Modern ecological and ethological studies can contribute to a more holistic understanding of the mechanisms governing the dynamic distribution of wolves in medieval northern Europe, and how these patterns can be related to varying ecological scenarios (Packham et al, 1992: 216-217). As has already been stated, wolves are extremely adaptable animals and can survive in virtually any type of habitat providing there is enough available prey and persecution is limited. Packs of two to forty-two animals form the basic units of a wolf population, with most lone individuals occupying a temporary status as they move to or from a pack (Fuller et al, 2003: 163-4). Numerous studies indicate a clear relationship between wolf density and prey abundance, with higher numbers of wolves occupying smaller territories in areas with higher densities of ungulates (ibid: 171). Of course, habitat and prey cannot be readily untangled; in a study of wolf territories in the western Alps, wolf selection of coniferous woodland was linked to the winter range of cervids – vegetation cover, slope and aspect were all important variables influencing ungulate distribution and thereby indirectly affecting wolf distribution (Marucco et al, 2001). Humans play an important role in influencing wolf distribution, particularly where both wolves and ungulates are heavily exploited or 'harvested'; in a survey of wolf distribution in semi-agricultural landscapes in Tuscany, wolves selected for lower densities of paved roads and a higher proportion of woodland cover and the availability of ravines, however the core areas of wolf distribution were related to prey density and included secure habitats such as private game reserves (Ciucci et al, 2001). Even in regions with comparatively high levels of urbanisation and human activity, wolf packs are able to survive provided there is enough prey and that human persecution is limited (Haight, Mladenoff and Wydeven, 1998). This is of immediate relevance to reconstructing wolf biogeography in medieval Britain and Scandinavia; the intensive exploitation of wild ungulates in the former from the late eleventh century, peaking in the thirteenth century (Young, 1979: 74-134), coupled with extensive hunting of wolves, also peaking in the thirteenth century, is contrasted with the latter region, where the level of ungulate and wolf exploitation is significantly lower at this time. On the Scandinavian Peninsula red and roe deer, elk and reindeer were available prey whilst imported fallow deer were typically confined to the Danish islands (Andrén, 1997). The variable levels of ungulate exploitation are related to contrasting hunting cultures, whilst the variable levels of wolf exploitation are related to human accessibility to wolf habitats and the inclination to sustain systematic persecution. The latter

appears to be linked to government encouragement and by extension political and economic power.

The difference between the two regions is topographical; the intensively managed landscapes of the British Isles had a comparatively smaller area of wilderness (i.e. land unsuitable for cultivation) than the Scandinavian Peninsula, although this area was reduced in both regions, partially as a result of human population growth, which is estimated to have tripled between the eleventh and mid-fourteenth century (Fossier, 1997: 245). This growth is reflected by the rise in settlement numbers and density in both regions, however in southern Scandinavia only an estimated 5% of the population appears to have been located in the limited number of mostly small towns (ten in Norway, fifteen in Sweden and between fifty and sixty in Denmark) (Benedictow, 1996: 155-6, 181-182). Nonetheless, in central and northern Scandinavia, by the end of the first millennium, farms and settlements had pushed to higher or more northerly locations relying predominantly on pastoral farming (Svensson, 1998). Of course, there were stretches of woodland without permanent settlement, even south of the *Limes Norrlandicus*, but these were slowly contracting (Price, 2000: 32). In the south, the expansion of settlements' outfields in the Viking Age contributed to the decline in woodland (Berglund et al, 1991: 431), although the main phases of clearance took place in the high medieval period (Mogren, 1998: 219). These patterns would continue up to the mid-fourteenth century when population decline and the desertion of settlements, farms, summer pastures and transhumance routes resulting from climate deterioration, famines, the Black Death and other epidemics, may have enabled Scandinavian wolf and wild ungulate populations to regenerate, although this reduction in human activity appears to have come too late for the English wolf population (Moe, Indrelid and Fasteland, 1988: 443; Nielssen, 1977; Callmer, 1991: 348; Rackham, 1996: 76).

The potential for wolf dispersal also differed between the two regions. Wolf home ranges and their seasonal variation can be immense; these are partially dependent on latitude and social relations within the pack as well as available resources (Marucco et al, 2001). Modern ecological analogues present a range of values: 80-240km^2 in southern Europe to 415-500 km^2 in northern Europe (Okarma et al, 1998: 847), whilst a recent report on Scandinavian wolf populations states annual home range values of 680-1700km^2 (Pedersen et al, 2001). Local variation results from a range of factors such as the sizes and composition of packs and the distribution of prey (Okarma et al, 1998: 851). When thinking about the movement of wolves in medieval landscapes both regional and local mobility must be acknowledged. An example of the latter can be illustrated by a study of wolf ecology in Abruzzo, Italy, which revealed the movement of wolves within the hinterland of settlements (Boitani, 1986; Zimen, 1981). In winter, wolves usually remained within the wooded area during the day. In the afternoon they became more active and at night moved into the valleys and human settlement areas, in some cases approaching the centre of a village. Towards dawn the wolves returned to the woods. If during the day, a wolf found itself away from its main woodland resting spot, it would normally spend the day resting in pockets of dense vegetation in the fields. In summer, the wolves rested at higher altitudes. This study illustrates the important of shelter for a wolf pack within a village-field-woodland-upland landscape and points to the possibility of similar behavioural patterns for wolves in medieval northern Europe. At the regional level, there is no easily comparable data for wolf dispersal in Britain, however recent studies in Scandinavia can provide a potential analogue for wolf mobility. Mapping the movement of five radio-collared young Swedish wolves in 1998 demonstrated their dynamic and varied mobility, ignoring political and ecological boundaries and crossing a variety of different landscapes (fig. 5) (Karlsson *et al*, 1999). Of course this pattern cannot be simply projected back into the early or high medieval periods as it invariably reflects a host of context-specific variables. Nonetheless, the potential for this mobility across the Scandinavian Peninsula can be linked to population regeneration, with animals moving between Sweden and Norway, and also between Russia and Finland, and between Finland and Sweden (*ibid*; Haglund, 1975: 42). Indeed, in 1828 the royal gamekeeper von Greiff wrote that it was impossible to exterminate wolves in Sweden due to the continuous belts of woods and mountainous regions from which they descended to settle down and breed (Brusewitz, 1969: 188).

The mobility of wolves is further illustrated by the difficulties encountered when hunting them. Successful hunting requires not only equipment and experience, but also accessibility. A study of rural communications in Wisconsin suggested that the fragmentation of large, remote wilderness tracts through the construction of firelanes and roads increased the access and efficiency of hunters and trappers (Thiel, 1985). The study concluded that (short of changing human attitudes) the relative distribution and effectiveness of communications within a given area would influence the sustainability of a wolf population, and this has been borne out in more recent work (Mladenoff *et al*, 1995). Certainly, hunting wolves in upland areas is extremely difficult; during the Norwegian wolf hunts at Evenstad in Østerdal, a helicopter was used on the mountainous woodland border between Hedmark and Oppland due to the impassability of the terrain (*Aftenposten*: morning edition, Wednesday, 26th February 2001, p2. 1st section). The difficulty of hunting wolves in mountainous terrain is also attested in Lapland (Henriksson, 1974: 49). Both expansive moors and mountains created obstacles to extensive human management, at times limiting contact between human communities and thereby providing a relatively sheltered environment for the wolf. In 1759, Testrup observed that in the (then relatively extensive) heath of Jutland, wolves hid in the high heathers and could not be driven away, menacing both travellers and shepherds (Olwig, 1984: 99). Whilst none of the above observations are unproblematic, they clearly demonstrate the complexity and potential diversity of wolf mobility in the landscapes of medieval northern Europe. Dividing wolf populations into 'Scotland', 'Wales', 'England', 'Sweden' and 'Norway' ignores the potential for this mobility; like the modern central Norwegian 'wolf zone' – a system designed to protect wolves in specified, and from 2000-2004 increasingly smaller, designated areas (and hunting them when they transgress the boundaries), representing an attempt to physically 'map' these predators onto the landscape – these are political and legal rather than ecological boundaries. In the case of medieval Britain, it may have been possible for wolves to move from Scotland down to England where the abundance of ungulates created a potential for high wolf densities. However, human persecution appears to have isolated the Scottish population, which continues to be documented several centuries after the last extant references to any wolves in England or Wales. In the Scandinavian Peninsula and Denmark, where wolf hunting did not really begin in earnest until the seventeenth century, there was a higher potential for wolf dispersal from adjoining regions such as (modern) Germany in the south and Finland and Russia in the north. Having reflected on the relevance of major observations from recent wolf studies in the context of medieval northern Europe, it is now possible to begin to incorporate the range of primary sources discussed above into a holistic synthesis.

Synthesis and conclusion

It is likely that wolves moved between different types of habitats, seasonally, and in response to a variety of factors such as changes in food supply, shelter and hunting pressure; changes within wolf populations must also be expected, but are difficult, if not impossible, to verify (Wing, 1993: 238). As discussed above, the strong positive correlation between wolf place-names and uplands has been interpreted as reflecting a prominent northern English wolf population at the time of the Conquest, however the documented presence of wolves in southern and eastern counties represents the mobility of individuals, perhaps even packs. Outside documentary sources, wolves appear in Old English poetry as animals haunting the battlefield but inhabiting wilderness, a motif also found in Old Norse literature. This association can be interpreted in both cultural and ecological terms. Courtly literature developing in the course of the twelfth century focused on a particular seigneurial view of the world, where activity was often juxtaposed between the civilised court and the wilderness, the latter often a 'forest' (Saunders, 1993). In this context, the French-speaking aristocracy in England and Scotland used *le forest* to refer to both woodland and a hunting reserve, whilst the Latin term *foresta* was predominantly used to refer to the latter (Gilbert, 1979: 19).

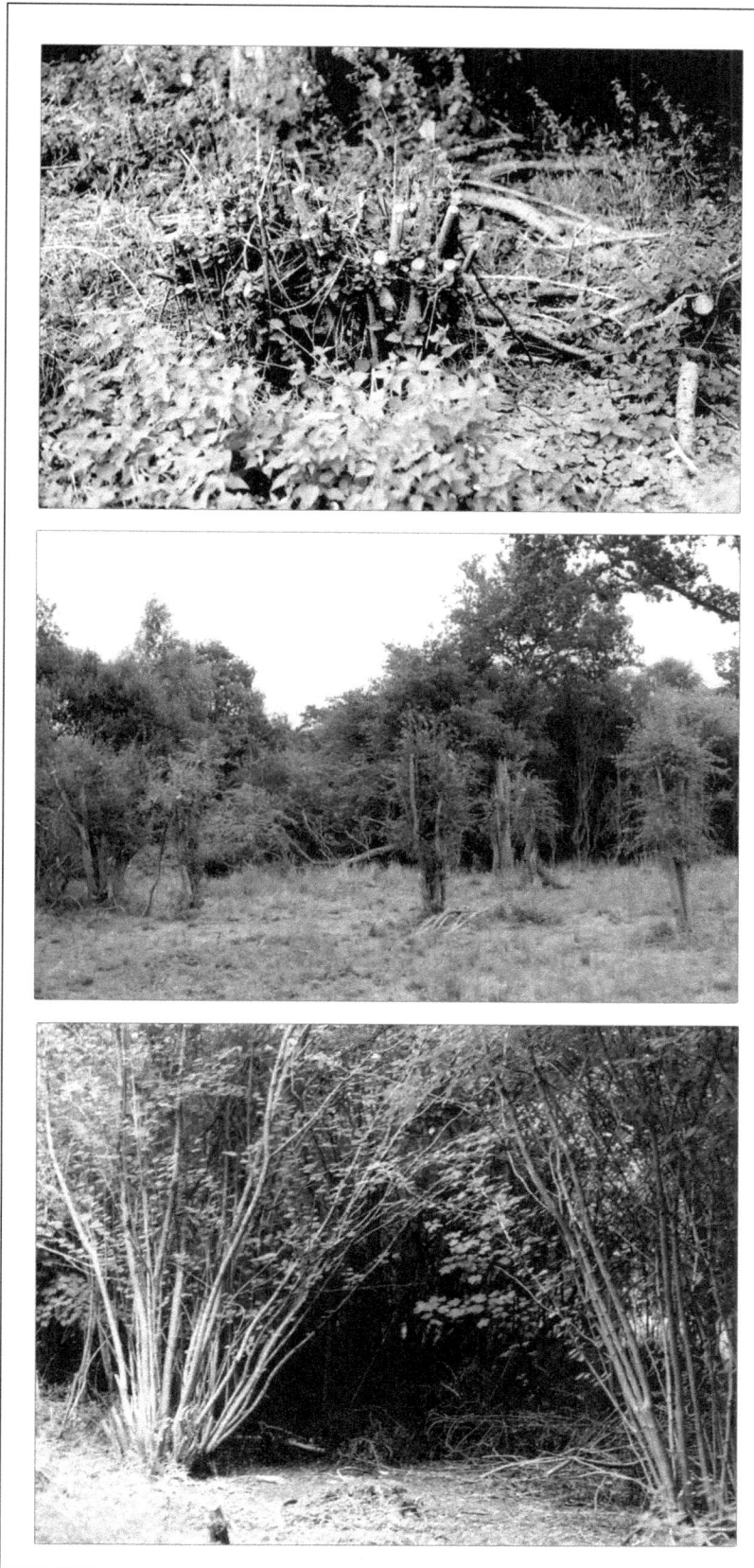

Figure 7.4: Three stages in the coppice cycle, Hatfield Forest (Photograph by A. G. Pluskowski)

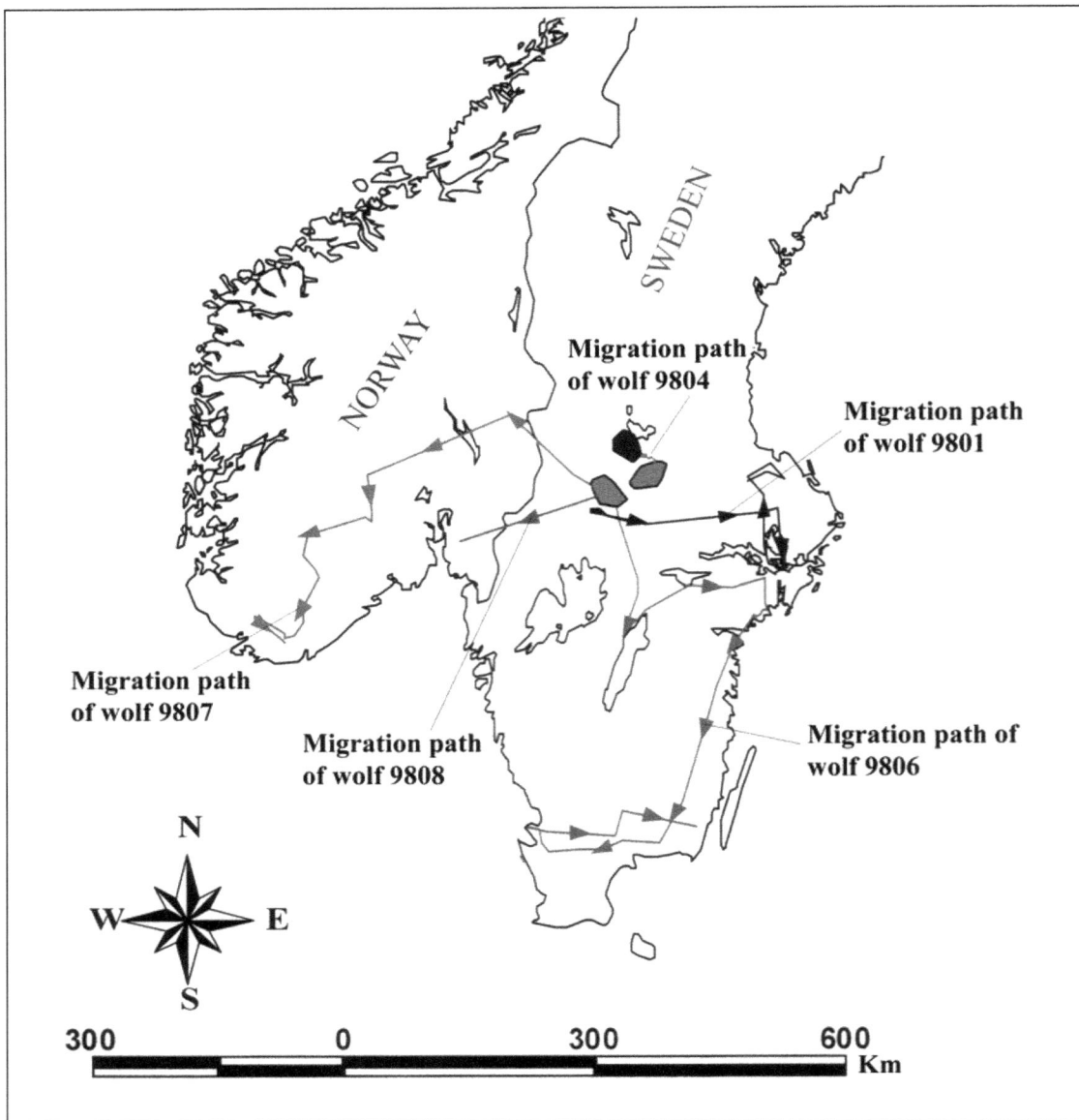

Figure 7.5: The movement of five radio-collared young Swedish wolves across the Scandinavian Peninsula in 1998 (aft. Karlsson et al, 1999)

Of course, neither legal *foresta* nor romance forests were areas of impenetrable woodland, but their resident populations of deer, which were the principle target of the elite hunt, required a certain amount of woodland, limited densities of human activity and of course attracted the attention of both human and lupine predators, and almost certainly played a significant role in determining the distribution of the latter. Deer farming was practised in medieval England (Birrell, 1992; Sykes 2001), south east Scotland (Gilbert, 1979), Denmark and parts of Sweden (Andrén, 1997). Whilst it is impossible to estimate the relative numbers of deer at any given time, the highest density of parks, many of which were used for containing and 'farming' deer, could be found in England estimated at numbering some 3200 in c. 1300 (Rackham, 1980: 191), followed by Denmark with at least fifty documented in c. 1230 (Andrén, 1997: 473), and finally

twelve parks in thirteenth century Scotland, although a more accurate indication of managed hunting culture in this region is represented by the presence of over eighty forests (Gilbert, 1979: 356-363). Unfortunately, a systematic archaeological survey of medieval parks in Scandinavia has yet to be undertaken although in Denmark, red, roe and fallow deer appear to have been frequently confined on islands: naturally bounded hunting grounds, free from unwanted predators (Andrén 1997).

On the mainland, the legislation of the English and Scottish crown, and later the Swedish kings, encouraged the systematic hunting of wolves. This attitude is paralleled by the virtual absence of wolves in the idealised seigneurial landscapes of medieval romance literature (Rooney, 1993); a case in point is the mid-fourteenth century *Tale of Gawain and the Green Knight* where wolves are encountered in 'the wilderness' but are not even mentioned in the hunting landscapes surrounding the castle, where the action focuses on deer, boar and foxes (line 720, Barron, 1998: 68-9). The links between medieval seigneurial ideals of hunting, and actual practises, need to be explored in more detail from an interdisciplinary perspective. Certainly the entries on the wolf in fifteenth century English hunting manuals such as the *Boke of St. Albans* and *The Master of Game* are more likely to be Continental borrowings rather than native documentary accounts, and cannot be taken as evidence for the presence of wolves in fifteenth century England, with a resulting date for their final extermination of 1485-1509 (Harting, 1990: 37), especially as Middle English hunting texts were more concerned with courtly etiquette than with the practicalities of hunting (Rooney, 1993: 8).

The popularity of wolves in Old Norse literature is more complex. Noting their typical absence in the *Riddarasögur* – a literary genre equivalent to English and Continental courtly romances – their presence frequently appears to reflect a historical interest in ancestral conceptualisations of wolves. The literary association between wolves and wilderness is supported 'on the ground' by palaeobotanical reconstructions of suitable habitats and projected populations of wild ungulates. At first glance, the central mountains of Norway stretching off into the north and the Swedish woods above the *Limes Norrlandicus* appear to have provided the most suitable habitats. Zooarchaeological evidence from the interior of the Scandinavian Peninsula certainly provides evidence for the presence of a diverse range of wild ungulates (Mikkelsen, 1994) supporting both human and lupine needs. However, the majority of wolf remains from medieval southern Scandinavia come from the fringes of the Peninsula – a number are from urban or proto-urban contexts and invariably reflect the treatment of wolves as commodities of one kind or another. No remains have been found at sites in the interior commonly associated with the hunting and trapping of animals such as elk and reindeer, although written accounts suggest wolves were hunted in the central and northern parts of the Peninsula. Given the difficulties of identification, this limited pattern may reveal something about the value of the wolf – which documents suggest was limited but nonetheless existent – and in turn it is likely these remains were not moved significant distances, and therefore they can contribute to a biogeographical sketch of wolf distribution in early and high medieval southern Scandinavia. It is likely that wolves were not solely restricted to the mountainous and relatively heavily wooded interior (where hunting would have been extremely difficult and costly), but also moved through relatively less densely wooded regions, in turn related to the distribution of, largely unmanaged, wild ungulates. Given the limited number and size of settlements on the Scandinavian Peninsula this is not surprising, and such potential mobility is supported by modern analogues. The situation in Denmark is more uncertain; wolf packs could have moved northwards from Germany, although wolf presence is documented on the Danish islands into the late Middle Ages (Aaris-Sørensen, 1977).

Thus, the association between wolves and wilderness should perhaps be redefined as the association between wolves and ungulates, typically wild but where unavailable, domestic. It is difficult to ascertain whether the abundance of livestock would have presented an easier target for wolves, as depredations are related to a range of ecological factors, although areas with abundant and diverse wild species seem to have few if any attacks on livestock. Transhumance practises certainly move potential prey from areas of relatively high human presence and activity to those with dramatically less human presence and activity, the latter favouring the wolf. But given the nature of shepherding practises in both medieval Britain and Scandinavia and the relative abundance of wild ungulates, it is much more likely that livestock were taken infrequently; the popularity of the wolf and sheep *topos* in literature and iconography can be related to its Biblical precedent and from there its usefulness as a metaphor in the symbolic repertoire of medieval communities (Pluskowski, forthcoming a).

It is possible to imagine that in medieval northern Europe, wolves inhabited a mosaic of landscapes at varying proximity to human settlements, although the most important factor influencing their distribution appears to have been concentrations of wild ungulates, in turn influenced by human groups in varying degrees which varied between Britain and Scandinavia. Whilst wolves are documented in both medieval and modern sources approaching urban centres, their persistent link with wilderness – land unsuitable for, or not used for cultivation – in literature, appears to reflect both ecological and conceptual realities. With the crystallisation of seigneurial hunting culture revolving around deer as the ultimate prey by the twelfth century, wolves were no longer welcome in idealised landscapes and this was paralleled by persistent royal-funded wolf extermination in England, facilitated by the improvement of communications and the contraction of suitable habitat, which prevented the English wolf population from recovering after the fourteenth century, and effectively isolated the Scottish population. In the Scandinavian Peninsula, despite human population growth and the development of the interior in the high medieval period, the comparatively limited accessibility to wolves, the lack of a widespread seigneurial hunting culture focusing on the control of wild ungulates and the geographical links with the Continent, enabled wolf populations to regenerate any damage they may have sustained by the late fourteenth century, only to face persistent extermination campaigns several hundred years later.

Acknowledgements

I would like to thank the Arts and Humanities Research Board, Trinity College Cambridge, Gonville & Caius College Cambridge and the Department of Archaeology, University of Cambridge for funding the research upon which this paper is based. I would also like to thank Dr Catherine Hills, Dr Preston Miracle, Paul Bibire for their continuing support and advice, Professors Anders Andren, Martin Jones and Oliver Rackham for their suggestions and the following for their extensive hospitality, interest and advice: Dr Włodek Jędrzejewski and Dr Bogumiła Jędrzejewska of the Mammal Research Institute at Białowieża, the team of the Schleswig Zooarchaeologische Arbeitsgruppe, particularly Dr Dirk Heinrich, the team of Grimsö wildlife research station, particularly Marcus Karlsson and Olof Liberg, as well as numerous colleagues and friends in the British isles, Scandinavia, central and eastern Europe who contributed in countless ways. I would also like to thank Philippa Patrick for her endless, tireless support through the maelstrom of Ph.D research and for proof reading this paper. Finally, I would like to thank my co-speakers at TAG who made the session and this volume possible, and special thanks to Krish Seetah for getting me there and back in one piece, for his boundless enthusiasm and for supporting the session.

Abbreviations

VCH   Victoria County History

References

Aaris–Sørensen, K. (1977). 'The sub-fossil wolf, Canis lupus L., in Denmark', Videnskabelige Meddeleslser fra Dansk Naturhistorisk Forening, 140, 129-146.

Andrén, A. (1997). 'Paradise lost: looking for deer parks in medieval Denmark and Sweden', in H. Andersson, P. Carelli and L. Ersgård (eds.), Visions of the Past. Trends and Traditions in Swedish Medieval Archaeology, Stockholm, Central Board of National Antiquities.

Aybes, C. and Yalden, D. W. (1995). 'Place-name evidence for the former distribution and status of wolves and beavers in Britain', Mammal Review, 25, 201-227.

Barron, W. R. J. (ed. and trans.) (1998). Sir Gawain and the Green Knight, Manchester, Manchester University Press.

Benedictow, O. J. (1996). 'The demography of Viking Age and the High Middle Ages in the Nordic countries', Scandinavian Journal of History, 21, 151-182.

Berglund, B. E. Larsson, L., Lewan, N., Olsson, G. A. and Skansjö, S. (1991). 'Ecological and social factors behind the landscape changes', in B. E. Berglund (ed.), The Cultural Landscape During 6000 Years in Southern Sweden - the Ystad Project, Ecological Bulletin 41, Copenhagen, Munksgaard.

Birrell, J. (1992). 'Deer and deer farming in medieval England', Agricultural History Review, 40, 2, 112-126.

Bökönyi, S. (1974). History of Domestic Mammals in Central and Eastern Europe, Budapest, Akadémiai Kiadó.

Boessneck, J. (ed.) (1979). Eketorp: Befestigung und Siedlung auf Öland, Schweden: die Fauna, Stockholm, Almqvist & Wiksell.

Boitani, L. (1986). Dalla parte del lupu, L'Airone di Giorgio Mondadori e Associati Spa, Milan, Italy.

Bradley, S. A. J. (ed.) (1995). Anglo-Saxon Poetry, London, Everyman.

Brusewitz, G. (1969). Hunting: Hunters, Game, Weapons, and Hunting Methods from the Remote Past to the Present Day, London, Allen and Unwin.

Byock, J. L. (1993). The Saga of the Volsungs: the Norse Epic of Sigurd the Dragon Slayer, Enfield Lock, Hisarlik Press.

Callmer, J. (1991). 'The process of village formation', in B. E. Berglund (ed.), The Cultural Landscape During 6000 Years in Southern Sweden - the Ystad Project, Ecological Bulletin 41, Copenhagen, Munksgaard.

Ciucci, P. Artoni, L. Tedesco, E. and Boitani, L. (2001). 'Ecology of a wolf pack in a semi-agricultural landscape in Tuscany, central Itay', in C. Sillero and M. Hoffmann (eds.) Canid Biology and Conservation Conference, 17-21 September 2001, Oxford, Oxford, Zoology Department, Wildlife Conservation Research Unit.

Coy, J. (1980). 'The animal bones', in J. Haslam (ed.), 'A Middle Saxon iron smelting site at Ramsbury, Wiltshire', Medieval Archaeology, 24, 41-51.

Dent, A. (1974). Lost Beasts of Britain, London, Harrap.

Dickins, B. (ed.) (1915). Runic and Heroic Poems of the Old Teutonic Peoples, Cambridge, Cambridge University Press.

Donner, R. (ed. and trans.) (2000). King Magnus Eriksson's Law of the Realm: a Medieval Swedish Code, Helsinki, Ius Gentium Association.

Faulkes, A. (ed. and trans.) (1987). Snorri Sturluson: Edda, London, Everyman.

Finberg, H. P. R. (1967). 'Anglo-Saxon England to 1042', in H. P. R. Finberg (ed.), The Agrarian History of England and Wales. I.II, AD 43-1042, Cambridge, Cambridge University Press.

Fisher, W. R. (1880). The Forest of Essex: its History, Laws, Administration and Ancient Customs, and the Wild Deer which Lived in it, London, Butterworths.

Fossier, R. (1997). 'The beginning of European expansion', in R. Fossier (ed.), The Cambridge Illustrated History of the Middle Ages, vol. 2, 950-1250, Cambridge, Cambridge University Press.

Fuller, T. K., Berg, W. E., Radde, G. L., Lenarz, M. S. and Joselyn G. G. (1992). 'A history and current estimate of wolf distribution and numbers in Minnesota', Wildlife Society Bulletin, 20, 42-55.

Fumagalli, V. (1995). *Landscapes of Fear. Perceptions of Nature and the City in the Middle Ages*, Cambridge, Polity Press.

Gilbert, J. M. (1979). *Hunting and Hunting Reserves in Medieval Scotland*, Edinburgh, Donald.

Haight, R. G. Mladenoff, D. J. and Wydeven, A. P. (1998). 'Modelling disjunct gray wolf populations in semi-wild landscapes', *Conservation Biology*, 12, 4, 879-888.

Haglund, B. (1975). 'The wolf in Fennoscandia', in D. H. Pimlott (ed.), *Proceedings of the First Working Meeting of Wolf Specialists and of the First International Conference on the Conservation of the Wolf, September 1973,* Morges, Interantional Union for Conservation of Nature and Natural Resources, 37-43.

Hart, C. (1971). *The Verderers and Forest Laws of Dean*, Newton Abbot, David and Charles.

Harting, J. E. (1994). *A Short History of the Wolf in Britain*, Whitstable, Pryor (reprint).

Hedges, R. E. M. Pettit, P. B. Bronk Ramsay, C. and Van Klinken, G. J. (1998). 'Radiocarbon dates from the Oxford AMS system, datelist 25', *Archaeometry*, 40, 2, 437-455.

Henriksson, H. (1974). *Early Norrland 6: Popular Hunting and Trapping in Norrland*, Stockholm, Almqvist & Wiksell. CHECK.

Ithel, J. W. (1860). *Annales Cambriæ*, London, Longmans.

Johansson, F. (1990). Benfynd från det medeltida Örebro, kv. Tryckeriet 10, *Statens historiska Museum, Osteologiska enheten rapport 1990*:6.

Karlsson, J., Widén, P-L., Andrén, H., Karlsson, J. (1999). *Årsrapport. Lodjursprojektet, Vargprojektet, Viltskadecenter, Grimsö forskningsstation*, Grimsö, Viltskade Center, Grimsö forskningsstation.

Larrington, C. (trans.) (1996). *The Poetic Edda*, Oxford, Oxford University Press.

Le Goff, J. 1990. *Medieval Civilization*, Oxford, Blackwell.

Lepiksaar, J. (1975). 'Über die Tierknochenfunde aus den mittelalterlichen Sidelungen Sudschwedens', in A. T. Clason (ed.) *Archaeozoological Studies*, Oxford, North-Holland/American Elsevier.

Lepiksaar, J. (1976). Djurrester från det medeltida Skara. *Västergötlands fornminnesförenings tidskrift* 1975-76.

Linnard, W. (1982). *Welsh Woods and Forests: History and Utilization*, Cardiff, National Museum of Wales.

Madox, T. (1969). *The History and Antiquities of the Exchequer of the Kings of England*, New York, Augustus M. Kelley.

Magnusson, M. and Pálsson, H. (eds. and trans.) (1970). *Njal's Saga*, Harmondsworth, Penguin Books.

Manchester, W. R. (1993). *A World Lit Only by Fire: the Medieval Mind and the Renaissance*, London, Macmillan.

Marucco, F. Ricci, S. Galli, T, Manghi, L. and Boitani, L. (2001). 'Winter habitat selection of wolves in the western Alps', in C. Sillero and M. Hoffmann (eds.), *Canid Biology and Conservation Conference, 17-21 September 2001, Oxford*, Oxford, Zoology Department, Wildlife Conservation Research Unit.

Mech, L. D. and Boitani, L. (2003). 'Wolf social ecology', in L. D. Mech and L. Boitani (eds.), *Wolves: Behavior, Ecology and Conservation*, Chicago, University of Chicago Press.

Mikkelsen, E. (1994). *Fangstprodukter i vikingtidens og middelalderens økonmi. Organiseringen av massefangst av villrein i Dovre*, Oslo, Universitetets Oldsaksamling.

Mladenoff, D. J. Sickley, T. A. Haight, R. G. and Wydeven, A. P. (1995). 'A regional landscape analysis and prediction of favorable gray wolf habitat in the Northern Great Lakes Region', *Conservation Biology*, 9, 279-294.

Moe, D. Indrelid, S. and Fasteland, A. (1988). 'The Halne area, Hardangervidda. Use of a high mountain area during 5000 years – an interdisciplinary case study', in H. H. Birks *et al* (eds.), *The Cultural Landscape, Past, Present and Future*, Cambridge, Cambridge University Press.

Mogren, M. (1998). 'The village, the forest and the archaeology of Ängersjo', in H. Andersson, L. Ersgård and E. Svensson (eds.), *Outland Use in Preindustrial Europe*, Stockholm, Institute of Archaeology, Lund University.

Mogren, M. (2002). 'Medieval state expansion and the outpost model – the case of the Swedish north', in G. Helmig, B. Scholkmann, M, Untermann (eds.), *Centre, Region, Periphery: Medieval Europe, Basel 2002*, Vol 1, Basel, Archäologische Bodenforschung Basel-Staft.

Nielssen, A. R. (1977). *Ødetida på Vestvågøya. Bosettingshistorien 1300-1600*, Thesis, University of Tromsø.

Norlund, P. (1948). *Nordiske fortidsminder. IV. bind. 1. hefte: Trelleborg*, Kobenhavn, I Kommission hos Gyldendalske Boghandel, Nordisk Forlag.

Okarma, H. Jędrzejewski, W. Schmidt, K. Śnieżko, S. Bunevich, A. N. and Jędrzejewska, B. (1998). 'Home ranges of wolves in Białowieża primeval forest, Poland, compared with other Eurasian populations', *Journal of Mammalogy*, 79, 3, 842-852.

Olwig, K. (1984). *Nature's Ideological Language, a Literary and Geographic Perspective on its Development and Preservation on Denmark's Jutland Heath*, London, Allen & Unwin.

Orchard, A. (1998). *Dictionary of Norse Myth and Legend*, London, Cassell.

Packham, J. R. Harding, D. J. L. Hilton, G. M. and Stuttard, R. A. (1992). *Functional Ecology of Woodlands and Forests*, London, Chapman & Hall.

Pedersen, H. C. Liberg, O. Sand, H. and Wabakken, P. (2001). 'The Scandinavian wolf research project (SKANDULV)', in C. Sillero and H. Hoffmann (eds.), *Canid Biology and Conservation Conference Abstracts, Oxford 17-21 September 2001*, Oxford, IUCN/SSC Canid Specialist Group, The Wildlife Conservation Research Unit of Oxford University, 91.

C. Philo and C. Wilbert (eds.) 2000. *Animal Spaces, Beastly Places: New Geographies of Human-Animal Relations*, London, Routledge

Pluskowski, A. G. (2003). *Beasts in the Woods: Medieval Responses to the Threatening Wild*, unpublished Ph.D. thesis, University of Cambridge.

Pluskowski, A. G. (2005). 'The tyranny of the gingerbread house: contextualising the fear of wolves in medieval northern Europe through material culture, ecology and folklore', *Current Swedish Archaeology* 13, 141-160.

Pluskowski, A. G. (forthcoming a). *Wolves and Wilderness in the Middle Ages*, Woodbridge, Boydell & Brewer (in preparation).

Pluskowski, A. G. (forthcoming b). 'Where are the wolves? Investigating the scarcity of European grey wolf (*Canis lupus lupus*) remains in medieval archaeological contexts and its implications, International *Journal of Osteoarchaeology* (forthcoming).

Price, N. S. (2000). 'The Scandinavian landscape: the people and environment', in W. W. Fitzhugh and E. I. Ward (eds.), *Vikings. The North Atlantic Saga*, London, Smithsonian Institution Press, 31-40.

Pulsiano, P. (ed.) (1993). *Medieval Scandinavia: an Encyclopedia*, New York, Garland.

Rackham, O. (1980). *Ancient Woodland: its History, Vegetation and Uses in England*, London, Edward Arnold.

Rackham, O. (1996). *Trees and Woodland in the British Landscape, the Complete History of Britain's Trees, Woods and Hedgerows*, London, Phoenix (2nd revised edition).

Rackham, O. (1997). *The History of the Countryside*, London, Phoenix Giant.

Reichstein, H. (1991). *Berichte über die Ausgrabungen in Haithabu Bericht 30. Die wildlebenden Säugetiere von Haithabu (Ausgrabungen 1966-1969 und 1979-1980)*, Neumünster, Karl Wachholtz Verlag.

Riley, H. T. (ed.) (1867). *Gesta abbatum monasterii Sancti Albani a Thoma Walsingham*, London, Longmans.

Rooney, A. (1993). *Hunting in Middle English Literature*, Cambridge, D.S. Brewer.

Saunders, C. (1993). *The Forest of Medieval Romance: Avernus, Broceliande, Arden*, London, Brewer.

Schia, E. (1991). *Oslo innerst i Viken: liv og virke i middelalderbyen*, Oslo, Aschehoug.

Schia, E. (1994). 'Urban Oslo and its relation to rural production in the hinterland – an archaeological view', in A. R. Hall and H. K. Kenward (eds.), *Urban-Rural Connexions: Perspectives From Environmental Archaeology*, Oxford, Oxbow.

Sobol, P. G. (1993). 'The shadow of reason: explanations of intelligent animal behaviour in the thirteenth century', in J. E. Salisbury (ed.), *The Medieval World of Nature: a Book of Essays*, New York, Garland.

Spiegel, H. (ed. and trans.) (1994). *Marie de France: Fables*, Toronto, University of Toronto Press.

Steane, J. (1985). *The Archaeology of Medieval England and Wales*, London, Croom Helm.

Steele, J. H. and Fernandez, P. J. (1991). 'History of rabies and global aspects', in G. M. Baer (ed.), *The Natural History of Rabies*, Boca Raton, CRC Press.

Svensson, E. (1998). *Människor i utmark*, Stockholm, Almqvist & Wiksell International.

Sykes, N. J. (2001). *The Norman Conquest: A Zooarchaeological Perspective*, unpublished Ph.D. thesis, University of Southampton.

Thiel, R. P. (1985). 'Relationship between road densities and wolf habitat suitability in Wisconsin', *American Midland Naturalist*, 113, 404-407.

Tschan, F. J. (ed. and trans.) (1959). *Adam of Bremen: History of the Archbishops of Hamburg-Bremen*, New York, Columbia University Press.

Vretemark, M. and Sten, S. (1995). 'Djurbenen från kv., Klaudia, Västerås', *Statens historiska museum, Osteologiska enheten, rapport 1995*, 11.

Wigh, B. (1998). 'Animal bones from the Viking town of Birka, Sweden', in E. Cameron (ed.), *Leather and Fur: Aspects of Early Medieval Trade and Technology*, London, Archetype Publications.

Wigh, B. (2001). *Animal Husbandry in the Viking Age Town of Birka and its Hinterland*, Stockholm, Birka Project Riksantikvarieambetet.

Wilson, A. M. (1977). *The Sinister Significance of Certain Birds and Beasts in Medieval English Literature and Art*, unpublished M.Litt dissertation, University of Cambridge.

Wing, E. S. (1993). 'The realm between wild and domestic', in A. Clason, S. Payne and H-P. Uerpmann (eds.), *Skeletons in her Cupboard: Festschrift for Juliet Clutton-Brock*, Oxford, Oxbow.

Wolsan, M. Bieniek, M. and Buchalczyk, T. (1992). 'The history and distributional and numerical changes of the wolf *Canis lupus* L. in Poland', in K. Bobek, K. Perzanowski and W. L. Regelin (eds.), *Global Trends in Wildlife Management, 18th IUGB Congress, Kraków 1987*, Kraków, Świat Press.

Yalden, D. W. (1999). *The History of British Mammals*, London, T & A. D. Poyser.

Young, C. R. (1979). *The Royal Forests of Medieval England*, Leicester, Leicester University Press.

Zimen, E. (1981). *The Wolf: A Species in Danger*, Delacourt, New York.

Perceptions versus reality: changing attitudes towards pets in medieval and post-medieval England

Richard Thomas

Introduction

In 1994 a survey of pet ownership within the European Union revealed that there were a startling 36 million pet dogs, 35 million pet cats and 173 other pet species (chiefly birds, rabbits, rodents, reptiles and fish) (Serpell, 1996: 13). A more recent survey has demonstrated that, in the United Kingdom alone, there is an estimated 7.5 million dog owners and only slightly fewer cat owners (anon, 2001a). Numerous charities and organisations exist to protect the rights of these animals and we pride ourselves on being an 'animal-loving' nation. Indeed, pet-keeping is, as Mann (1975: 1) notes, "a major leisure activity bringing pleasure, companionship and often a sense of security to a very large number of people". Yet, while our perception is that we live in a society that treats animals with respect and dignity, the reality appears to be somewhat different. For example, a recent study has concluded that "cruelty to animals is deep-rooted in UK society", with reported incidents including shooting and kicking cats, and tying fireworks to their tails (anon, 2001b).

In this paper, the perceptions and realities of keeping animals as pets in medieval and post-medieval England will be explored using a combination of contemporary literary and artistic evidence, and zooarchaeological data.

The literary and artistic evidence

As Noske (1989: 45) notes, medieval attitudes regarding humanity, and nature in general, were strongly influenced by the Church. Only man was created in God's own image and given dominion over all other living creatures (Genesis 1:26, 28; 9:3). The medieval Church sought to maintain this division, particularly in its disassociation from Classical pagan beliefs, where animals and humans were often considered to be interchangeable. Consequently, representations of the devil in this period frequently appear as a mixture of human and animal, and the keeping of companion animals was reviled (Noske, 1989: 46; Russell, 1984: 209; Serpell and Paul, 1994: 133). Later prejudice towards pet-keeping also reflected a reaction against bestiality and the witch-hunts of the sixteenth century, where the possession of an "animal familiar was sufficient to arouse suspicions of witchcraft" (Serpell and Paul, 1994: 133).

It is perhaps unsurprisingly, therefore, that medieval sources record little affection for animals (pets or otherwise). For example, Thomas Aquinas, a thirteenth century philosopher-theologian, wrote that, "people cannot show animals charity (love) or even friendship, because animals are not rational creatures and fellowship is based on reason" (cited in Salisbury, 1994: 11). Such feelings were particularly emphasised by religious establishments, as exemplified by the letter from the Archdeacon of Ely to the abbess of a convent in 1345 forbidding the keeping of dogs or birds within the walls of the nunnery (Serpell, 1996: 48). Even in the early fifteenth century, negative attitudes towards close relationships with animals persisted. In *The Master of the Game*, Edward Duke of York wrote that, 'if any beast had the Devil's spirit in him, without doubt it is the cat' (cited in McNelis, 1997: 71).

The principal purpose for which pet animals – in the modern sense of the term – were kept by households appears to have been much more functional. Cats were recorded as being used for catching rodents as a tenth-century Welsh law illustrates, recording the purpose of a cat as, "to hear, to kill, to have her claws whole, to nurse and not devour her kittens" (cited in Salisbury, 1994: 14). Dogs were also viewed in a similarly utilitarian way. In a twelfth-century bestiary the various functions of dogs are described as including: tracking wild creatures, guarding sheep, protecting the homes of their master and hunting (Salisbury, 1994: 18).

Exceptions to this functionalist viewpoint existed, however, although it is apparent that the majority of these pertain to members of aristocratic households. While this may reflect greater opportunities amongst the elite to engage in leisure pursuits, it might equally be the result of biases in the evidence, since lower classes of society were less frequently portrayed. For example, a ninth-century poem, written in the margin of a manuscript by a Welsh monk, reveals real affection towards a cat called Pangur Bán (Thomas, 1983: 109). Thomas à Becket is also recorded as having pet monkeys in his entourage in the twelfth century, whilst touring France as Henry II's ambassador, and Henry III was so attached to his pet dog that he carried it around in a basket (Serpell, 1996: 47, 49). Illustrative evidence reveals further sentimental attitudes to pet animals, such as the *Queen Mary Psalter* (*c.*1310-1320), which features two couples seated together on a bench, with one woman holding a lap-dog under her arm (Warner 1912: 217). In Peter de Langtoft's early-fourteenth century *Chronicle of England* there is an image of the oft-maligned King John tenderly caressing a dog, with another sitting behind him (Wright, 1866).

Even during the early modern period in England, animal pets were seen as 'morally suspect' and one seventeenth-century moralist noted that "over familiar usage of any brute creation is to be abhorred" (cited in Thomas, 1983:

40). In 1607 Edward Topsell, author of a history of 'fourefooted beastes', declared the cat to be an "unclean and impure beast that liveth only upon vermin and by ravening" (Thomas, 1983: 109). Many of the dogs kept for working purposes in this period also received a rather ignominious end once they had outlived their usefulness. For example, a late seventeenth century farmer recorded how his dog Quon was killed and baked for grease (Thomas, 1983: 102). Following the Renaissance, attitudes to animals appear to have hardened somewhat. This period saw an expansion in the exploitation of natural resources, increased mechanisation, and a greater knowledge of anatomy, all of which may have contributed to René Descartes' conjecture that animals were automata, capable of 'complex behaviour' only in a purely mechanistic sense; such animals could not reason, nor experience pain, and various experiments were undertaken to demonstrate this fact (Thomas, 1983: 33-35).

However, as Thomas (1983: 102) notes, it was not the 'necessary animals' but the 'unnecessary' ones, such as the small lap-dogs, that received "real affection and the highest status". Indeed, Serpell (1996, 49) states that "by the sixteenth century, the fashion for lap-dogs achieved unprecedented levels of popularity", despite continuing criticism of the practice. The Stuarts in particular were so obsessed with them that in 1617 James I was accused of loving his dogs more than his subjects (Thomas, 1983: 102). By the Stuart period there were plenty of cat-lovers too, with one merchant in the 1630s making holes in the doors of his house to allow his cats to freely roam throughout (Thomas, 1983: 109). Thus, "by 1700 all the symptoms of obsessive pet-keeping were evident" and the late sixteenth/seventeenth century even witnessed a change in law to class pets as private property in response to the view that they were kept for "private emotional gratification" (Thomas, 1983: 111-12, 117).

From the eighteenth century, fondness for pets was more regularly expressed in literary genres, such as Christopher Smart's eulogy, "for I will consider my cat Jeoffry" (Williams, 1980: 87-90). In the same period, graves of certain pets also began to be covered with elaborate tombstones, such as the monument containing an epitaph to Serpent – a 'favorite dog of Lady Stepney's' in 1750 (Feeke, 2000: 12). While the sufficient regularity with which pet animals appeared in artistic form in this period, probably relates to their status value as much as devotion to a particular animal (Craske, 2000: 41-2), it appears that the view of animals as soulless machines incapable of feeling, was beginning to change.

It was not until the latter half of the nineteenth century, however, that current attitudes to pet-keeping and animal welfare in general, emerged (Serpell and Paul, 1994; Serpell, 1996; Burt, 2000). The sentimental sculptural representations of dogs by Joseph Gott (1786-1860) and the formation of organisations such as the Society for the Prevention of Cruelty to Animals in 1824, which later became the RSPCA, provide good exemplars of this paradigm shift (Craske, 2000; Ritvo, 1994: 108).

Defining pets

Prior to the examination of the available archaeological evidence, it is essential to consider which animals might have constituted pets in the medieval and post-medieval period. It is perhaps all too easy to impose our own cultural values on the past and assume that cats and dogs were the principal pets. Whilst the past treatment of these animals cannot be ignored, particularly since the examples noted above tend chiefly to relate to these animals, there are also a number of less obvious species that require consideration.

In farming communities, for example, in which close associations are likely to have developed with domestic animals, it is certainly possible that animals such as cows and sheep were treated as pets – although ultimately slaughtered for meat (Harris, 1986:177-8). The Romans are known to have kept ravens as pets and even taught them to talk, a practice that appears to have continued into the post-medieval period (Maltby, 1979: 73). Illustrative evidence, in the form of the fourteenth-century Luttrell Psalter, also depicts a lady with a pet squirrel on her shoulder (Woolgar, 1999: plate 73) and Edward Topsell (cited in Thomas, 1983: 110) remarks that, "apart from their tendency to devour woollen garments, they were 'sweet, sportful beasts and . . . very pleasant playfellows in house'". In the middle of the seventeenth century, William Cowper wrote a poem following the death of his 8½-year-old pet hare (Rhodes, 1988: 58-60) and by the eighteenth century Thomas (1983: 110-11) had identified the keeping of pet mice, hedgehogs, bats, toads and a diverse range of caged birds.

In the later medieval and post-medieval periods, we also have to consider the possibility of imported animals as pets. Certainly, from the thirteenth century, monkeys and parrots, amongst other exotic species, were imported into Britain as pets as extensive trade routes developed (Thomas, 1983: 110; Albarella et al., 1997: 51; Albarella, in press). The importation of tortoises from North Africa can also be traced back to the early seventeenth century (Highfield, 1989).

The archaeological evidence

While contemporary literary and artistic evidence can provide a glimpse of attitudes towards pet keeping in the medieval and post-medieval periods, such pieces of evidence should not be considered in isolation, their interpretation is not unproblematic. These data typically reflect the opinion of one person at a specific point in time and they are unlikely, therefore, to be representative of more general attitudes. One means of overcoming this problem is by comparing such evidence with archaeological data – in this instance the preserved remains of the animals and their excavated context.

Although it is difficult to attribute 'attitude' and 'intent' within the archaeological record, it is possible to analyse the remains of those animals that may have actually been treated as pets. Such data can also provide the opportunity to examine trends in a more quantitative manner, over a broader period of time and across a, potentially, wider range of social groups.

Identifying pets and attitudes towards them

Prior to the examination of the zooarchaeological evidence, it is imperative to consider which aspects of a faunal assemablage might enable the identification of pets, and attitudes towards them. Undoubtedly, the first task is to recognise the presence and relative abundance of those taxa that might have represented "companion animals" (O'Connor, 2003: 81). While the identification of such species can indicate the presence of potential pet animals on archaeological sites, it does not reveal anything about how they were treated and whether they were indeed pets, or just represented animals that were living on or around a site, exploited for a commodity (*e.g.* fur), or kept for a purely functional purpose (*e.g.* catching rodents, hunting, security). Indeed, perhaps the only instance in which the presence of pet animals might be inferred from species representation alone is by the identification of exotic taxa. The next step, therefore, is to consider the excavated context from which the animal bones derived.

If the bones of a potential pet animal are found disarticulated, in deposits that are clearly associated with household waste, then it might be surmised that, in death at least, it was not treated any differently from rubbish. Conversely, if the articulated remains of such animals are found within discrete burials, one possible interpretation is that they represent the careful disposal of a pet. Obviously, one of the principal problems with identifying pets using this approach is that deposits are often disturbed and redeposited. Consequently, what was originally a discrete deposit containing a burial may later be incorporated with more general household rubbish. Moreover, as O'Connor (2003: 82) notes, "the deliberate placement of an animal corpse will generally only be recognisable *in situ*" and therefore requires adequate recording by excavators. These contexts may, meanwhile, only inform us how the animal was treated in death, not in life. While the burial of a loved pet is a fairly widespread practice in contemporary society this may well have been exceptional in the past. The fact that the burial could also represent inedible animals, or those with a symbolic status, should not be excluded either. Thus, we need to seek other indicators.

As O'Connor (2003: 82) notes, it is generally the case that animals kept as pets are not eaten, "other than in cultures in which the young of livestock kept for food are adopted as pets until their time comes for the chop". Consequently, the identification of butchery marks on the bones of potential pet animals might indicate that they were exploited for a purpose other than companionship. For example, cut marks on metapodials, mandibles and crania can indicate skinning. Cut and chop marks on the long bones might suggest dismemberment, and possibly flesh removal for consumption by humans or other animals. Interpretations of industrial scale exploitation of pet animal by-products can also be inferred by combining butchery evidence with age data. Given a standard population of pets at a site over a period of time, one would perhaps expect a preponderance of adult animals, together with a few younger specimens that represent natural mortality. However, a site on which a high proportion of very immature, butchered bones were recovered might indicate the processing of these animals for a particular commodity (*e.g.* fur or skin).

The health status of particular animals might also indicate whether they were treated as pets. High proportions of immature animals could indicate a stressed population, or a policy of deliberate culling. For example, it is recorded that dogs were banned from being kept in Exeter in 1423 because they were thought to be a major health hazard, and watchmen were empowered to kill them (Maltby, 1979: 64). A further means of directly assessing the health of animals kept as pets is through the identification of bone pathologies. The presence of fractures in all stages of healing, particularly on the vertebrae and ribs, can provide a good indicator of animal maltreatment, for example (Teegen, 2005: 34). Caution must be exercised, however, to ensure that these are not the result of conditions which can lead to grater susceptibility to fracture such as osteodystrophia fibrosa (Jubb and Kennedy, 1970: 35-38). Living conditions might also be inferred from the presence of such conditions as rickets or osteomalacia – caused by a lack of sunlight or vitamin D – which results in the bowing of long bones. Conversely, the presence of bone pathologies that will have severely limited the functional value of an animal, or evidence of healed breaks, may provide an indication of animals kept for companionship.

Biometrical analysis can also be used to explore malnutrition in populations of animals. It is generally accepted that while teeth are less sensitive to nutritional deficiencies, periods of malnutrition during skeletal development can have a profound effect on the size of post-cranial bones (Davies, 2005: 85). Given datasets from two populations of animals, therefore, malnourishment might be identifiable if the teeth of both samples are similar in size, but one of them has relatively smaller post-cranial bones. Unfortunately, this method is not applicable to all species, since the bones of some animals that might have constituted pets – such as dogs – can vary widely in size and shape. Cats, however, do not exhibit such genetic diversity and therefore could be analysed in this way. Harcourt (1974) has already tried to use metrical data as a guide to understanding the purpose for which animals were kept, with small Roman dogs being interpreted as pets on the assumption that they would have been too small to serve any useful purpose.

As Maltby (1979: 64) notes, however, this approach is flawed since it is impossible from measurements alone to determine the purpose to which a dog was put, since animals of similar size may have had widely different functions.

The medieval and post-medieval evidence

In this section, the faunal evidence from a range of medieval and post-medieval sites (urban, rural and elite) is considered (*Figure 8.1*), to establish whether there are any identifiable archaeological correlates to the changing attitudes towards pet animals outlined above. This largely takes the form of a preliminary, qualitative survey of existing published data, although a more detailed quantitative analysis is currently in progress.

It is pertinent to begin by considering the evidence for the two most likely pets, namely cat and dog. *Table 8.1* demonstrates that these two animals generally comprise only a small proportion of the domestic fauna, typically ranging from less than one to seven percent. It is also apparent that cats are generally less well represented than dogs, a pattern that has been identified on medieval Scottish and Irish sites (McCormick, 1988: 221; Smith, 1998: 862), although this might reflect the fact that the smaller bones of cat are more likely to be missed during excavation. For both cat and dog, there are, in fact, no clearly discernible temporal patterns in their proportion at different sites. The most immediately noticeable problem with these data, however, is the very small number of sites with phases that extend beyond the seventeenth and eighteenth centuries – significantly problematic since it is in the later periods that changes in the attitudes towards pet animals might be identifiable. Irrespective of this problem, it is vital to address the data from earlier periods more closely to determine if pet animals can be identified in the archaeological record and whether it is possible to infer how they were perceived and treated.

On the archaeological sites selected for study, cats and dogs are frequently represented by partial skeletons (*Table 8.1*). Unfortunately, at many sites the lack of *in situ* recording of articulated animal skeletons means that it is often difficult to re-assemble all the individuals – a problem noted at both Dudley Castle, West Midlands (Thomas, 2002: 324), and Exeter, Devon (Maltby, 1979: 63). Where these animals appear as articulated skeletons, the possibility exists that they represent reverently buried pets. However, this is not always the case. At Dudley Castle, the contexts within which partial skeletons of both dogs and cats were recovered also contained domestic rubbish, suggesting that the animals were buried, or disposed of, with little ceremony (Thomas, 2002: 324). For example, a medieval garderobe deposit contained the skeletons of at least four dogs and two cats (Thomas, 2002: 328). A similar interpretation was drawn at the urban site of Exeter, where the animals appeared to have been "buried in or cast upon rubbish heaps" after they had died (Maltby, 1979: 62). At Middleton Stoney,

Oxfordshire, twelve partially complete cat skeletons, of which all but one was immature, were recovered from a medieval latrine shaft (Levitan, 1984: 118). Similarly, at least five cats were also disposed of in a late medieval cesspit in Skeldergate, York (O'Connor, 1984: 24-5).

One rather more unusual case has been identified in early post-medieval deposits from The Bedern Foundry, York. Here, the fill of a late fifteenth- to early sixteenth-century post-hole in a wall construction trench contained the partial skeleton of a cat, together with several hens (Bond and O'Connor, 1999: 368). The author also refers to a similar (unpublished) instance at Broadgate East, Lincoln (Bond and O'Connor, 1999: 368). While these could represent the careful burial of pets, it is striking that that in both cases cats and hens were buried together within a foundation deposit. One can only presume this represents some commemorative ritual during the construction of the building.

Exceptions to this pattern of disposing complete carcasses have been observed at Lincoln (Dobney *et al.*, 1996). Here it was noted, in both medieval and post-medieval urban deposits, that cat and dog bones were only represented by isolated specimens. Whether this reflects the fact that they were originally buried (or at least discarded) as complete skeletons and later disturbed is not apparent. For the most part, however, the predominance of partial skeletons, in rather ignominious locations, is more representative of a functional method of disposal than careful, reverential burial.

The incidence of butchery marks on the bones of cats and dogs is generally low in the medieval and post-medieval period, however, it does occur. At Dudley Castle, for example, 9% of all dog bones exhibited some form of butchery (Thomas, 2002: 325). Interestingly, all the specimens from this site that had recordable marks were isolated and disarticulated. Certainly, some of those marks were inflicted as a result of dismemberment; such as the presence of cut marks on the anterior surface of the atlas and around the greater trochanter of the femur. The majority of cut marks, however, were located on the shafts of the long bones and on the pelvis, and are, thus, more characteristic of flesh removal. Only one cut mark suggestive of skinning was identified at Dudley Castle and this was located just above the distal articulation of a metapodial. Similar instances of non-skinning related butchery marks have been identified on dog bones from a number of medieval sites, including: Faccombe Netherton, Hampshire (Sadler 1990); West Cotton, Northamptonshire (Albarella and Davis, 1994); Camber Castle, East Sussex (Connell *et al.*, 1997); and in Norwich, Castle Mall (Albarella *et al.*, 1997) and Dragon Hall (Murray and Albarella, 2000). At Launceston Castle, Cornwall, a butchered dog bone was also identified in a phase dating as late as 1660-1939 (Albarella and Davis, 1996: 9-10). No obvious temporal patterns in butchery frequency were identified in this study (*Table 8.1*).

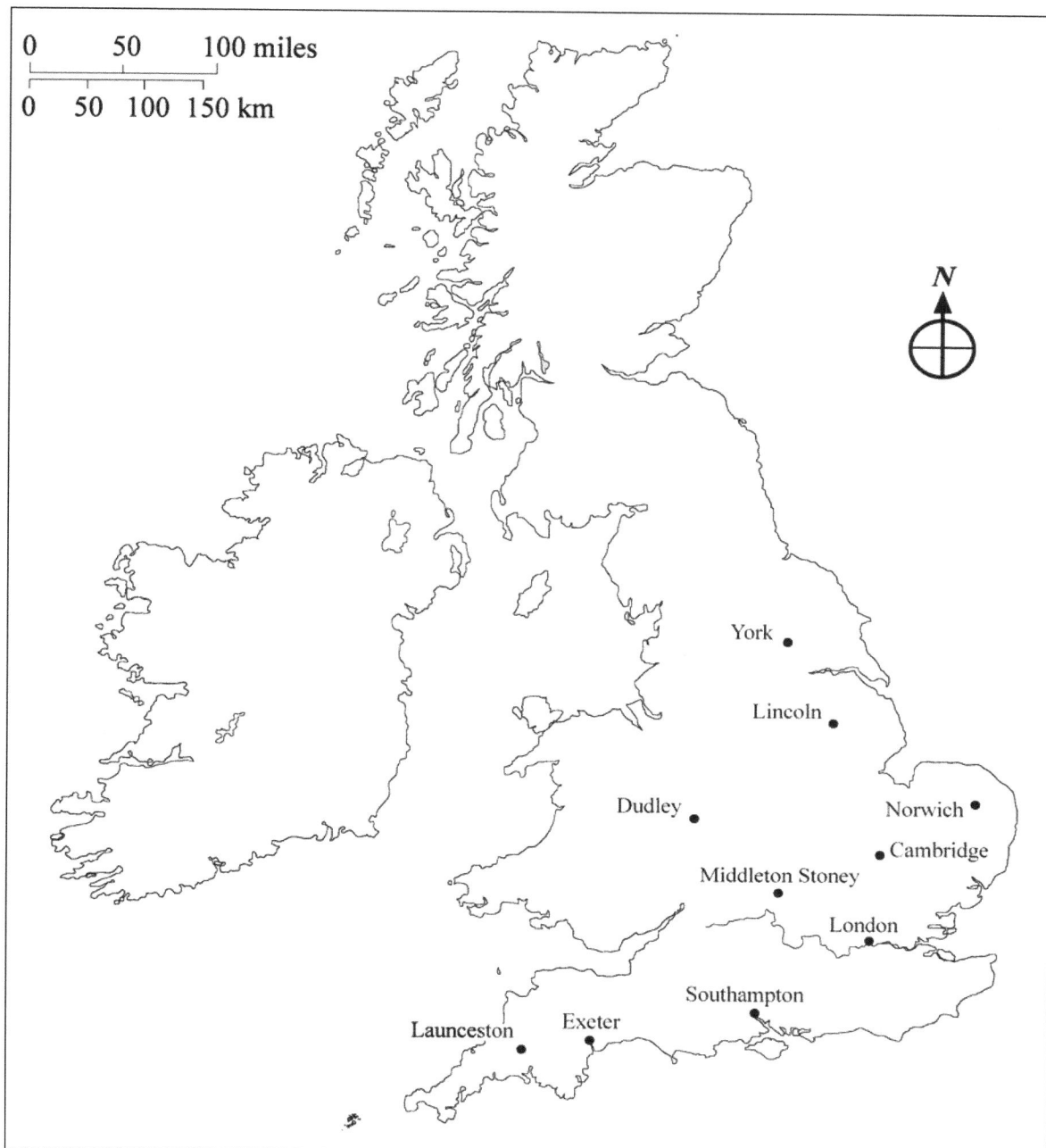

Figure 8.1 Location map of the principal archaeological sites discussed in this paper

While it is historically recorded that dog meat was consumed by people in times of stress (e.g. Thomas, 1983: 116; Wilson and Edwards, 1993: 51), this is probably an unlikely explanation to account for the widespread presence of butchered bones on archaeological sites, especially given the religious proscriptions on this matter (Deuteronomy 14:3-6; Leviticus 11:27). Whilst the butchery of dogs for their fat for cosmetic or medical purposes is a possibility (Gidney, 1996), a more viable suggestion is that some of the dog carcasses were knackered and "recycled as food for their companions" (Wilson and Edwards, 1993: 54; Thomas and Locock 2000). If such a practice existed in the medieval and post-medieval periods then the zooarchaeological evidence would suggest that it was a fairly widespread local 'industry', despite its absence from the historical documents.

In contrast, the reported incidences of cat butchery more frequently relate to skinning. For example, four percent of cat bones from Dudley Castle were recorded with cut marks (all from the fourteenth century), located on the labial side of a mandible and the distal epiphyses of unfused long bones (Thomas, 2002: 329). At Bene't Court, Cambridgeshire, the butchered/skinned remains of 79 cats, of which half were under 6 months of age, were also identified (Luff and Moreno Garcia, 1995). The frequency with which cats were skinned is perhaps

Site	Dog				Cat				
	NISP	%Domestic mammals	Partial skel NISP	Butchered NISP	NISP	NISP Domestic mammals	%Domestic mammals	Partial skel NISP	Butchered NISP
Exeter Md1 (1000-1150)	14	0.55	14	0	23	2544	0.90	0	0
Exeter Md2 (1100-1200)	14	0.26	0	0	126	5370	2.35	53	0
Exeter Md3 (1000-1200)	7	0.49	7	0	103	1439	7.16	35	0
Exeter Md4 (1150-1250)	0	0.00	0	0	23	324	7.10	21	0
Exeter Md5 (1200-1250)	0	0.00	0	0	21	764	2.75	0	0
Exeter Md6 (1250-1300)	20	0.48	13	0	92	4184	2.20	0	0
Exeter Md7 (1200-1300)	1	2.27	0	0	10	44	22.73	0	0
Exeter Md8 (1250-1350)	4	0.87	0	0	8	462	1.73	0	0
Exeter Md9 (1300-1350)	7	0.70	7	0	21	995	2.11	0	0
Exeter Md10 (1350-1500)	2	0.73	0	0	8	275	2.91	0	0
Exeter PM1 (1500-600)	72	1.99	0	0	462	3617	12.77	0	0
Exeter PM2 (1550-650)	9	3.04	0	0	10	296	3.38	0	0
Exeter PM3 (1660-700)	290	19.24	22	0	25	1507	1.66	0	0
Exeter PM4 (1660-800)	67	4.68	56	0	64	1433	4.47	10	0
Launceston 2 (c.10?5-c.1104)	2	40.00	0	0	0	5	0.00	0	0
Launceston 3 (c.1104-c.1175)	1	0.63	0	0	0	158.5	0.00	0	0
Launceston 4 (c.11?5-c.1227)	14	11.62	0	0	1	120.5	0.83	0	0
Launceston 5 (mid 13th century)	6	4.56	0	0	0	131.5	0.00	0	0
Launceston 6 (late 13th century)	17	1.29	0	0	7	1319	0.53	0	0
Launceston 8 (15th century)	23	0.80	0	0	8	2877	0.28	0	1
Launceston 9 (16th century-1650)	60	4.59	0	0	2	1307.5	0.15	0	0
Launceston 10+11 (1660-1939)	55	3.64	0	1	5.5	1512	0.36	0	0
Lincoln HMED (1250-1400)	5	1.20	0	0	5	416	1.20	0	0
Lincoln LMED (1400-1500)	0	0.00	0	0	22	401	5.49	0	0
Lincoln PM1 (1500-1600)	0	0.00	0	0	11	381	2.89	0	0
Lincoln PM2 (1600-1750)	30	1.26	0	0	141	2381	5.92	0	0
Dragon Hall (10th-11th)	1	0.91	0	0	1	110	0.91	0	0
Dragon Hall (11th-12th)	1	0.45	0	0	5	223	2.24	0	0
Dragon Hall (12th-m13th)	3	0.90	0	0	10	335	2.99	0	0
Dragon Hall (m13th-m14th)	17	3.48	0	1	12	489	2.45	0	0
Dragon Hall (m14th-m15th)	0	0.00	0	0	1	56	1.79	0	0
Dragon Hall (m15th-m16th)	1	0.97	0	0	1	103	0.97	0	0
Dragon Hall (m16th-m17th)	0	0.00	0	0	3	236	1.27	0	0
Thetford (10th-11th)	27	2.23	12	0	11	1210	0.91	3	0
Thetford (11th-12th)	7	1.56	0	0	10	448	2.23	7	0
Barnard's Castle (1095-1130)	2	2.33	0	0	0	86	0.00	0	0
Barnard's Castle (1130-1175)	1	0.11	0	0	1	881	0.11	0	0
Barnard's Castle (1130-1471)	1	0.16	0	0	33	621	5.31	0	0
Barnard's Castle (1471-1569)	115	19.10	0	0	2	602	0.33	0	0
Barnard's Castle (1569-1630)	47	85.45	0	0	1	55	1.82	0	0
Castle Mall 2 (late 11th-early12th)	67	7.84	31.5	3	40.5	855	4.74	20	4
Castle Mall 3 (late 11th-12th)	7.5	4.55	0	0	3	165	1.82	0	0
Castle Mall 4 (late 12th-mid 14th)	10.5	2.58	0	0	25.5	406.5	6.27	12.5	1
Castle Mall 5 (mid-late 14th-mid 16th)	10	1.04	5	0	35	957.5	3.66	24.5	0
Castle Mall 6 (late 16th-18th)	82.5	4.90	13.5	2	84	1683.5	4.99	0	1
West Cotton (c.1100-1250)	42	2.23	0	0	52	1879.5	2.77	0	2
West Cotton (c.1250-1400)	38	3.22	0	1	17	1178.5	1.44	0	0
West Cotton (c.1300-1450)	16.5	2.64	0	3	11	626	1.76	0	2
West Cotton (c.1450-1550)	10	2.11	0	0	2	474	0.42	0	0
West Cotton (c.1550-1800)	1	1.03	0	0	0	97	0.00	0	0
Dudley Castle 5 (1262-1321)	8.25	0.90	0	0	4	921.25	0.43	0	0
Dudley Castle 6 (1321-1397)	113.75	6.75	14	10	12.5	1684.75	0.74	0	2
Dudley Castle 7 (1397-1533)	83	2.90	19	7	52.5	2858.5	1.84	12	0
Dudley Castle 8 (1433-1647)	9.75	0.91	0	2	15	1077.25	1.39	0	0
Dudley Castle 8/9 (1533-1750)	2	0.27	0	0	3.25	735.25	0.44	0	0

Table 8.1 Analysis of cat and dog bone finds from a range of medieval and post-medieval sites in England

unsurprising since the cat's short gestation period and the large litter size would have provided "a constant and easily available source of pelts" (McCormick, 1988: 226) At Castle Mall, Norwich, cut marks suggestive of skinning were identified on the metapodials, cranium and phalanges, and a high proportion of immature cats with unfused bones was also recorded (Albarella *et al.*, 1997). However, in the last phase of occupation (late sixteenth – eighteenth centuries), while cut marks were still identified, the proportion of immature cats decreases – an intriguing trend considering the emergence of increasingly sentimental attitudes to these animals in the early modern period. The remaining sites that were examined in this study revealed no other obvious temporal variation in the proportion of butchered cat bones over time (*Table 8.1*), although the small sample sizes renders meaningless any conclusions drawn from this observation.

All told, the butchery marks present on cat and dog bones would seem to suggest that they were treated as a commodity rather than companions in the medieval and post-medieval periods. Yet, it must be borne in mind that this sort of evidence can only tell us about attitudes to these animals in death, not life. One of the interesting features of pet-keeping is that the same species can be treated as working animals, commodities and pets; consequently, as far as the archaeological recognition of this practice is concerned, other evidence requires consideration.

With respect to the maltreatment of cats and dogs, at Middleton Stoney, a fractured fibula that had fused to the tibia shaft was recognised, together with a humerus exhibiting exostoses on the proximal epiphysis that may have resulted from a blow or a kick (Levitan, 1984: 118). From the same site, a dog tibia was also tentatively identified with rickets (Levitan, 1984: 118). At twelfth-century Exeter, a dog femur was found with irregular bone growth around the distal epiphysis, which was a result of minor trauma (Maltby, 1979: 64). A sixteenth-century tibia from the same site also exhibited an unset fracture, which had been displaced at a 45° angle (Maltby, 1979: 64). While the presence of fractures generally seems to be low, those elements that are most likely to bear testament to animal abuse – the ribs and vertebrae (Teegen, 2005: 34) – are all too frequently not recorded because of difficulties in identification. The lack of modern comparative data for fracture prevalence in populations of abused and non-abused animals similarly hinders a detailed analysis of this issue (Thomas and Mainland, 2005: 4).

In an attempt to examine levels of nutrition in cats from medieval deposits at Coppergate, York, Bond and O'Connor (1999: 411-12) compared the relative size of the post-cranial bones and teeth against a modern reference specimen. This study revealed that while the teeth were of comparable size, the post-cranial bones of the archaeological sample were relatively smaller, leading the authors to conclude that the cats from York were probably, "less well nourished during the important early months of growth" (Bond and O'Connor, 1999: 412). While beyond the geographic scope of this present paper, it is interesting to note that in an attempt to examine the nutritional plane of cats in Ireland, McCormick (1988: 221) observed that early Christian period rural cats tended to be larger than those on medieval urban sites, leading the author to conclude that the former were "well bred and cared for as prized pets", while the latter were not (McCormick, 1988: 223).

Out of the other possible pet species in our period of study, ravens have occasionally been found on archaeological sites of medieval and post-medieval date. At Exeter, for example, 91 fragments of raven from some 20 individuals were identified (Maltby, 1979: 73), many of which derived from partial skeletons. This evidence led the author to suggest that the "practice of keeping tame ravens continued [from the Roman period] until the post-medieval period" (Maltby, 1979: 73). Raven bones have also been found in twelfth- to thirteenth-century deposits at The General Accident Site, Tanner Row, York (O'Connor, 1988). While the status of this animal as a pet is historically documented, these birds are accomplished scavengers and, as O'Connor (1993: 159) notes, they were ubiquitous in medieval towns throughout Europe. It is not beyond reason, therefore, that the presence of these birds in the archaeological record indicates natural mortality, or the deliberate killing of a pest, rather than pet-keeping.

Red squirrels are also occasionally found, as with four specimens in deposits dating from the later medieval period at Dudley Castle (Thomas, 2002: 89). Since these animals are extremely secretive forest inhabitants, they were almost certainly brought to the site through human agency. However, it is impossible to determine whether they represented the disarticulated remains of a number of buried pets, or bones removed with the skins in the exploitation of fur. The latter has been demonstrated, archaeologically at The Bedern, York, where squirrel comprised 35.7% of a fourteenth-century deposit, consisting primarily of metapodials and phalanges (Bond and O'Connor, 1999: 366).

With respect to some of the other possible pet species, while examples of their occurrence can be cited at a number of archaeological sites, their identification as pets is problematic. How can, for example, partial skeletons of hedgehogs, mice, bats and toads and especially the disarticulated remains of formerly pet domestic animals be distinguished from commensal species, or animals exploited for some other purpose? Archaeology is probably unable to provide an answer to this question.

Evidence for the importation of exotic animals that may have been kept as pets is rather limited, but it does exist. At Castle Mall, Norwich, for example, two bones of a parrot were identified in fifteenth-century deposits (Albarella et al., 1997). Barbary apes (Macaca sylvana) have been recovered from a context dating to c. 1300 at Southampton (Noddle, 1975: 334) and medieval/post-medieval deposits from London (Pipe, 1992), while a South American capuchin monkey (Cebus nigrivittatus) was retrieved from seventeenth-century London (Armitage, 1983). This evidence suggests of an interest in keeping unusual animals as pets, or at least curiosities, brought back with sailors from their travels. As Albarella (in press) notes, the acquisition of unusual animals often signified the high social status of their owners and provided a 'metaphor of power' over the natural world, as much as a desire for companionship. By the nineteenth century, archaeological evidence for tortoises exists (e.g. Thomas, 2003), which presumably reflects the growing commercialisation of the pet trade and the mass importation of these animals from Africa (Highfield, 1989).

Discussion and Conclusion

Serpell (1996, 23) has noted that the 'current proliferation' of pets is unprecedented and that historically, pet-owners have been a minority. This brief examination of the historical and archaeological evidence would seem to support this assertion. The numbers of cats and dogs found on archaeological sites in England in the medieval and post-medieval period is generally low and there appears to be no unequivocal evidence that these animals were in fact kept as pets. Both cat and dog skeletons tend to be recovered from contexts suggesting rubbish disposal rather than reverential burial, and the frequent occurrence of butchery marks indicates their exploitation as an economic commodity. Multiple roles might be evident: cats may have been largely kept for controlling rodent populations and for their pelts, while dogs may have been utilised for a wide range of functions including, guarding, hunting and a source of meat. Many of these animals may also have been strays or feral.

From the seventeenth and eighteenth century onwards it is clear from the literary and artistic evidence that a softening of attitudes towards pet animals began to occur, or was at least perceived to have occurred. However, this is not borne out in the archaeological record and throughout the post-medieval period cats and dogs continued to be buried in rather ignominious circumstances and treated in a fairly utilitarian way. The only real direct archaeological evidence for changing attitudes to animals is the appearance of new species – such as parrots and tortoises – which indicates an interest in keeping animals for pleasure or, at the very least, curiosity or status.

Perhaps the identification of such a change is unsurprising. As far as the archaeological evidence is concerned, pet animals could easily become incorporated within standard domestic refuse, particularly if they were initially buried in shallow graves, or they may have even been buried away from settlements – frequently the primary focus of archaeological excavation – and therefore not recovered. Certainly, more careful recording of articulated animal skeletons by excavators might better enable pet remains to be identified archaeologically. However, more faunal analyses from sites dated to the later post-medieval period are also required to test whether there are, in fact, no archaeological correlates to the changing attitudes evident from other lines of enquiry.

Zooarchaeological data are not without limitations either, since they are much better equipped at providing information about attitudes to animals in death than in life. It is not beyond consideration, for example, that "emotional and materialistic concerns were both important" (Serpell, 1996, xiv). Consequently, even though an animal may have been a cherished pet in life, it may have been exploited for economic gain upon death. Unfortunately, as far as the archaeological record is concerned, it is only the latter process that is likely to leave a visible trace.

Finally, drawing on the literary and artistic evidence, one might presume that the keeping of pet animals was a practice limited to the upper levels of society; the very same people that commissioned such texts/imagery. In contrast, the majority of animals may well have been used in a working capacity, and inhabited a lower social sphere, and will have been exploited in both life and death. Evidently, more detailed research – particularly on later post-medieval sites – is required to give these animals a much clearer history.

Acknowledgements

I would like to thank Jen Browning, Neil Christie, Annie Grant and Heidi Thomas for their helpful comments on an earlier draft of this paper. My thanks also to Umberto Albarella for kindly allowing me sight of his forthcoming paper. My thanks also to Umberto Albarella for kindly allowing me sight of his forthcoming paper and to Joe Skinner for producing *Figure 8.1*.

References

Albarella, U. (in press). 'Companions of our travel: the archaeological evidence of animals in exile', in S. Hartmann (ed.), *Flora and Fauna in their Medieval Environment*, Frankfurt an Main, Verlag Peter Lang.

Albarella, U. and Davis, S. (1994). *The Saxon and Medieval Animal Bones Excavated 1985-1989 from West Cotton, Northamptonshire*, London, AML Report 17/94.

Albarella, U. Beech, M. and Mulville, J. (1997). *The Saxon, Medieval and Post-Medieval Mammal and Bird Bones Excavated 1989-1991 from Castle Mall, Norwich, Norfolk*, London, AML Report 72/97.

Anon. (2001a). 'Look what the cat's brought in'. http://www.abdn.ac.uk/mammal/catkills.htm (last viewed 10/12/03)

Anon. (2001b). 'Britons have 'throwaway' attitudes to pets'. http://news.bbc.co.uk/1/low/uk/1409612.stm (last viewed 10/12/03)

Armitage, P. (1981), 'Jawbone of a South American monkey from Brooks Wharf, City of London', *The London Archaeologist* 4, 10, 262-70.

Baker, J. and Brothwell, D. (1980). *Animal Diseases in Archaeology*, London, Academic Press.

Bond, J. and O'Connor, T. P. (1989). *Bones from Medieval Deposits at 16-22 Coppergate*, The Archaeology of York 15/5, London, Council for British Archaeology.

Burt, J. (2000). 'The effect of pets in the nineteenth and early twentieth century, in S. Feeke' (ed.), *Hounds in Leash. The Dog in 18th and 19th Century Sculpture*, Leeds, Henry Moore Institute, 54-61.

Connell, B. and Davis, S. J. M. (1997). *Animal Bones from Camber Castle, East Sussex, 1963-1983 Excavations*, London, AML report 107/97.

Craske, M. (2000). 'Representations of domestic animals in Britain 1730-1840', in S. Feeke (ed.), *Hounds in Leash. The Dog in 18th and 19th Century Sculpture*, Leeds, Henry Moore Institute, 40-54.

Davies, J. J. (2005). 'Oral pathology, nutritional deficiencies and mineral depletion in domesticates – a literature review', in J. Davies., M. Fabiš., I. Mainland., M. Richards and R. Thomas (eds.), *Diet and Health in Past Animal Populations: Current Research and Future Directions*, Oxford, Oxbow, 80-88.

Dobney, K. Jaques, S. D. and Irving, B. G. (1996). *Of Butchers and Breeds: Report on Vertebrate Remains from Various Sites in the City of Lincoln*, Lincoln Archaeological Studies No. 5, Nottingham, Technical Print Services.

Feeke, S. (2000). 'An introduction to the exhibition', in S. Feeke (ed.), *Hounds in Leash. The Dog in 18th and*

19ᵗʰ Century Sculpture, Leeds, Henry Moore Institute, 5-12.

Gidney, L. (1996). 'The cosmetic and quasi-medicinal use of dog fat', *Organ*, 11, 8-9.

Harcourt, R. A. (1974). 'The dog in prehistoric and early historic Britain', *Journal of Archaeological Science*, 1, 151-175.

Harris, M. (1986). *Good to Eat: Riddles of Food and Culture*, London, Allen & Unwin.

Highfield, A. C. (1989). 'Tortoises of North Africa; taxonomy, nomenclature, phylogeny and evolution with notes on field studies in Tunisia', *Journal of Chelonian Herpetology*, 1, 1-12

Jubb, K. V. F. and Kennedy, P. C. (1970). *Pathology of Domestic Animals. Volume I*, New York and London, Academic Press.

Levitan, B. (1984). 'The vertebrate remains', in S. Rahtz and T. Rowley (eds.), *Middleton Stoney: Excavation and Survey in a North Oxfordshire Parish, 1970-1982*, Oxford, Department for External Studies, 108-148.

Luff, R. M. and Moreno Garcia, M. (1995). 'Killing cats in the medieval period: an unusual episode in the history of Cambridge, England', *Archaeofauna*, 4, 93-114.

Maltby, M. (1979). *The Animal Bones from Exeter 1971-1975*, Sheffield, Exeter Archaeological Reports 2.

Manning, A. and Serpell, J. (1994). *Animals and Human Society: Changing Perspectives*, New York and London, Routledge.

Mann, P. G. H. (1975). 'Introduction', in R. S. Anderson (ed.), *Pet Animals and Society*, London, Baillière Tindall, 1-7.

McCormick, F. (1988). 'The domesticated cat in early Christian and medieval Ireland', in G. MacNiocaill and P. F. Wallace (eds.), *Keimelia: Studies in Medieval Archaeology and History in Memory of Tom Delaney*, Galway, Galway University Press, 218-228.

McNelis, J. I. (1997). 'A greyhound should have 'Eres in þe manere of a serpent': Bestiary material in the hunting manuals *Livre de chasse* and *The Master of the Game*', in L. A. J. R. Houwen (ed.), *Animals and the Symbolic in Medieval Art and Literature*, Groningen, Egbert Forsten, 67-75.

Murray, E. and Albarella, U. (2000). *Mammal and Bird Bone Excavated 1997-8 from Dragon Hall, Norwich, Norfolk*, Birmingham, Birmingham University Field Archaeology Unit Project No. 715.

Noddle, B. (1975). 'The animal bones', in C. Platt and R. Coleman-Smith (eds.), *Excavations in Medieval Southampton 1953-1969. Volume 1: The Excavation Reports*, Leicester, Leicester University Press, 332-339.

Noske, B. (1989). *Humans and Other Animals: Beyond the Boundaries of Anthropology*, London, Pluto Press.

O'Connor, T. P. (1982). *Animal Bones from Flaxengate, Lincoln, c.870-1500*, London, Council for British Archaeology for the Lincoln Archaeological Trust.

O'Connor, T. P. (1984). *Selected Groups of Bones from Skeldergate and Walmgate*, The Archaeology of York 15/1, London, Council for British Archaeology.

O'Connor, T. P. (1988). *Bones from the General Accident Site, Tanner Row*, The Archaeology of York 15/2, London, Council for British Archaeology.

O'Connor, T. P. (1993). 'Birds and the scavenger niche', *Archaeofauna*, 2, 155-162.

O'Connor, T. P. (2003). *The Analysis of Urban Animal Bone Assemblages: A Handbook for Archaeologists*, York, Council for British Archaeology for the York Archaeological Trust.

Pipe, A. (1992). 'A note on exotic animals from medieval and post-medieval London', *Anthropozoologica* 16, 189-191.

Rhodes, N. (1988). *William Cowper: Selected Poems*, Manchester, Carcanet Press Ltd.

Ritvo, H. (1994). 'Animals in nineteenth century Britain: Complicated attitudes and competing categories', in A. Manning and J. Serpell, J. (eds.), *Animals and Human Society: Changing Perspectives*, New York & London, Routledge, 106-126.

Russell, J. B. (1984). *Lucifer: The Devil in the Middle Ages*, Ithaca and London, Cornell University Press.

Sadler, P. (1990). 'Faunal remains', in J. Fairbrother (ed.), *Faccombe Netherton, Excavations of a Saxon and Medieval Complex II*, London, British Museum Occasional Papers No. 74, 462-508.

Salisbury, J. E. (1994). *The Beast Within: Animals in the Middle Ages*, London, Routledge.

Serpell, J. (1996). *In the Company of Animals: A Study of Human-Animal Relationships* (Canto edition), Cambridge, Cambridge University Press.

Serpell, J. and Paul, E. (1994). 'Pets and the development of positive attitudes to animals', in A. Manning and J. Serpell, J. (eds.), *Animals and Human Society: Changing Perspectives*, New York & London, Routledge, 127-144.

Smith, C. (1998). 'Dogs, cats and horses in the Scottish medieval town', *Proceedings of the Scottish Antiquaries Society*, 128, 859-885.

Teegen, W. (2005). 'Rib and vertebral fractures in medieval dogs from Haithabu, Starigard and Schleswig', in J. Davies., M. Fabiš., I. Mainland., M. Richards and R. Thomas (eds.), *Diet and Health in Past Animal Populations: Current Research and Future Directions*, Oxford, Oxbow, 34-38.

Thomas, K. (1983). *Man and the Natural World: Changing Attitudes in England 1500-1800*, London, Allen Lane.

Thomas, R. (2002). *Animals, Economy and Status: The Integration of Historical and Zooarchaeological Evidence in the Study of a Medieval Castle*. University of Birmingham, Unpublished Ph.D. thesis.

Thomas, R. (2003). *The 19ᵗʰ - 20ᵗʰ Century Animal Bones from Stafford Castle: an Educational Collection and a Zooarchaeological Investigation*, Unpublished report for Stafford Borough Council.

Thomas, R. and Mainland, I. (2005). 'Introduction: animal diet and health - current perspectives and future directions', in J. Davies., M. Fabiš., I. Mainland., M. Richards and R. Thomas (eds.), *Diet and Health in Past Animal Populations: Current Research and Future Directions*, Oxford, Oxbow, 1-7.

Warner, G. (1912). *Queen Mary's Psalter: Miniatures and Drawings by an English Artist of the 14th Century Reproduced from Royal MS. 2 B VII in the British Museum*, London, Longmans & Co.

Williams, K. (1980). *The Poetical Verse of Christopher Smart 1: Jubilate Agno*, Oxford, Clarendon Press.

Wilson, B. and Edwards, P. (1993). 'Butchery of horse and dog at Witney Palace, Oxfordshire, and the knackering and feeding of meat to hounds during the post-medieval period', *Post-Medieval Archaeology*, 27, 43-56.

Woolgar, C. M. (1999). *The Great Household in Late Medieval England*, New Haven and London, Yale University Press.

Wright, T. (1866). *The Chronicle of Pierre de Langtoft, in French Verse, from the Earliest Period to the Death of King Edward I*, London, Longmans.

Art, Archaeology, Religion and Dead Fish:
A Medieval Case Study from Northern England

Sue Stallibrass

Introduction

This paper looks at the multiple roles that animals can play in people's lives, taking a single site as a case study. The archaeological material is described and considered in traditional ways. These concentrate in turn on evidence for what the past environment was like, evidence for how it was exploited economically, evidence for artefact manufacture and evidence for ritual deposition. These interpretations are all based on the same very small group of vertebrate remains, although they also draw upon other lines of evidence including the stratigraphy of the site, medieval art, ethnographic studies and a familiarity with modern Christian beliefs and practices.

The paper then argues that this current style of thinking is probably highly inappropriate. It divides activities and belief systems into several separate categories, whereas the people using the site may have had more holistic views of themselves and the world around them. To an archaeologist, it can be tempting to view butchery waste as simply a convenient raw material for artefact manufacture. To the people involved in creating and using the artefacts as a means of communication with their deity, it may have been very significant that the raw materials derived from their means of subsistence.

The conclusion is that we should approach our studies of faunal remains with many more questions than those relating simply to utilitarian functions, taphonomy and site formation processes. In effect, this paper aims to put thoughts about living people (and how *they* thought) back into faunal studies.

Caveat

The interpretations of this site and its archaeological finds have been helped enormously by the fact that we already know from historic sources that it was of religious significance to the people who built and used it. We also know the nature of that religion i.e. Christianity, and we are still familiar with many of the beliefs and religious practices and ceremonies that are associated with it. This is a huge advantage: normally archaeologists have to guess whether or not a site had religious significance, and are completely ignorant about the nature of the religious beliefs and practices that may have been associated with it. This paper is written in a style that attempts to consider the religious aspects in an archaeological manner.

The site and the contexts producing animal bone material

In 1997 the site of a small medieval chapel at Chevington, Northumberland was excavated by a team from The Archaeological Practice (University of Newcastle) led by Alan Williams and Phil Woods. The location of the site was known from historic references although the building itself had been raised to the ground at an unknown date. Pottery associated with the use of the chapel dates to the thirteenth and fourteenth centuries, a period when local sovereignty was disputed by the Scots and the English. It is not known when the chapel went out of use. The site and its environs were due to be completely destroyed by the extension of an opencast coalmine and the archaeological work was undertaken through normal planning procedures. A client report was lodged with the Northumberland Sites and Monuments Record, but the excavations are unpublished. The site lies approximately five kilometres inland from the North Sea coast in an area of low-lying land that has poor agricultural qualities. The drift geology is glacial boulder clay that is poorly drained and it is not well suited to arable production. The current terrestrial landuse concentrates on cattle pasture and coal mining. The adjacent North Sea is a rich source of marine fish such as herring and members of the cod family, and is still exploited from fishing ports further up and down the coast.

A very small amount of animal bone was recovered by hand during the excavation, totalling six kilograms in weight (and this includes a small amount of material from roundhouses and ditches predating the construction of the chapel). Animal bone was recovered from deposits outside and inside the chapel. Internal contexts producing animal bones included three small pits that were thought, at the time of excavation, to have supported scaffolding during the chapel's construction phase. Two of these pits were located against the inner face of the south chancel wall and one was against the east wall of the nave (see *Figure 9.1*). The floor levels of the chapel had been disturbed in places and it is not clear whether or not the pits were ever sealed by the chapel floor. This makes it slightly uncertain as to whether they were dug during the construction of the chapel or during its use but the excavators are confident that they date to the medieval period. Some very similar faunal material, presumably deriving from these features, was recovered from associated post-medieval disturbances including a robber trench adjacent to the chancel arch and a recent waterpipe trench in the same location.

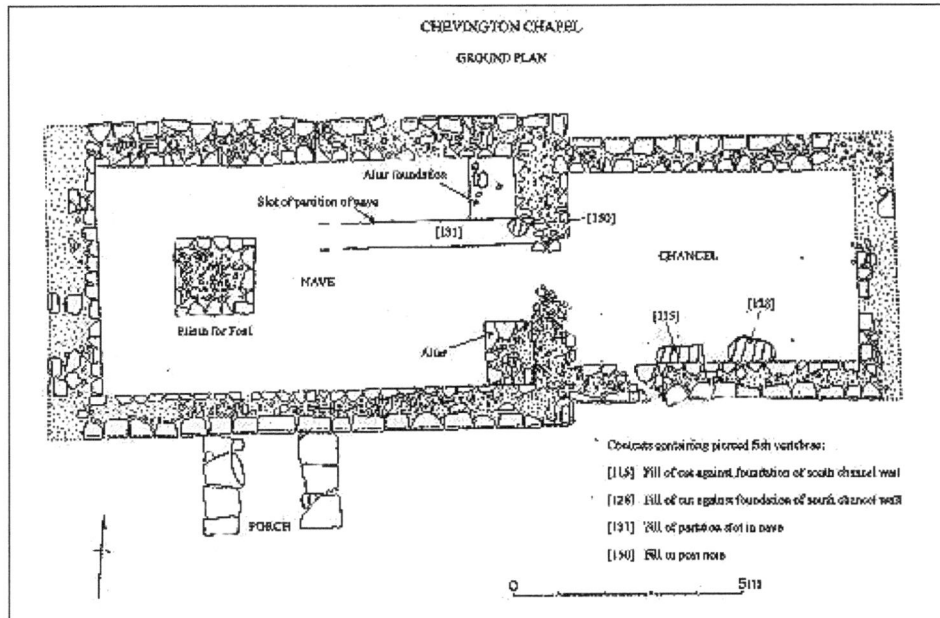

Figure 9.1: Plan of Chevington Chapel, Northumberland showing locations of medieval contexts producing fish vertebrae

The nature of the animal bone material

The material from outside of the chapel and from most of the internal deposits consists mainly of fragmentary bones of domestic mammals such as cattle, sheep and pig. Several show clear butchery marks. The animal bones recovered from the pits within the chapel building (and from the later features that cut through them) are very different. These consist almost entirely of fish vertebrae, plus a few fragments of cattle bone. Only one other fish bone was recovered from the site: a broken head bone from an unidentified species, found in the floor of the nave

The fish vertebrae were kindly identified by Dr Alison Locker and all derive from marine species. Nearly all of them are from gadids (the cod family) and most of the bones that could be identified to species level derive from ling (*Molva molva*) with a few from cod (*Gadus morhua*). There is also one vertebra from an elasmobranch (shark type). The vertebrae all derive from the upper and middle parts of the spinal column. There are no tail vertebrae. The ling vertebrae are all considerably larger than those from a modern reference specimen of the same species that was nearly one metre in length.

The elasmobranch vertebra is naturally lacking in any spinous processes and is also naturally perforated through its centre. In effect, it is a 'ready-made' bead. Gadid vertebrae, in contrast, normally have spinous processes and no central perforation. In the material recovered from Chevington Chapel, every gadid vertebra has been modified to look crudely like the elasmobranch vertebra by having the spinous processes removed and the centre artificially perforated (see *Figure 9.2*). Tool marks could

not be seen on the central perforations when examined through a binocular microscope at times ten magnification; the surfaces having been polished smooth. Similarly, the rough edges where the spinous processes have been broken off have been smoothed off and polished as though they have been rubbed with soft material or handled by people. The pattern of surface alteration is not consistent with abrasion through contact with sediment and appears to have occurred prior to burial.

Three of the groups of fish bones are each associated with a single modified cattle bone (see *Figure 9.3*). One of these groups came from a disturbed context (a late post-medieval pipe trench close to the chancel arch) and only produced four fish vertebrae plus one cattle bone. Of the two pits against the south chancel wall, one contained at least forty-two fish vertebrae plus one cattle femur bone and the other contained at least 105 fish vertebrae. Since the excavated material was not sieved, the original numbers of fish vertebrae may have been considerably greater than those recovered. Precise numbers are difficult to establish as some of the vertebrae (which are quite fragile) have broken, although most of the bones recovered are complete. Two of the cattle bone fragments are heads of femurs. These have both been cut off to produce a hemisphere of bone that has been perforated through the centre in the style of a spindle whorl (see *Figure 9.3*). The third cattle bone comprises most of the distal trochlea of a humerus. This barrel-shaped fragment has similarly been cut off the bone to give a flat surface on one side and a convex 'dome' on the other, and has also been perforated through the centre. Unlike the femur heads, this fragment is not symmetrical and would be useless as a spindle whorl.

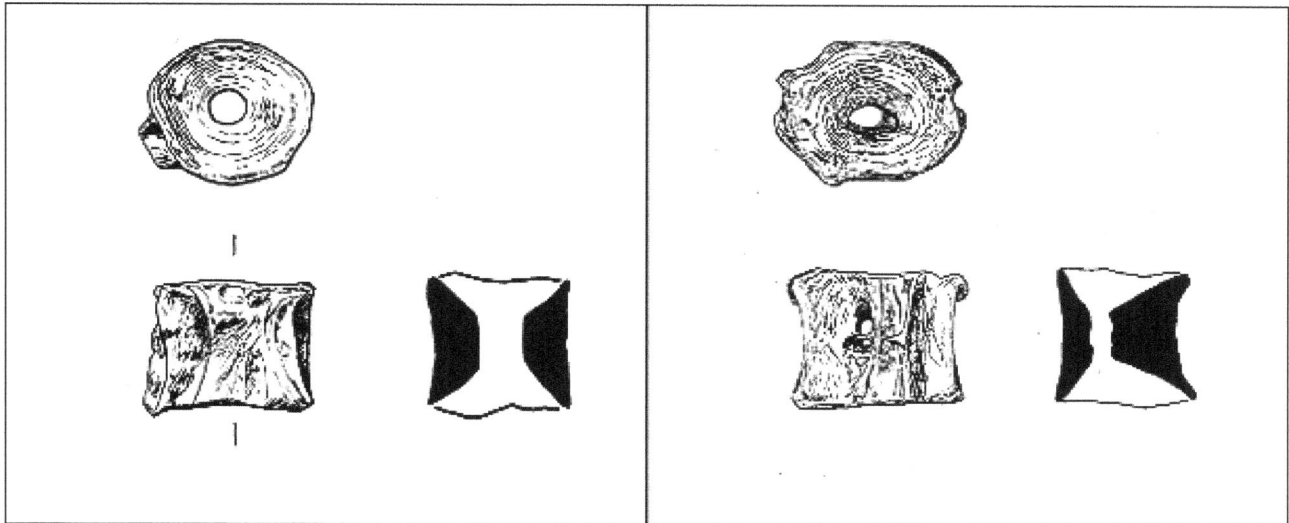

Figure 9.2: Two of the modified ling vertebrae each viewed from one end, from the side and in section. Note the crudely symmetrical forms, following the removal of spinous processes. The central, artificial perforations vary in size and shape. Diameters of vertebrae approximately 23 and 25 mm

Interpretation of the animal bones found outside of the chapel and in the nave floor

Most of the bones were found outside in the graveyard, with a few small bones in the floor of the nave. They all appear to be normal food refuse. Although we might find it surprising that people would eat in a churchyard and throw away their rubbish there, medieval churchyards were the location for many social activities including holidays (holy days) and festivals. In effect, they were open-air village halls. People may well have prepared food at the site as well as consumed it there.

An alternative explanation for the presence of food remains relates to the unsettled politics of the area, when it was fought over by the Scots and the English. Local civilians, or soldiers from either side of the dispute may have taken shelter at the site, and would have needed to eat to survive.

Environmental interpretation of the fish vertebrae found within the chapel

The fish vertebrae provide information about the environment and how it was exploited, regardless of what happened to them later. Traditionally, ling and other gadids tend to be caught out at sea with lines and hooks (Locker 2001). Although some gadids do come closer inshore in some locations at certain times of the year, it is almost certain that these fish were caught out at sea from boats for two reasons: ling tend to stay in deep water and the local coastline is very shallow. By analogy with Hartlepool further down the coast, the fishermen would probably have had to travel ten to twenty miles out into the North Sea, even if the fish shoals had been directly

offshore rather than located further north or south (data from Sharpe 1816, cited in Locker 2001).

The ling vertebrae all derive from fish that were well over one metre in length, indicating the availability of large gadids in the North Sea prior to the recent drastic reductions in numbers and sizes of fish caused by over-exploitation in the twentieth and twenty-first centuries.

Economic interpretation of the fish vertebrae found within the chapel

The lack of tail vertebrae is characteristic of fish that have been opened up for preservation (Locker 2001). When large fish such as gadids are prepared it is common practice to chop off the head, to cut the fish's body open along one side most of the way down from the head end, and to open out the fish like a double page spread in a book. This provides a large surface area to be dried, salted, smoked or pickled. There is no need to cut the thin tail end of the body open, and the tail vertebrae remain *in situ*. The exposed upper and middle vertebrae can be discarded, together with the head bones, and it is noteworthy that only one head bone and no tailbones of any fish were recovered from the chapel site. This implies that the initial processing of the fish took place elsewhere.

It is clear that people who lived at or visited Chevington had access to fish processing waste. Given that the site is only five kilometres inland, it is likely that the people were actively involved in the processing themselves. Since fishing is traditionally a community or family occupation, it is also likely that the same people or their close relatives actually caught the fish as well.

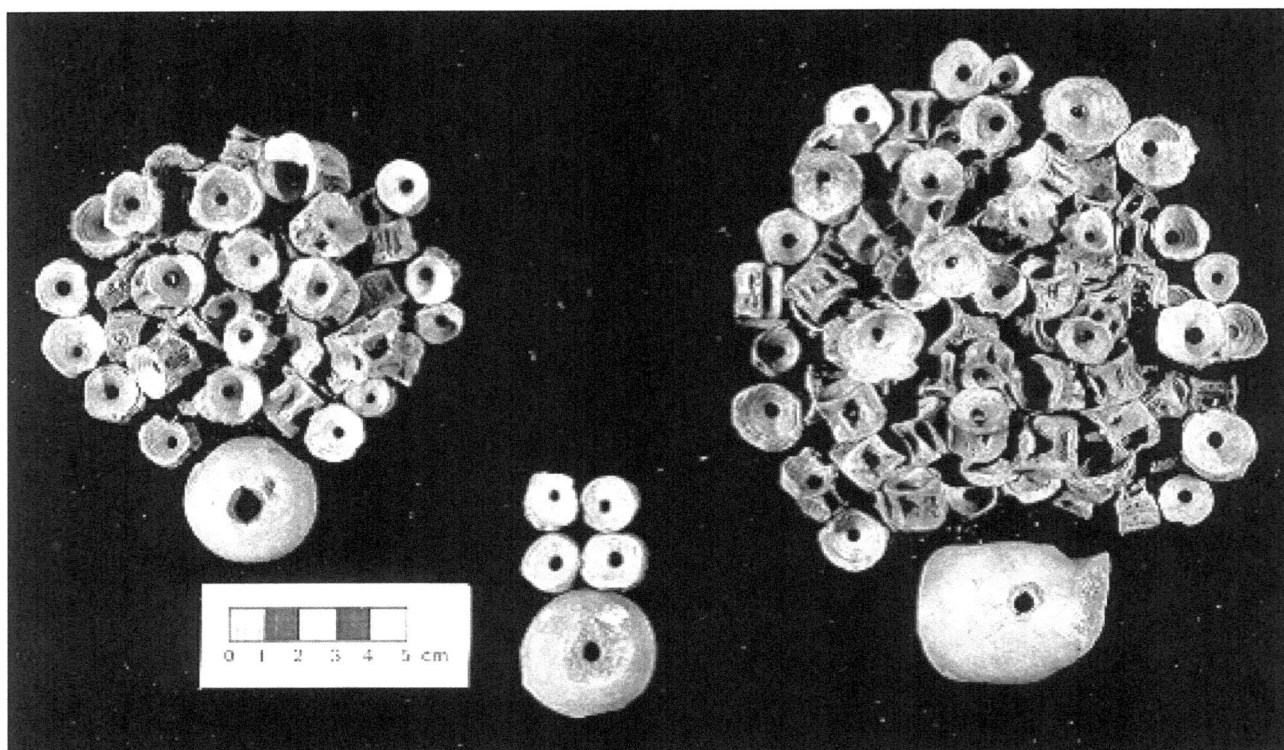

Figure 9.3: The three groups of perforated fish vertebrae and modified cattle bones. Left: 42 vertebrae plus one cattle femur head from one of the pits against the south chancel wall. Centre: four vertebrae plus one cattle femur head from a modern pipe trench through the chancel arch, probably redeposited from the adjacent pit beside a putative altar base. Right: 105 vertebrae plus one cattle distal humerus fragment from the second pit against the south chancel wall.

From an economic perspective, the local land would not have been very productive arable farmland, although it would have been suitable (as it is now) for cattle pasture. The presence of large supplies of fish stock nearby in the North Sea provided an alternative source of food; one that could not only be used locally, but which could also be exploited as a tradable commodity. Since these marine fish are migratory, their exploitation was probably seasonal. Dead fish need rapid processing to prevent the meat from spoiling. It is not thought likely that fishermen in this period had suitable boats for long distance sea transport of live fish, and so their capture was probably restricted to the times when they were located offshore.

During the medieval and post-medieval periods, fish was an important part of the diet for Christians i.e. the whole population of England and Scotland. Fish could be eaten on 'meat free' days of the week and during Lent, a period when Christians undergo voluntary food restrictions in memory of the martyrdom of their god's half-human son. Marine fish was a major component of this part of Christians' diets. Once it has been processed and dried or cured, fish can be stored for up to two years, making it highly transportable. It is likely that the people living in the vicinity of Chevington chapel during the medieval and post-medieval periods combined farming with fishing, although it is not possible to ascertain which took up more time or which provided more resources.

Artefactual interpretation of the fish vertebrae and cattle bones found within the chapel

Every bone in this part of the collection has been perforated centrally. With the exception of the elasmobranch vertebra that is naturally symmetrical, none of the fish vertebrae or cattle bone fragments are perfectly balanced, but each and every one has been modified until it approximates a symmetrical form. The fish vertebrae resemble beads and it is possible that their internal perforations have been smoothed by the polishing action of threads running through them. This would explain the lack of tool marks.

If the fish vertebrae were strung together on threads, what could have been their function? The vertebrae are fragile items and would soon have been destroyed if used for anything (such as net spacers) that would have exposed them to physical damage. In fact, in order to survive any usage prior to burial they must have been kept in a relatively protected environment such as hanging on a wall or inside some sort of container.

The perforated cattle bones are clearly deliberate artefacts. Whilst the two femur heads could have been used as spindle whorls, this is not a possibility for the humerus trochlea. Given that each of these three fragments was found in association with a group of perforated fish vertebrae, it is parsimonious to assume that all three had the same function and that, in some way, that function was intimately related to that of the vertebrae. The smoothing observed on the outside of the fish vertebrae is consistent with the effects of frequent handling or contact with clothing, and the smoothing of the internal perforations is consistent with the passage of an internal thread.

One possible explanation of the modification and association of the fish and cattle bones is that they were the components of rosaries or paternosters. These composite artefacts, similar to worry beads used in many modern cultures, are designed to aid concentration when reciting prayers associated with the Christian religion. Each bead is passed along the thread by hand in accompaniment to the recitation of a short set prayer. During the medieval period, Christian religious ceremonies and activities in Britain (including prayers) utilised the Latin language. The same prayers are still used today, although they are currently usually said in English. In the case of rosaries, which are associated with the Catholic sect of Christians, prayers are often addressed to the mother (named Mary) of the Christian god and the relevant prayer is called an *Ave Maria* (Latin) or Hail Mary (English). Paternosters are used mainly to address the god directly as *Pater Noster* (Latin) or Our Father (English). Rosaries, in fact, combine the two prayers and aid the recitation of one hundred and fifty *Ave Marias* in sets of ten, separated by single Paternosters. This sequence is often reflected by the arrangement of the beads upon the thread, with groups of ten beads separated by a single bead.

The numbers of beads on rosaries and paternosters can vary, although rosaries usually have a multiple of eleven. Early rosaries and paternosters were simply strings of beads. Sometimes these had a single, larger bead at the base where the two ends of the thread were held together. Later, at some time during the medieval or post-medieval period, it became common for the basal bead to be replaced by a cross, symbolising the martyrdom of the son of the Christian god, Jesus Christ (see *Figure 9.4*).

During the medieval period, England was a Christian country, and most people were Catholics, although this situation changed during the later medieval/early post-medieval period, when Tudor monarchs declared and maintained their independence from the Catholic Church. Currently, most Catholics (including children) own their own, personal, rosary which has been blessed by a priest and which they carry around with them or keep in a safe place. It is likely that most medieval people, too, owned their own rosaries.

The medieval manufacture of rosaries

Rosaries have been made from a great variety of natural and manufactured materials. The thread can be made of vegetable fibres such as flax, hemp or bast, or from animal fibres and tissues such as spun wool, hair or sinews. Basically, anything that can be used or modified as a bead is suitable raw material. Known medieval and early post-medieval examples include beads made of wood, bone, shell, soft forms of rock such as shale and cannel coal, and precious stones (Winston-Allen 1997), as well as manufactured ceramics and glass. Nuno Gonçalves' famous fifteenth century polyptych 'The Veneration of St Vincent' in the Museu de Arte Antiga in Lisbon shows at least two rosaries (Royal Academy of Arts 1955). One is made of immaculately uniform spherical beads made of some hard, dark material and is held by a female member of the court of King Alfonso V. The second appears to be made of shark vertebrae and is held by a fisherman. It may be significant that St Vincent is a patron saint of fishermen. Unfortunately, the patronage or dedication of the chapel at Chevington is unknown.

If the Chevington material does derive from rosaries, why should they have been buried in pits within the chapel? Circumstantial evidence supporting the concept that these modified bones were buried deliberately in the chapel, in sacred contexts, comes from the position of the font. Like rosaries, baptismal fonts are blessed and should not be disposed of in secular locations. When the rough stone foundation platform for the font at the west end of the chapel's nave was excavated, it revealed a pit directly beneath it that contained a deliberately buried earlier font. This is quite a common practice and may also relate to the association of baptismal fonts with cycles of birth, death and rebirth as well as to a desire to keep obsolete sacred objects within a sanctified area (see Stocker 1997).

The locations of the pits containing the modified fish and cattle bones appear to be similarly non-random. The chancel is the most sacred area of a Christian church or chapel, being the area in which priests perform ceremonies and in which the most precious religious artefacts and icons are kept or displayed. At Chevington, two of the bone-containing pits were located here. In the nave area, there was evidence for two stone structures built up against the wall dividing the chancel from the nave, one on either side of the linking archway. Using architectural analogies, these features have been interpreted by the excavators as the bases of altars. The animal bones from the nave came from a pit immediately adjacent to one of these altars? and from associated disturbed contexts. The most obvious conclusion is that the pits were dug in specially chosen locations, in particularly sacred areas of the chapel. Rather than being scaffold supports that just happened to have highly specific material disposed in them, they appear to have been purpose-made containers for the deposits containing the modified animal bones, similar to the pit dug for the obsolete font.

Figure 9.4: 21ˢᵗ Century French rosary of wood and synthetic thread demonstrating arrangement of five sets of ten beads separated by single beads.

Two potential explanations for the burial of rosaries in the chapel are suggested here. Both relate to the fact that rosaries are blessed by priests and cannot, therefore, be discarded with secular waste but must either be kept as personal belongings or disposed of in sacred locations.

The first, and possibly less likely, suggestion concerns the period when the Church of England persecuted Catholics following Henry VIII's break with Rome. A rosary, with its distinctive sequencing of ten beads followed by a single bead or knot was an obvious piece of evidence that its owner practised Catholicism. Such incriminating evidence would have had to have been kept hidden from searchers, and burial within the chapel would have been a safe and appropriate method of disposal and concealment. However, this explanation relies on a date of burial that post-dates the Reformation of AD 1534. Although the stratigraphic evidence has suffered from some truncation and disturbance, which means that it is not possible to ascertain exactly when the pits were cut, the remaining stratigraphy and associated ceramics do indicate that the pits were dug in the medieval period rather than later.

The second explanation refers to a practice that was common in the medieval period, and which still occurs today in some Christian groups. A rosary, which has been blessed and which is intimately associated with Mary the mother of the Christian god, can be donated to her in order to call for her assistance. Alternatively, it can be given to her in gratitude for something good that had happened (or for preventing something bad from happening). Whilst the Christian god himself is viewed as omnipotent, his mother is viewed as a more approachable personage, who can be appealed to, to mitigate on an individual's behalf. Much as votive offerings in other religions are placed in temples, in front of religious statues and idols, or thrown into sacred waters, Catholics sometimes place rosaries on statues of Mary or on or under altars. The burial of the putative rosaries in Chevington Chapel may relate to offerings made during the use of the chapel as a Catholic place of worship.

How do the environmental, economic, artefactual, artistic, religious and stratigraphic lines of evidence relate to one another? More importantly, what did it all mean to the people who used the chapel in the medieval period?

The organisation of the text above reflects modern archaeologists' preoccupation with scientific methodology and it attempts to clarify what is evidence and what is interpretation. This explicit separation of fact and fancy is essential if the data are to be recorded and presented in a manner that is open to reinterpretation. But does the concomitant fragmentation of both the data and the discussions prevent any real appreciation of their significance and how they might inter-relate?

A taphonomic line of enquiry can collate the disparate lines of evidence into a narrative sequence, albeit one that is centred on the bones themselves rather than on any people who may have interacted with them.

A taphonomic sequence can be summarised as:

1   Large gadid fish are living out at sea.
2   Some of these fish are caught and taken back to land.
3   The fish (now dead) are beheaded, gutted and filleted and the waste parts are disposed of.
3a N.B. no direct evidence: the filleted fish are preserved in some way e.g. by drying, salting or smoking and are either stored for deferred consumption locally or traded elsewhere, presumably in return for another commodity, for services or for cash.
4   Some of the discarded fish vertebrae and a few discarded cattle bones are collected as raw material for the manufacture of artefacts.
5   The modified vertebrae and cattle bone fragments are strung together in groups to be used as rosaries or paternosters.
6   Some of the rosaries or paternosters are ritually placed in specially dug small pits in sacred areas of the Christian 'temple'.

This perfunctory sequence explains how the fish bones were obtained, transformed and deposited. But it lacks any understanding of *why* the fish and cattle bones were treated in this way or *who* transformed them from unwanted, smelly waste, to an artefact used in religious devotion.

Sea fishing is usually a cooperative venture involving men and boys from a community or a family. It requires considerable capital investment in the purchase or construction of a boat, plus a long-term commitment to the maintenance of the boat and associated equipment (nets, lines, oars, sails, etc). The fishing itself can be a dangerous task, involving considerable hardship and risk of failure, damage and death. To succeed, people have to rely on skill, experience, help from each other and divine providence.

Fish processing is usually undertaken by female members of a community or family (often termed 'fish wives'). The tasks often take place out of doors, where the unwanted fish heads, guts and bones can be discarded *in situ*. It can be boring, tiring and messy work, but can also be a highly sociable activity. Whoever modified the fish vertebrae and cattle bones clearly had access to both types of bone waste: one derived from local sea fishing, one from (presumably local) cattle husbandry. The modification did not require any particular skills or equipment, other than a drill or awl of some kind to make the perforations, and a heavy blade to cut through the cattle bones. In other words, the same person or members of the same family could have caught the fish, processed them, cooked them, eaten them, used some of the waste bones to make beads, and used a rosary or paternoster for some time before burying it in a sacred location. Wood and other raw materials would probably have been available, but whoever made these beads chose to use fish vertebrae and cattle bones. Was this simply because they were easily available, or did the person who made them consider them significant? What could be more appropriate when pleading on behalf of a loved one, than a devotional object made out of that person's source of life, livelihood and potential death? Nuno Gonçalves thought it appropriate for the fisherman in the St Vincent polyptych to have a paternoster made out of fish vertebrae, and the clarity and detail of the painting demonstrate that he was clearly familiar with their form.

Conclusion

The discussion presented here is almost certainly flawed, and can be criticised for being a 'Just So' story: a plausible but unproven explanation. Balanced against this are its advantages. It places an emphasis on the personal involvement of people with the archaeological record. It illustrates ways in which their perceptions of animals can change and take on new significance. These, surely, are more accurate representations of people in the past than mechanistic descriptions of an archaeological record devoid of people and their motives.

This study has benefited enormously from the prior knowledge that this site was a Christian 'temple' and also from some familiarity with current and medieval Christian practices. Although many archaeologists and faunal analysts are happy to consider structured deposition as a cause of patterning in the archaeological record, an ignorance of the thought processes in the minds of the people depositing the material tends to restrict interpretations of such patterning to mechanical descriptions of 'site formation processes'. It is almost as though we consider the site to have formed itself when, as archaeologists, we should really be most interested in who was at the site, what they were doing, and why they were doing it. Instead of this, a structured deposit is often described as though it were an end in itself: a rote performance by unknown and unknowable people obeying predetermined rules. Although we cannot always know the religious affiliation and significance of structures and deposits created in the past we should, at the very least, expect people to have been involved with their surroundings. Not just physically, but emotionally and conceptually as well.

What I hope to have demonstrated in this paper is that, by combining a range of types of evidence: art, archaeology, religion and dead fish, and by considering not only what has happened to the archaeological material but also who used it and what they might have been thinking at the time, we can begin to see how apparently different aspects of life are, in fact, just that: different aspects of a single life. To someone, or to some family in the past, these archaeological artefacts were live fish being caught in a dangerous sea, dead smelly animals needing gutting and processing, supper, something to trade, raw materials for making some beads, a precious rosary to be kept safe at all times and handled at times of prayer and, finally, a special devotional offering to a divinity. To us as archaeologists, it is easy to regard fish as always being fish, but to the people at Chevington in the medieval period, the role of those fish was always changing and their significance was transformed from prey to prayer.

Acknowledgements

This paper has benefited from comments from several people and I am grateful to them all, but I should particularly like to thank Lindsay Allason-Jones of the Hancock Museum, University of Newcastle, who undertook the initial research into the use and manufacture of rosaries. Alan Williams has been very helpful providing site plans and contextual information, and the line drawings of fish vertebrae are by Adrian Bailey, then of The Archaeological Practice. The black and white photograph of the three groups of fish and cattle bones was taken by Ian Qualtrough of the Department of Geography, University of Liverpool. I am enormously indebted to Omri Lernau who introduced me to the St Vincent polyptych. I also thank the editor of this volume Aleks Pluskowski for including this paper, which was presented at a later (unpublished) conference and for his patience with its late delivery.

This paper has thrown up several aspects that I was previously rather ignorant about, and I have probably made many mistakes. I hope that readers will forgive the errors and any sins of omission, and I would be grateful for any comments or information that could help me to rectify them.

References

Locker, A. (2001). *The Role of Stored Fish in England 900–1750AD; the Evidence from Historical and Archaeological Data*, Sofia, Publishing Group Ltd. N.B. The original (date 2000) PhD thesis of the same title containing colour versions of graphs is available through Inter-Library Loans from the University of Southampton.

Royal Academy of Arts (1955). *A Thousand Years of Portuguese Art, Portuguese Art 800–1800*, London, Exhibition Catalogue 1955–56.

Stocker, D. (1997). 'Fons et origo. The symbolic death, burial and resurrection of English font stones', *Church Archaeology*, 1, 17–25.

Winston-Allen, A. (1997). *Stories of the Rose. The Making of the Rosary in the Middle Ages*, Pennsylvania, Pennsylvanian State University Press.

www.ingramcontent.com/pod-product-compliance
Lightning Source LLC
Chambersburg PA
CBHW061003030426
42334CB00033B/3351